ISBN 978-1-332-11167-1
PIBN 10286154

Forgotten Books is a registered trademark of FB &c Ltd.
Copyright © 2017 FB &c Ltd.
FB &c Ltd, Dalton House, 60 Windsor Avenue, London, SW19 2RR.
Company number 08720141. Registered in England and Wales.

For support please visit www.forgottenbooks.com

1 MONTH OF
FREE
READING

at

www.ForgottenBooks.com

By purchasing this book you are eligible for one month membership to ForgottenBooks.com, giving you unlimited access to our entire collection of over 700,000 titles via our web site and mobile apps.

To claim your free month visit:
www.forgottenbooks.com/free286154

English
Français
Deutsche
Italiano
Español
Português

www.forgottenbooks.com

Mythology Photography **Fiction**
Fishing Christianity **Art** Cooking
Essays Buddhism Freemasonry
Medicine **Biology** Music **Ancient**
Egypt Evolution Carpentry Physics
Dance Geology **Mathematics** Fitness
Shakespeare **Folklore** Yoga Marketing
Confidence Immortality Biographies
Poetry **Psychology** Witchcraft
Electronics Chemistry History **Law**
Accounting **Philosophy** Anthropology
Alchemy Drama Quantum Mechanics
Atheism Sexual Health **Ancient History**
Entrepreneurship Languages Sport
Paleontology Needlework Islam
Metaphysics Investment Archaeology
Parenting Statistics Criminology
Motivational

Certain Principles in Evanson's "Dissonance of the "Four generally received Evangelists," &c. examined

IN

EIGHT DISCOURSES

DELIVERED BEFORE

THE UNIVERSITY OF OXFORD,

AT ST. MARY'S,

IN THE YEAR MDCCCX.

AT

THE LECTURE

FOUNDED BY

THE LATE REV. JOHN BAMPTON,

' CANON OF SALISBURY.

BY

THOMAS FALCONER, A.M.

OF CORPUS CHRISTI COLLEGE, OXFORD.

OXFORD,

At the University Press, for the Author.

Sold by Messrs. LONGMAN, HURST, REES, and ORME, London; and
J. UPHAM, Bath.

1811.

TO

THE REV. W. WHITEHALL DAVIES,

OF

BROUGHTON, FLINTSHIRE,

I INSCRIBE

THIS VOLUME

AS

A MEMORIAL

OF

ENDURING FRIENDSHIP.

T. F.

Bath,
March 17, 1811.

PREFACE.

PERHAPS an obfcure ftudent of the hiftory of religious controverfies may be fomewhere found, who will not think the information unneceffary, that a book entitled " The Dif- " fonance of the Four generally received Evan- " gelifts, &c. by the Rev. E. Evanfon," which fuggefted the principal fubjects of difcuffion in the following Lectures, was firft publifhed in the year 1792; that Dr. Prieftley, in the year 1793, replied to this work in " Letters " to a Young Man;" that Mr. E. addreffed " A Letter to Dr. Prieftley's Young Man" in the following year, and in a Poftfcript anim- adverted on another opponent, the Rev. D. Simpfon; that a fecond edition of " The Dif- " fonance" was publifhed in 1805; that the doctrines and principles and arguments of

" The Diffonance" were ftill neglected by the eftablifhed Clergy, with the exception of Mr. Simpfon, till fome of thefe were repeated (and they were merely repeated) in a Vifitation Sermon at Danbury in 1806, when this Sermon was examined in certain anonymous " Stric- " tures," and alfo in a moft able Letter to the author, the Rev. F. Stone, A. M. by the Rev. E. Nares, Rector of Biddenden; and laftly, that in 1807 a Canon of the New Teftament was publifhed, according to the felection of Mr. Evanfon in his " Diffonance." It is fomewhat remarkable, that an attempt, like Mr. E's, to annul the teftimony of the ancient Chriftians, as Chriftians, to the genuinefs and authenticity of the Gofpels, did not excite more folicitude and exertion. This work had engaged my attention foon after its firft publication, and at an early period of my life; and when I refumed this occupation, I found that the remains of this controverfial effay contained arguments which I had no occafion to ftrengthen, and were written in a ftyle which I could not fubfequently improve. I did not purfue the enquiry at that time, becaufe I daily expected that more experienced controverfialifts would appear in the field with armour of proof[a]. Mr. E. might have confidered himfelf as fortunate that he was not oppofed by the late Bifhop of Clonfert, (the pious, the learned, and the fuffering Chriftian,) who was of opinion, that this fophiftical book fhould be examined and anfwered. Whilft I thus ftate to advantage the importance of the object of my own labours, the reader will fympathize in my regret, that what was thought worthy the powers of his mind was attempted by any other.

It is neceffary to remark, that the Difcourfe on the Greek language was finifhed feveral months before the publication of a difquifition on a part of the fame fubject in the " Herculanenfia:"

---

[a] To guard againft mifreprefentation I wifh to obferve, that my Difcourfes comprife a much fmaller extent of enquiry than Dr. Prieftley's Letter, which contains a large proportion of very admirable argument; and, if I fhould not have my meaning diftorted by a calumnious gang of local inquifitors and familiars, I would fay, that what I have done may be confidered as fupplementary to the *orthodox parts* of Dr. Prieftley's reply.

The Truftees of the late Canon Bampton's benefaction require each Candidate for the appointment to the Lecture to preach before the Univerfity within the year preceding the election. The Difcourfe on November 5, 1808, which is fubjoined, is this probationary academical exercife.

I am obliged to the fingular patience of more than one friend, who perufed, oftener than once, nearly all the difcourfes in manufcript; and if I have adopted only fome of their corrections, or inferted only fome of their fuggefted additions, (which, if collected together, would not occupy the fpace of more than three or four pages at the utmoft,) I admit that the work is thus rendered lefs perfect : but I wifhed as well to fuftain alone the whole cenfure, as to lay an undivided claim to the whole of the approbation of the public. With refpect to the Difcourfe on the fifth of November, as originally publifhed, I am refponfible for every fentiment and expreffion, and, with one exception, for every fact. I have been fince reminded, that Archbifhop Tillotfon, in his fermon on the fame

occafion, had preferved the curious information refpecting Sir Everard Digby.

The fubjects felected by the preachers of
this Lecture, from the time of its inftitution,
will fhew, that the want of merit in the prefent Lectures, or in any that may foon follow,
is not to be afcribed to the preoccupation of
all the beft topics by our predeceffors.

I beg leave, in concluding, to explain the
apparent neglect of preceding writers. I have
been fo ftudious, perhaps culpably ftudious, of
originality, if not of novelty of reply, to many
objections, that I forbore to confult other au--
thors; and indeed, where I wifhed to have
extrinfic aid, it was often more eafy to invent
an argument for the occafion, than to procure
the book, to examine a reference, or to pene-
trate to the conclufion of a comment.

EXTRACT

FROM

THE LAST WILL AND TESTAMENT

OF THE LATE

REV. JOHN BAMPTON,

CANON OF SALISBURY.

———— " I give and bequeath my Lands and
" Eſtates to the Chancellor, Maſters, and Scholars
" of the Univerſity of Oxford for ever, to have and
" to hold all and ſingular the ſaid Lands or Eſtates
" upon truſt, and to the intents and purpoſes herein-
" after mentioned ; that is to ſay, I will and appoint
" that the Vice-Chancellor of the Univerſity of Ox-
" ford for the time being ſhall take and receive all
" the rents, iſſues, and profits thereof, and (after all
" taxes, reparations, and neceſſary deductions made)
" that he pay all the remainder to the endowment
" of eight Divinity Lecture Sermons, to be eſta-
" bliſhed for ever in the ſaid Univerſity, and to be
" performed in the manner following :

" I direct and appoint, that, upon the firſt Tueſ-
" day in Eaſter Term, a Lecturer be yearly choſen

" by the Heads of Colleges only, and by no others,
" in the room adjoining to the Printing-Houfe,
" between the hours of ten in the morning and
" two in the afternoon, to preach eight Divinity
" Lecture Sermons, the year following, at St.
" Mary's in Oxford, between the commencement
" of the laft month in Lent Term, and the end of
" the third week in Act Term.

" Alfo I direct and appoint, that the eight Di-
" vinity Lecture Sermons fhall be preached upon
" either of the following Subjects—to confirm and
" eftablifh the Chriftian Faith, and to confute all
" heretics and fchifmatics—upon the divine au-
" thority of the holy Scriptures—upon the autho-
" rity of the writings of the primitive Fathers, as
" to the faith and practice of the primitive Church
" —upon the Divinity of our Lord and Saviour
" Jefus Chrift—upon the Divinity of the Holy
" Ghoft—upon the Articles of the Chriftian Faith,
" as comprehended in the Apoftles' and Nicene
" Creeds.

" Alfo I direct, that thirty copies of the eight
" Divinity Lecture Sermons fhall be always print-
" ed, within two months after they are preached,
" and one copy fhall be given to the Chancellor
" of the Univerfity, and one copy to the Head of
" every College, and one copy to the Mayor of the
" city of Oxford, and one copy to be put into the
" Bodleian Library ; and the expence of printing
" them fhall be paid out of the revenue of the
" Land or Eftates given for eftablifhing the Divi-

" nity Lecture Sermons ; and the Preacher shall
" not be paid, nor be entitled to the revenue, be-
" fore they are printed.

" Also I direct and appoint, that no person shall
" be qualified to preach the Divinity Lecture Ser-
" mons, unless he hath taken the Degree of Master
" of Arts at least, in one of the two Univerfities
" of Oxford or Cambridge; and that the same per-
" son shall never preach the Divinity Lecture Ser-
" mons twice."

NAMES OF LECTURERS, &c.

1780. JAMES BANDINEL, D. D. of Jefus College;
Public Orator of the Univerfity. The author
firſt eſtabliſhes " the truth and authority of the
" Scriptures;—for the authenticity of the hiſ-
" tory being acknowledged, and the faƈts which
" are therein recorded being granted, the teſti-
" mony of *miracles* and *prophecies,* joined to the
" *excellence of the doƈtrines,* is a clear and com-
" plete demonſtration of our Saviour's divine
" commiſſion." P. 37.

1781. Timothy Neve, D. D. Chaplain of Merton College.
" The great point which the author has prin-
" cipally attempted to illuſtrate is, that well
" known, but too much negleƈted truth, that
" Jefus Chriſt is the Saviour of the world, and
" the Redeemer of mankind."

1782. Robert Holmes, M. A. Fellow of New College.
" On the prophecies and teſtimony of John the
" Baptiſt, and the parallel prophecies of Jefus
" Chriſt."

1783. John Cobb, D. D. Fellow of St. John's College.
The ſubjeƈts difcuſſed are; " An inquiry after
" happinefs; natural religion; the Gofpel; re-
" pentance; faith; profeſſional faith; praƈtical
" faith; the Chriſtian's privileges."

1784. Jofeph White, B. D. Fellow of Wadham College;
" A comparifon of Mahometifm and Chriſtia-
" nity in their hiſtory, their evidence, and their
" effeƈts."

1785. Ralph Churton, M. A. Fellow of Brafe Nofe College; " On the prophecies refpecting the de-
" ftruction of Jerufalem."

1786. George Croft, M. A. late Fellow of Univerfity
College; " The ufe and abufe of reafon; ob-
" jections againft infpiration confidered; the au-
" thority of the ancient Fathers examined; on
" the conduct of the firft Reformers; the charge
" of intolerance in the Church of England re-
" futed; objections againft the Liturgy an-
" fwered; on the evils of feparation; conjec-
" tural remarks upon prophecies to be fulfilled
" hereafter."

1787. William Hawkins, M. A. late Fellow of Pembroke
College ; " On Scripture Myfteries."

1788. Richard Shepherd, D. D. of Corpus Chrifti College; " The ground and credibility of the Chrif-
" tian Religion."

1789. Edward Tatham, D. D. of Lincoln College; " The
" Chart and Scale of ,Truth."

1790. Henry Kett, M. A. Fellow of Trinity College.
" The object" of thefe Lectures is " to rectify
" the mifreprefentations of Mr. Gibbon and
" Dr. Prieftley with refpect to the biftory of the
" primitive Church."

1791. Robert Morres, M. A. late Fellow of Brafe Nofe
College; On " faith in general; faith in divine
" teftimony no fubject of queftion; internal evi-
" dence of the Gofpel; effects of faith; reli-
" gious eftablifhments; herefies."

1792. John Eveleigh, D. D. Provoſt of Oriel College.
" I ſhall endeavour," ſays the learned author,
" firſt to ſtate regularly the ſubſtance of our
" religion from its earlieſt declarations in the
" Scriptures of both the Old and New Teſta-
" ment to its complete publication after the re-
" ſurrection of Chriſt; ſecondly, to give a ſketch
" of the hiſtory of our religion from its com-
" plete publication after the reſurrection of
" Chriſt to the preſent times, confining however
" this ſketch, towards the concluſion, to the
" particular hiſtory of our own Church; thirdly,
" to ſtate in a ſummary manner the arguments
" adducible in proof of the truth of our reli-
" gion; and fourthly, to point out the general
" ſources of objection againſt it."

1793. James Williamſon, B. D. of Queen's College;
" The truth, inſpiration, authority and evidence
" of the Scriptures confidered and defended."

1794. Thomas Wintle, B. D. of Pembroke College;
" The expediency, prediction, and accompliſh-
" ment of the Chriſtian redemption illuſtrated."

1795. Daniel Veyfie, B. D. Fellow of Oriel College;
" The doctrine of Atonement illuſtrated and de-
" fended."

1796. Robert Gray, M. A. late of St. Mary Hall; " On
" the principles upon which the reformation of
" the Church of England was eſtabliſhed."

1797. William Finch, LL. D. late Fellow of St. John's
College; " The objections of infidel hiſtorians
" and other writers againſt Chriſtianity confi-
" dered."

b

1798. Charles Henry Hall, B. D. late Student of Chrift Church. " It is the purpofe of thefe difcourfes " to confider at large what is meant by the " fcriptural expreffion, ' fulnefs of time ;' or, in " other words, to point out the previous fteps " by which God Almighty gradually prepared " the way for the introduction and promulga- " tion of the Gofpel." See the Preface.

1799. William Barrow, LL.D. of Queen's College. Thefe Lectures contain " anfwers to fome popular " objections againft the neceffity or the credi- " bility of the Chriftian revelation."

1800. George Richards, M. A. late Fellow of Oriel Col- lege; " The divine origin of prophecy illuftrated " and defended."

1801. George Stanley Faber, M. A. Fellow of Lincoln College; " Horæ Mofaicæ; or, a view of the " Mofaical records with refpect to their coin- " cidence with profane antiquity, their internal " credibility, and their connection with Chrif- " tianity."

1802. George Frederic Nott, B. D. Fellow of All Souls College; " Religious Enthufiafm confidered."

1803. John Farrer, M. A. of Queen's College; " On the " miffion and character of Chrift, and on the " Beatitudes."

1804. Richard Laurence, LL. D. of Univerfity College; " An attempt to illuftrate thofe Articles of the " Church of England which the Calvinifts im- " properly confider as Calviniftical."

1805. Edward Nares, M. A. late Fellow of Merton College ; " A view of the evidences of Chriftianity
" at the clofe of the pretended age of reafon."

1806. John Browne, M. A. late Fellow of Corpus Chrifti
College. In thefe Lectures the following principle is varioufly applied in the vindication of
religion; that " there has been an infancy of
" the fpecies, analogous to that of the indivi-
" duals of whom it is compofed, and that the
" infancy of human nature required a different
" mode of treatment from that which was fuit-
" able to its advanced ftate."

1807. Thomas Le Mefurier, M. A. late Fellow of New
College; " The nature and guilt of Schifm con-
" fidered with a particular reference to the prin-
" ciples of the Reformation."

1808. John Penrofe, M. A. of Corpus Chrifti College;
" An attempt to prove the truth of Chriftianity
" from the wifdom difplayed in its original efta-
" blifhment, and from the hiftory of falfe and
" corrupted fyftems of religion."

1809. J. B. S. Carwithen, M. A. of St. Mary Hall ; " A
" view of the Brahminical religion in its confir-
" mation of the truth of the facred hiftory, and
" in its influence on the moral character."

SERMON I.

I Cor. ii. 5.

That your faith fhould not fland in the wifdom of men, but in the power of God.

SEVERAL eminent theological writers have fuggefted an hypothefis, that Providence felected the firft teachers of Chriftianity from perfons, not merely defective in attainments, but alfo in mental capacity. Thefe writers do not indeed depreciate the ufe of human learning in the prefent time, but maintain, that neither learning nor human abilities were employed, as inftruments of converfion, at the commencement of the miniftry of the Apoftles. The very poffibility of the employment of liberal learning in this manner is excluded by the hypothefis, which fuppofes, that the firft teachers of Chriftianity were not only deftitute, but not even fufceptible of improvement by education ; that therefore they could not ufe, as means of propagating Chriftianity,

B

the fecular wifdom, which they had not natural ability to acquire. They cannot indeed
deny, that Paul and Apollos poffeffed both
eloquence and learning; but they feem to be
reftrained by a fuperftitious reluctance from
admitting, that thefe acquired qualifications
were applied to the inftruction of the primitive converts, left perhaps they fhould appear
to admit the neceffity, or even ufeful concurrence, of thefe aids, as fecondary caufes, in advancing the progrefs of the Chriftian religion.

They, who fuppofe that St. Paul fufpended
the full exercife of his natural abilities, and
circumfcribed the difplay of his eloquence and
learning, feem to imagine, that the ufe of fuch
powers was injurious to the miraculous evidence of Chriftianity, as if thofe powers were
not equally the gift of God, with any infpired faculties whatfoever. They alfo exclude, by this reafoning, the adaptation of
means, already exifting, to an end defigned to
be promoted; and forget, that the Almighty
does not act by the intervention of miraculous
endowments, when thofe beftowed by Him
in the natural courfe of his bounty are adequate to the purpofes of his wifdom. Thefe
purpofes were equally manifefted in the preaching and actions of the Apoftle to the Gentiles,

to whatever fource, whether to nature, or to infpiration, the means, by which thefe purpofes were accomplifhed, are to be referred. It feems to be the object of fuch reafoners to deduce the wifdom of the Almighty from a total difcrepancy and unfitnefs between the end, which was to be attained, and the means, which were to be employed. They would prove, that our Lord defignedly preferred the twelve, as men not only of uncultivated, but of weak underftandings. But if *all* thofe, who promulgated the Gofpel to the world, were not perfons of this defcription, the argument, which is derived from the infufficiency of the agent oppofed to the greatnefs of the effect, is defective and illufory. No other ftandard is propofed of the imperfection of the capacities of the firft teachers of the Gofpel, befides " the erroneous views, which they " formed of their Mafter's doctrine, intentions, " and kingdom, when he was with them " upon earth." How much foever they might mifunderftand thefe fubjects, the mifconception of them was an error common to a great part of their nation, and could not fo much be confidered as a teft of " natural incapa- " city," as a meafure of their prejudices and paffions, which fuperfeded the exercife of their

reafon. The fplendid exception of St. Paul
muft fubvert all fpeculations, which are founded upon the hypothefis, that the Almighty
provided incompetent phyfical means in order
to diftinguifh his own agency, as if His wifdom and power required the contraft of the
wifdom and power of thofe, to whom He
himfelf had not difpenfed the ordinary meafure of intellectual ability. In conformity with
this unworthy theory we might have expected to fee an illiterate Galilean miraculoufly
enabled to reafon, without premeditation, and
even inftantaneoufly, before the philofophic
tribunal of Stoics and Epicureans, affembled
at the Areopagus. But inftead of fuch a fudden communication of knowledge, or infpiration of qualifications for the particular occafion, an eloquent and learned Jew of Tarfus
was felected to be the Apoftle of the eloquent
and learned Gentiles. It is obferved by the
philofophical Greek [a] geographer of antiquity,
that every kind of knowledge was cultivated
with fo much ardour at Tarfus, that it fur-
paffed Athens and Alexandria, and every other

[a] Strab. Geog. lib. xiv. p. 673. This passage has been
often referred to ; but if I had been fatisfied with the
particulars ufually cited, I fhould not have found the moft
curious part of the account.

feat of ſcience that could be named, and that it differed from them all in this reſpect, that its learned men were all citizens, with a ſmall intermixture of ſtrangers ; ſo that St. Paul might aver with propriety and truth, that he was " a citizen of no mean city." When the inhabitants of Lyſtra applied to him the title of Mercury, " becauſe he was " the chief ſpeaker," are we to underſtand that this appellation was deſcriptive of his eloquence, or ſimply intended to diſtinguiſh his ſpeaking from the comparative ſilence of his aſſociate ? To the Jews he relates with juſtifiable ſatisfaction the advantages of the Jewiſh part of his education under Gamaliel, and in his orations at Athens and Cæſarea he does not heſitate to diſplay the erudition of the ſchools of Tarſus.

This argument, drawn from the ſuppoſed defective capacities of the Apoſtles, has been ſtill further extended, in contradiction to facts with an innocent and fanciful credulity, which may extenuate the imprudence of the author, but expoſes Chriſtianity to new objections. It has been ſaid [b], that if we compare " the " excellence and ſublimity of the doctrine and

[b] See Maclaine's Anſwer to Soame Jenyns.

" precepts of the Gofpel with the rank and " capacities of its teachers, we then are " brought into the fphere of miracles." But the rank and capacity of St. Paul were much too great to prefent fuch a contraft. Excellence characterizes all the writings of this Apoftle, and fublimity is not the cafual ornament of a few paffages only ; but in the proportion that his natural abilities exceeded thofe of the Galilean teachers, in the fame degree do they fhew the infufficiency of this ftandard of revelation. It would follow from this reafoning, that the more we degrade the intellectual abilities of the firft teachers of the Gofpel, the further we recede from the probability of forgery and impofture ; and that, upon the intimation of fuch fufpicions from an adverfary, we may confidently direct him to compare the excellence and fublimity of the precepts and doctrines of the Gofpel with the capacities of its original teachers. But great as we may be willing to fuppofe this difparity to have been, what do we really know of the abilities of the firft teachers of Chriftianity ? They purfued indeed humble occupations ; they were vilified in the popular adage, that " no good thing could come out " of Galilee ;" and of two of the chief apo-

ftles, Peter and John, it is ſaid, that they were
" unlearned and ignorant." If the paſſages
in the epiſtle to the Corinthians relate to the
preachers of Chriſtianity, we muſt further
deſcribe them as " things baſe," " weak,"
" fooliſh," and " deſpiſed." But according to
this interpretation St. Paul would include
himſelf among thoſe, who were not merely
in the eſtimation of men weak and fooliſh,
but abſolutely ſuch in reſpect to natural capacity. We might with equal propriety affirm, that among the firſt converts were the
poor only, and the illiterate, when the Apo-
ſtle declares, that " the wiſe after the fleſh,"
" the noble," and " the mighty," who were
called, were " not many," as aſſert, that the
Apoſtles were not ignorant only, but incapable of intellectual improvement. It ſeems
not to have been attended to, that the want of
that worldly intereſt and conſequence, which
is derived from wealth or power, were more
likely to depreſs them lower in the opinion of
mankind, and to expoſe them to greater neglect
and contempt, than mere mental inferiority.

We may examine this argument in another
light. Whatever may have been the other
ſubjects on which Inſpiration may have operated, we cannot conceive, that the weak in

underftanding have in any cafe been purpofely
felected to fhew its nature and effects. In the
inftance of a written fyftem of inftruction
mental deficiency in the author would be no
fecurity againft impofture, but would certainly
perplex and involve the fubject in additional
intricacies. It would tend to prove, that a writer of more ability might be able to make the
diftinction between infpiration and ordinary
human endowments lefs perceptible. If this
confequence is not to be admitted, why are we
to appreciate the excellence and fublimity of
the doctrines and precepts of the Gofpel by an
oppofition of the incapacity of its teachers ?
If, on the other hand, no comparifon can be
made, and none certainly can be made, between the extent of the wifdom of man and
the fuggeftions of infpiration, it will not depend upon the degree of his intellect, be it
more or be it lefs, whether we are or are not
brought " into the fphere of miracles."

But in the ftatement of the fact, that the
firft teachers were either Galileans, or perfons
of defective abilities, an exception occurs,
which has been neglected in the zeal to augment the neceffity of miraculous interpofition.
A portion of the world was inftructed neither
by Galileans, nor by perfons of " natural in-

"'capacity," even if we exclude the labours of the learned Apoftle of Tarfus. They were inftructed through the medium of written documents, compofed by men, whofe underftandings cannot be reduced to the ftandard of the hypothefis, and the place of whofe birth we cannot correctly affign to the region of Galilee. The neceffity of infpiration cannot vary with the inequalities of human capacity, and infpiration itfelf can be referred to human capacity only as being fomething, whofe dictates could not originate from the powers of man, but which thofe powers are adapted to communicate.

We may now adjuft the ftatement of the argument in this manner, according to the hypothefis and according to the fact. One portion of the world was converted by Jews, who are fuppofed to have been men of " na-" tural incapacity;" another portion was converted by a Jew, who poffeffed an intellect of no ordinary meafure, improved by the inftruction of learned preceptors, and the learned intercourfe of his native city. But whatever fuperiority the fublimity and excellence of doctrines or precepts may have, as vifible effects of infpiration, when contrafted with the incapacity of the teachers, who de-

livered them, this criterion is not applicable
to the example of St. Paul, nor can we equal-
ize this difference of ability by the evasive
assumption, that in the service of Christianity
he also might become, like others, a mere
passive channel of inspiration.

We are not at liberty, I conceive, to illus-
trate the words of the text by any conjectural
explanation respecting the conduct of St. Paul,
whether he might apply the whole of the powers which he possessed, or whether he restrain-
ed his eloquence and suppressed his erudition,
in his personal teaching. We know that when
he affirms that " his speech and his preaching
" were not with enticing words of man's wif-
" dom," he could not allude to eloquence;
for in this epistle he has given the first, perhaps, and most perfect specimen of its application to subjects arising out of the Christian
dispensation. He could not mean to disparage
the use of argument by his apostrophe, " where
" is the disputer of this world?" when he
shews himself, whenever it is required, to be
a great master of the art of reasoning. Men
did not know God by means of the wisdom
of this world; and St. Paul does not ignorantly
censure the philosophy of his own, or any other
age, in these expressions, but decides upon its

nature and incompetency from a learned ac-
quaintance with its tenets. The doctrine of
Chrift crucified, which he oppofed to this wifdom, was fufficient to counterbalance any cafual effects of the eloquence with which he
might have fpoken of its benefits to mankind;
for it was ftill regarded as foolifhnefs by the
Greeks, the authors and cultivators of this wifdom, the difciples of the Lyceum and the Aca-
demy, of Zeno and of Epicurus. He defcribes
his preaching among the Corinthians in his refolution not " to know any thing among them,
" fave Jefus Chrift, and him crucified;" intimating however that he could have accommodated his manner and teaching to hearers,
who might have expected him to adapt his
reafonings to rules of captious difputation, and
to conform his ftyle to examples of delufive
oratory.

It appears then, that the natural abilities
of the firft teachers of Chriftianity, whatever
they might have been originally, were not
changed by the influence of infpiration; fo
that, on one hand, the loweft meafure of underftanding was not defigned to prefent a contraft to infpiration; nor, on the other, was the
greateft neceffary to affift or to difplay its nature or its powers. The preaching of an elo-

quent and learned Apoftle to the eloquent and learned Gentiles could not furprize or delude them into the reception of Chriftianity, for eloquence and learning were not novelties to a Grecian auditory, and therefore thefe qualifications would have availed but little, if thefe hearers had not difcerned, in the fubject of his preaching, fomething, which their own enquiries enabled them to decide was not the invention of an accomplifhed teacher, nor owed its exiftence to " the wifdom of man."

If we examine the four Gofpels, we fhall not perhaps find in them either the powers of St. Paul, or the unlettered ignorance of Galileans. We may obferve, that although they all proceeded from " the fame fpirit of truth," yet thefe narratives of nearly the fame facts have not been reduced by the controul of infpiration to an uniformity of ftyle and manner, fo as to exclude the appearance of peculiarities of the writers, arifing from difference of difpofition, of habits, of education, in fhort, of natural abilities.

In the depreciation of the capacities of the firft teachers of the Gofpel, thefe teachers are apparently confounded with the Evangelifts; and what is alledged refpecting one is applied without difcrimination to the other. But is

there any reaſon to think that mankind were
not then inſtructed, as they have been ſince,
by perſons of various abilities and acquire-
ments, as inſpiration neither communicated
human learning, where it had not been previouſly attained, nor did it obliterate what had
been formerly ſtored in the memory. It neither annihilated that improvement of the faculties, which reſults from their exerciſe and
application, nor reduced the mind to its original rudeneſs. The gift of tongues is not
an exception, as I conceive, to this remark.
The knowledge of languages is not itſelf learning, but the means of communication; not
the thing to be communicated, which may, or
may not, be learning.

If indeed it ſhould be imagined, that after
a lapſe of time it might be neceſſary that the
Goſpel ſhould be preached by perſons of ſuperior qualifications, this reaſoning cannot be
reconciled to the known inequality of abilities
among the contemporary teachers. It is not
perhaps eaſy to explain, how the neceſſity of
employing the eloquent and the learned, in dif-
fuſing the Goſpel, ſhould ariſe from the change
of circumſtances in the lapſe of time. The A-
poſtles in general were commanded to preach
the Goſpel "every where," "to every creature,"

" to all nations," without any other reſtriction, than that they ſhould commence their labours at Jeruſalem. Some of the epiſtles of St. Paul are thought to have preceded the publication of the Goſpels ; the time, therefore, when learning was to be more properly applied to the inſtruction of mankind, coincides with the period, when the leſs educated Apoſtles were engaged in preaching the ſame Goſpel in other parts of the world. But the portion of time, which had elapſed ſince the promulgation of Chriſtianity, had made no alteration in the ſtate of the world, as to the progreſs of literature. The nations of Greece and Aſia were not ex-tending their knowledge, nor advancing in civilization by the introduction of new arts. About the period of the birth of our Saviour literature and the arts had nearly reached, at Rome particularly, that perfection of which, un-der the circumſtances of the empire, they were ſuſceptible. The nations above mentioned had neither receded nor advanced in thoſe reſpects, which might ſeem to require more than ordi-nary attainments and abilities in the primitive teachers of Chriſtianity. Beſides, the converts in theſe countries were numerous long before the concluſion of the firſt century. The in-terval of time therefore, which the argument

comprifes, is much too narrow, and the change
of circumftances too fmall, to enable us to determine the neceflity or propriety of employing the learned and eloquent in the apoftolical
miffions.

By feparating fecular wifdom from infpiration we fhould diftinguifh, and perhaps not ad-
vantageoufly, the teachers of the evangelical
from the great teacher of the Jewifh difpenfation. What could create the incompatibility of
one with the other under the Gofpel? Nothing
can be difcovered in the nature of infpiration,
or of human knowledge, which will explain it.
All the various wifdom of the Egyptians did
not interfere, as far as we can difcern, with the
infpiration of Mofes, nor could the erudition
of Daniel, nor the natural abilities of the other
prophets, be fuppofed to obfcure or to augment the fplendour of their divine illumination. They preferved indeed, as the Evangelifts preferve, a difference of ftyle and manner, which appear to be their own. The
learning and acquired knowledge of Solomon
were confpicuous, as well as the wifdom,
which he received from God. But as all
knowledge is the gift of God, the wifdom of
the Almighty was as much manifefted in the
choice of perfons, on whom this gift had been

previoufly beftowed, as it would have been by a fubfequent infpiration of fuch a proportion of human knowledge, as was neceflary to enable the Apoftles to perform the duties of teachers of the Gofpel.

The expreffions of St. Paul, " the wifdom " of men," have been paradoxically inter- preted, and arbitrarily applied by a writer, the principles of whofe work, " The Diffonance " of the four generally received Evangelifts, " &c." it is my intention to attempt to analyze in the ufual feries of thefe Lectures. He has explained the phrafe, as denoting not merely the early evidence of the Chriftian Fathers in eftablifhing the authenticity of the books of the New Teftament, but alfo the human learn- ing by which that evidence has been collected and examined. He condemns upon this au- thority " the pious fraud," as he terms it, " of " the Fathers of the Church," and the ftudies of modern critics. " c Obferving," he fays, " from St. Paul's mode of preaching the Gof- " pel to the Corinthians, that the faith of a wife " and rational Chriftian ought to ftand not in " the wifdom of men, but in the power of " God," he rejects all the teftimony, and all

c Evanfon's Letter to Dr. Prieftley's Young Man, p. 4, 5.

the enquiries of writers " from Serapion to Mi-
" chaelis." The words of St. Paul, in which
he defcribes his own manner of preaching the
Gofpel, are then referred, not, as the analogy
required, to the character of the prefent narratives of the Evangelifts, but to the teftimony
on which thefe narratives have been fince
received as authentic. But it is evident that
thefe words were written at a time ante-
cedent to the exiftence of any fuch evidence,
for this fpecies of evidence neceffarily pre-
fuppofes a written document. Can it be imagined that St. Paul intended prophetically to
admonifh Chriftians of every age not to attend
to the external teftimony of the Gofpels, which
the writers were then compofing, when he
muft at the fame time impeach the teftimony
of the Corinthians themfelves and all others,
who were able to atteft, from perfonal knowledge, the authenticity of this Epiftle ?

It is alfo affirmed, " that all the external
" [d] evidence, which the cafe admits, is fo
" fcanty and defective, that it is not poffible
" to prove the authenticity of any of the evan-
" gelical hiftories upon that ground only;"

[d] Evanfon's Letter to Dr. Prieftley's Young Man, Pref.
p. 1.

and it is expected, " that the feveral objection-
" able paffages fhould be clearly reconciled, as
" the Scriptures really exift, without recur-
" ring to any human authority, or to conjec
" tures unwarranted by the Gofpels them-
" felves." That the external teftimony is
" fcanty and defective." is an affertion which
is incorrect, in whatever way we explain it.
It is incorrect, whether we underftand that it
implies, that the cafe did not from its nature
admit fufficient evidence, or, that what was
known to many, has been attefted by few.
We have not indeed all the original evidence;
for much, that was written, has perifhed.   At
prefent I fhall only obferve, that the Gofpel
was taught orally during a period of eight years,
During this interval the number of witneffes
of this teaching muft have been increafing by
the acceffion of new converts, and their families.   The Gofpels therefore were committed
to writing, when their contents could be
verified, not by determining the identity of
autographs, but by comparing the preaching,
to which the Chriftians had been habituated,
with the written narrative.   At this time alfo
there muft have been alive many believers at
Jerufalem, contemporary with our Saviour,
who muft have remembered not only the latter

events of his hiftory, but his teaching in their
fynagogues, and in the Temple. This circumftance effentially diftinguifhes the authentication of the evangelical, from the authentication of every other hiftory. The teftimony
of the firft converts would prove, what their
contemporaries would be fo much interefted
in knowing, that fuch a Gofpel was the fame
with that, by the preaching of which they had
been converted to Chriftianity, or according to
which the firft Chriftians had been educated,
before it was committed to writing. How
much more fatisfactory would this be than a
mere affurance, that fuch a writing was certainly an apoftolical autograph ! We may infift likewife upon the facility with which the
written narrative could be thus verified, even
by fuch converts as the adverfaries of Chriftianity term mean and ignorant perfons. The
original evidence then was fimple and copious;
and that which we now have cannot be denominated fcanty, when, even in the fhort
letter of [e] Polycarp, he either cites or refers to
more than one half of the books, which conftitute the prefent volume of the New Teftament. Our next enquiry is, whether it is de-

[e] Powel's Difc. p. 70.

fective ? And this involves a queftion, how far the citation by contemporary writers of paf- fages from various parts of a book, is evidence of the genuinenefs and authenticity of the whole ? It might indeed be fuppofed, how- ever rafhly, that the citations themfelves were the only genuine parts of the work; but this could be faid of the Gofpels with lefs detri- ment to their credibility, than of any other writings whatever. They have a fource of cre- dibility peculiar to themfelves, arifing from their form of compofition. The identification of the doctrines with the facts of the Gof- pels, by augmenting the intimacy of the con- nection of one with the other, has rendered a forgery of detached parts more difficult than it would have been, if the Gofpels had con- fifted merely of a fyftem of moral precepts, fevered from the narrative, and had not re- ferred to the general character of the divine perfon, who delivered them. For the fame reafon they, who would attempt to mutilate the Gofpels on the pretext of the want of au- thenticity, would find it difficult to conceal the chafm which would be produced by the abftraction of even no very confiderable portion of the narrative. The external evidence there- fore muft be rejected, if at all, for reafons, which are better fupported than any, that are drawn from its fcantinefs, or defects. We may indeed rather fufpect that " wifdom of man," by which, after a lapfe of fo many centuries, it has now been difcovered, that the evidence, on which the authenticity of the Gofpels has been received, is defective in kind, and infufficient in degree, and therefore cannot produce rational conviction; and that there is other evidence, better adapted to the underftanding of mankind, and which we are directed in Scripture to apply, not only as a teft of authenticity, but alfo as a criterion of Revelation itfelf.

It is alledged, that another method is indicated for attaining certainty on thefe fubjects; " the power of God," by which the author of " The Diffonance" underftands " the " teftimony of prophecy." But no example is, or perhaps can be, adduced, of the ufe of this expreffion in this manner from the writings of St. Paul, or from any other part of Scripture. It was obferved before, that the mere phrafe, " the wifdom of man," conftituted the fole fcriptural authority refpecting the incompetency of external evidence in general; and here, " the power of God" is fuppofed, by the fame arbitrary expofition, to denote not only fome fuperior teftimony, but particularly that of prophecy. " The Diffonance" however is a work, which fully illuftrates the pofition, that perverfion of intellect is marked by requiring more proof than particular fubjects will admit; as natural incapacity or great ignorance are indicated, by being fatisfied with infufficient or with inapplicable teftimony.

The reduction of the Canon of the New Teftament to its juft extent by the direction of Scripture and the light of prophecy, muft derive its claim to attention, after the expiration of eighteen centuries, folely from our reverence for the alledged fanction of the attempt. The invalidation of the authenticity of the books of which the canon at prefent confifts, has been undertaken in order to remove paffages, the interpretation of which does not favour the Socinian fyftem ; and it is perhaps more eafy to alledge defects in the external evidence, and to intimate fufpicions of extenfive forgery, than to pervert the meaning of fo large a portion, which thofe paffages form of the individual books, and to withftand. an explication of them founded on that general analogy, which fubfifts in the different parts of the unmutilated record.

It will be my object in this inveftigation to

refer a large mafs of minute and independent objections to fome general topics of difcuffion, and trace them to their principles. I propofe therefore to examine the paffages of Scripture relative to the application of prophecy, as a ftandard of the authenticity of the facred writings; to determine the fufficiency of the external evidence, when compared with prophecy, for the authority of thefe works; to enquire whether the publication of fpurious and fictitious books had, at the time, any influence in perplexing the queftion refpecting the genuinenefs of the Scriptures; to afcertain the grounds on which we receive the two firft chapters of St. Matthew's Gofpel; to inveftigate in what manner, if in any, the eftablifhment of Chriftianity in the time of Conftantine, as the religion of the ftate, tended to facilitate the corruption of the written Gofpels; and to reconcile the fuppofed anachronifms in the language of the Gofpels by an hiftorical fketch of the diffufion of the Greek tongue among various parts of the world. Thefe fubjects are not altogether new; but it is not my intention to arrange, or abbreviate, or repeat the arguments and enquiries, of preceding writers. It is fcarcely neceffary to remark, that a complete examination of " The

" Diffonance" cannot be comprifed in thefe
Lectures from the minutenefs of fome parts,
and the extent of others. Thefe therefore
may perhaps be referved for another place.

The peculiarity, which diftinguifhes the
mode, adopted in that work, from every other
mode of determining the Canon of the New
Teftament, is the abfolute rejection of one
branch of evidence, to which much importance has been always juftly attributed, the external or hiftorical teftimony. All facts feem
to admit the fame fpecies of proof; but the
author of " The Diffonance" affirms, that
" facts of different natures, to render them cre-
" dible, require very different kinds of tefti-
" mony." It may not be unneceffary to confider the application of this principle to two
hiftorical facts, the truth of which depends on
this variety of evidence. Thefe facts are,
" the invafion of Greece by Xerxes," and
" the deliverance of the Ifraelites from Egypt."
The reafon affigned for admitting the former
f fact to be true is, that the Greek " Hiftorians,
" who have recorded it, could have no fup-
" pofeable motive to falfify as to the main fact
" itfelf." It muft indeed be allowed, that

f Evanfon's Letter to Dr. Prieftley's Young Man, p. 6.

where the evidence is contemporary with the
events, and particularly, where it is the evidence of perfons, who have had fome fhare in
producing them, it may happen, that their accounts, according to the nature of the events,
may be exaggerated through vanity, or mifreprefented through a fpirit of animofity to a
contrary party. This is a defect to which perfonal evidence may, in general, be liable; but,
on the other hand, the truth of great events is
fecured by their publicity being in proportion
to the magnitude of their objects, to the number of agents, and the time occupied in their
preparation and accomplifhment. This publicity is not fuppofed to prevent partiality altogether from operating upon the mind of the
hiftorian, but it expofes him to detection by a
comparifon of other narratives, originating in
the importance of the events and the facility
of obtaining information. If we regard the
Evangelifts merely as contemporary witneffes,
we cannot difcover any occafion on which
they could glory in their Mafter, that would
not be counterbalanced by the circumftance
of his death. Chrift crucified was " a ftum-
" bling-block" to their countrymen, and
" foolifhnefs" to the philofophic ftranger, notwithftanding the dignity of our Lord's defcent,

and the perfection of his moral character. It is difficult to discover what worldly interest could be promoted by those doctrines, which it is the object of " The Diffonance" to prove to be spurious interpolations. Indeed it would be difficult to shew, that Christianity was not in every form unfavourable to the temporal welfare of its disciples, till the reign of Constantine, a period much too distant for the supposed impostors to derive or to expect any advantage from their corruptions of the Gospels.

That the truth or falsehood of the invasion of Greece by Xerxes is of no consequence to individuals of these times, is a position which cannot be admitted. It may not be of importance to us; that is, our political or any other condition are not affected by the former existence of such a place as Troy, or by such an event as the Trojan war; but it is of much importance to the general credibility of history that these facts should be received as true. It may have the semblance of paradox to assert, that the truth of the facts recorded in the New Testament has any dependence upon the truth of such facts as the war of Troy, or the invasion of Greece. But history has been always believed on the same kind of evidence.

Even fable itſelf has not been always introduced to falſify hiſtory, but ſometimes to be
its form of communication, and on other occaſions to complete its imperfect chronicles.
When therefore we endeavour, on ſpeculative
grounds, to invalidate the veracity of perſons,
who had the beſt opportunity of knowing the
facts which they commemorate, what will
prevent the application of 'the ſame doubts to
the evidence of the credibility of the New
Teſtament? The aſſiſtance of the Holy Spirit
conſiſted in calling all things to the remembrance of our Lord's diſciples; not in ſuper-
ſeding the former employment of their faculties, but in renewing the impreſſions formerly
made, and in diſtinguiſhing their teſtimony, not
by its kind, but by its ſuperior fulneſs and accuracy. When our Saviour ſaid, " The Holy
" Ghoſt, whom the Father will ſend in my
" name, he ſhall teach you all things, and
" bring all things to your remembrance what-
" ſoever I have ſaid unto you;" he did not
however aſſign this as the only cauſe of the
force of their teſtimony, but combined it with
another, " Ye alſo ſhall bear witneſs of me,
" becauſe ye have been with me from the
" beginning."

The miraculous facts recorded of the Exo-

dus of the Ifraelites are received by the Author
of " The Diffonance" merely on account of
" the teftimony ᵍ which the fpirit of prophecy
" bears to the general truth of the Pentateuch,
" and the divine authority of the Jewifh re-
" ligion." This is the different kind of teftimony, by which the truth of the miraculous
facts of the ancient facred hiftory is faid to be
confirmed, in oppofition to the evidence of the
facts of the Heathen annals. But where this
teftimony of the fpirit of prophecy is to be
found, in what words it is communicated, and
in what manner it is applied, are queftions,
which I propofe foon to difcufs.

At prefent I fhall vindicate the minutenefs,
with which I fhall be found frequently to have
purfued the reply to various objections, that
may feem to derive their importance folely
from fuch an examination. For I apprehend,
that a falfe dignity is not rarely affumed in controverfial difcuffions, and is fuftained by a con-
temptuous difregard of objections, which it is
perhaps more eafy to ftigmatize with epithets
of reproach, than to analyze by regular argument. If objections be intricate, they
may be difentangled; if futile, their ineffici-

ᵍ Evanfon's Letter to Dr. Prieftley's Young Man, p. 7.

ency may be expofed; if abfurd, their abfurdity may be demonftrated. Contempt is too
often the refuge of ignorance in diftrefs; but
even if it were the effect of better knowledge, and fuperior ability, it is moft impro-
perly applied to the fubject of religion, both
as it is dogmatical and irreverent. Contempt
is neither the proof nor the fign of fuperiority;
and in what inftance may not reafon and argument be fubftituted for expreffions of contempt? If an adverfary be difpofed to affign
to it all the polemical value which we can
expect, it can never amount to more than the
fimple oppofition of a negative. Would extenfive knowledge and fuperior ability appear lefs confpicuoufly to vulgar obfervers, in
a direct examination, than when they are to
be inferred from fupercilious neglect? If an
objection be neglected, who can diftinguifh
whether it is neglected becaufe it is contemned only, or becaufe it is unanfwerable?
This ambiguity, which is as favourable to one
party as to the other, can be removed only by
a formal inveftigation. Sophiftry and ignorance may be obvious to the experienced rea-
foner, or the learned enquirer; yet contempt
cannot be judicioufly employed to detach the
adherents of fcepticifm, who are perhaps more

fatisfied, that, as nothing but contempt is oppofed to what has influenced their minds, they
themfelves have juſt reafoning and accurate
knowledge on their fide.   But no objection is
unworthy the confideration of the moſt able,
or the moſt learned.   Different perfons are fo
varioufly impreffed by different objections,
that it is impoffible to affirm, that the moſt
frivolous are the moſt harmlefs.   Prejudice
may fo far counteract the effect of liberal attainments, as to reduce improved minds to the
level of thofe, which are rude and undifciplined ; and conjectures and infinuations may
perplex with doubts, underftandings, which,
when employed on other fubjects, appear to be
vigorous, and cultivated, and enlarged.

SERMON II.

REV. xix. 10.

For the testimony of Jesus is the spirit of prophecy.

IT may be justly questioned, whether the Almighty has ever employed prophecy to authenticate any of the writings, in which the revelation of his will has been communicated to mankind. If this had been one of the purposes of this testimony, we might have expected, that it would consist of a distinct collection of predictions, and not of a few indeterminate passages of scripture; and, that it would not be resolvable into a still more indefinite form, "the general spirit of prophecy."

It is the object of the author of " The Dif- " sonance" (in obedience, as he professes, to an inspired command) to reject all the proofs of written revelation, which are founded " on " mere human testimony." The words of the text, according to this interpretation, contain the injunction, by which we are directed to

apply to prophecy, as to the ftandard of revelation, and the criterion of the authenticity of
the writings, in which it is conveyed.

Thofe miracles, which are admitted by this
writer to have any validity, as proofs, are faid
to derive their credibility, as facts, from their
affociation with predictions; and, without this
combination, they are declared to be infufficient means of conviction. He fuppofes, that
a " he can prove, not only from the dictates of
" human reafon, but from the voice of revela-
" tion, that miracles, of themfelves, do not
" afford even to the fpectators a fufficiently
" firm and fatisfactory foundation for their re-
" ligious faith." I propofe therefore to confider, although perhaps not ftrictly according
to this arrangement, whether the evidence of
miracles is affected by its connection with
prophecy; to examine the reafons, which are
adduced in fupport of the fuperiority of the
proof by prophecy, above that by miracles;
the grounds on which we receive thefe two
fpecies of evidence, and the prophetic paffages
of the infpired writers, which are faid to conftitute the criterion of authentic fcripture.

a Evanfon's Letter to Dr. Prieftley's Young Man, p.
12.

When we are referred to fcripture, as the authority for the rejection of miracles, becaufe mankind might have been " deluded and de-" ceived by fuch evidence," we muft enquire in what language of fcripture the evidence, arifing from miracles, is thus condemned; in what circumftances their defects, as proofs, are faid to confift, and whether prophecy alters or corrects them.

" With regard to miracles under the Old " Covenant," it is faid [b], " that God himfelf, " by his prophet Mofes, cautioned the Jews " againft receiving the religious doctrines of " any pretended prophet, though he fhould " even work miracles to convince them, be-" caufe they would be liable to be deluded " and deceived by fuch evidence. ' If there ' arife among you a prophet, or a dreamer of ' dreams, and giveth thee a fign or a wonder, ' and the fign or the wonder come to pafs, ' whereof he fpake unto thee, faying, Let us ' go after other gods, which thou haft not ' known, and let us ferve them; thou fhalt ' not hearken unto the words of that prophet, ' or that dreamer of dreams, for the Lord your ' God proveth you, to know whether ye love

[b] Diff. Pref. p. viii. 2d edit.

D

' the Lord your God with all your heart and
' with all your foul." The fufficiency of the
evidence of miracles, fo far from being invali-
'dated, is afferted in this injunction of Mofes.
He feems to refer to it familiarly, as the beft
fpecies of evidence; as the evidence to which
they had been habituated, and the foundation
on which their faith is fuppofed at this time
to be eftablifhed. The temptation therefore
confifted in witneffing the fame evidence applied to a contrary purpofe; that evidence,
whofe force they had before acknowledged,
now adduced to evince their firmnefs, to difcover the principle of their profeffions, to afcertain whether they were ready to transfer
their obedience to another mafter, whofe
power they might erroneoufly eftimate from
the miracles of his pretended minifters. But
if we argue from the explanation of the author of " The Diffonance," we may fay, that;
as the object of the Almighty was to afcertain
the influence of his favours and mercies on
the minds of the Ifraelites, what proof could
be expected of their fidelity, when a teft was
to be applied, which was, in the eftimation of
the Almighty himfelf, inadequate and fallacious? Was not this alfo a late period of their
hiftory to promulgate a caution againft the

evidence of miracles derived from its intrinfic imperfections? The Ifraelites had been long accuftomed to the vifible and extraordinary difplay of the power of the Almighty, and are now, for the firft time, informed, that miracles. may delude their fenfes, and miflead their underftandings. What could be the guilt, in the eye of God, of thofe men, who refufed to admit, as evidences of his will, thofe figns and wonders, to which He himfelf had not communicated authority or reality? According to the impious principle which I am oppofing, miracles are divefted of their awful character, and deprived of their proper influence upon the fenfes and underftanding of mankind, and are reduced to fomething lower, as to dignity, and weaker, as to effect, than ordinary events. But in this very paffage of fcripture, in which miracles are faid to be delufive and fallacious, they are introduced in combination with prophecy, and therefore the diftinction of miracles with, and of miracles without, preceding predictions, (by which we are faid to be enabled to difcriminate real from fictitious wonders,) is not to be deduced from the authority of this paffage.

Nor do I conceive, even if it fhould be ad-

mitted to be a correct remark, that God "hath
" never refted the credit of his fupernatural
" revelation to his creatures upon mere mira-
" cles alone, even to thofe fpectators of them,
" who were chiefly intended to be convinced
" of its truth and certainty," that we fhould
be at liberty to frame an inductive argument
from the general obfervation. We could not
infer (as it would almoft feem, according to
this reafoning, that we might infer) that we
had here difcovered a law, which the Almighty had prefcribed to himfelf in confirm-
ing the communication of his will to mankind, in the fame manner as we may collect
the laws, by which he continues the exiftence, and regulates the operations, of the material world. The language and fpirit of the
remark imply, that the Almighty did not eftablifh miracles alone as the foundation of belief, becaufe they were of a nature not to juftify fuch a degree of confidence in the reprefentations of the fenfes. Are we then to imagine that the fpectators might truft to the impreffions made upon their fenfes, when the
miracle was accompanied with prophecy; but
that a miracle, without this fecurity for its
reality, is to be confidered as of uncertain exiftence? But when it is affumed that the

fenfes may be deluded, the addition of prophecy would not be any confirmation of the miraculous act. The uncertainty ftill remains the fame. Whether the fpectator affirm that the miraculous act coincides with the prophecy, or is contradictory to it, his teftimony may be difputed. As we are fuppofed to be incompetent judges of the reality of a miracle, fo are we of the exiftence of all fenfible objects; and therefore the moft conclufive proceeding would be, to queftion the exiftence of the prophecy itfelf, the reality of which, as well as that of the miracle, can be proved only by the evidence of the fenfes. And why fhould this evidence be regarded as unqueftionable in one cafe, and liable to fallacy in the other?

With refpect to thofe perfons who derive, from hiftorical records, the conviction of the truth of the early facts of this nature, the author of "The Diffonance" would refer them folely to prophecy, as the foundation of their credit. He "receives the miraculous facts "recorded of the Exodus of the Ifraelites on "the teftimony which the fpirit of prophecy "bears to the general truth of the Pentateuch, "and to the divine authority of the Jewifh "religion; but otherwife he would have re-.

" ferred" thofe facts " to the fame clafs with
" the early fables of the Romans, and all thofe
" wonderful circumftances, which are faid to
" have attended the origin of every other na-
" tion recorded in ancient hiftory." It is to
be obferved, that in the miracles performed
by Mofes immediately preceding the departure of the Ifraelites from Egypt, the accomplifhment fucceeded the prediction with the
interpofition of a very fhort interval. When
indeed the prophecy is delivered in one age,
and the tranfactions, to which it refers, take
place after the revolution of many fucceeding
ages, we may then be fatisfied that they are
not contemporary fictions. But if the prediction and the accomplifhment be feparated
by an inconfiderable portion of time, and are
both recorded by the fame writer, as in the
inftances of the miracles wrought by Mofes,
which attended the Exod of the Ifraelites, in
this cafe the evidence of prophecy can add no
weight to that of miracles. The writer may
be able to adjuft the miracles to the prophecy,
or the prophecy to the miracles, as the interval comprehends fo very fmall a portion of
futurity. The record of the miracle, unconnected with the delivery of prophecy, would
have been equally fatisfactory, as a proof, and

obligatory upon the conduct. If the one will
not convince, conviction cannot be expected
from the other. This, it must be acknowledged, is the weakeft cafe in prophecy that
can be fpecified, becaufe the fhortnefs of the
intervening period brings the accomplifhment
and the prediction into the fame record, and
under the controul of the fame writer. I wifh
however to guard my meaning from mifap-
prehenfion by obferving, that although the
length or fhortnefs of the interval fhould
really make no difference whatever with refpect to the powers and evidences of prophecy, yet, when the prophecy and the fact
are recorded in the fame writing, the queftion
of the priority of the prophecy may be difputed with more plaufibility than when the
periods between each are longer, and one perfon records the prophecy, and another the
fulfilment.

In order to evince the effects of the fuperior
influence of prophecy, it is obferved in " The
" Diffonance," that " the Jews were conti-
" nually apoftatizing to idolatry, notwith-
" ftanding the numerous miracles recorded in
" their hiftory, and the occafional fuperna-
" tural interpofition of divine power, and yet
" were thoroughly convinced of the truth and

" divine origin, and authority of the Mofaic
" covenant, upon their fo forcibly feeling the
" fevere completion of the prophecies in their
" Babylonifh captivity." That a nation would
be permanently influenced by the fufferings
of captivity, and that their conduct would be
altered upon thofe reflections, which a ftate of
general fuffering would neceffarily produce,
is probable and natural. But it is not the
defign of the author to explain the reformation of the Jewifh people in fo fimple a manner. We are expected, if not entirely to
overlook the neceffary effects of a long pref-
fure of calamity upon the mind, yet to refer
this conviction of the Jews refpecting the
truth and divine origin of the Mofaic covenant, and their abandonment of idolatry, to
two caufes inftead of one : firft, to the influence of their reflections on the completion of
their prophecies ; and, fecondly, to the evils
of their late condition. If the real caufe of
their apoftafy to idolatry had been, their
doubts refpecting the truth and divine origin
of the Mofaic covenant, it might perhaps have
been accounted for, perhaps even vindicated,
upon the principles of " The Diffonance," by
alledging the want of other evidence than
miracles. But this want of evidence was not

the caufe of their apoftafy; neither is it probable that an accumulation of prophecies.
would have prevented it.

.It would appear from the expreffions of the
preceding citation, as if the former generations were required to receive and acknow-
ledge. the truth and divine origin of the Mofaic covenant upon one kind of proof, and the
latter upon another. But, if we place on one
fide the accumulated teftimony, which the
Almighty gave of himfelf, and, on the other,
the intermarriages of the Jews with the idolatrous nations, we may then be convinced,
that thefe conneftions, continued through feveral generations, were fufficiently powerful
to counteraft the operation of the commands.
of the Almighty, and to obliterate for a time
the evidence of the revelation of his will. The
Jews perfifted in their difobedience to the important precept, not to contraft alliances with
the families of idolatrous ftrangers, from the
time of their firft fettlement in the land promifed to their forefathers, to the conclufion of
their captivity. This land too they were enabled to occupy by the means of miracles, and
in conformity with prophecy. That they were
at length reclaimed from idolatry by their re-
fleftions on thofe prophecies, which were ac-

complifhed in their punifhment, is not confirmed by any hiftorical facts. It is a reafon,
which is not affigned in the account of their
conduct at that time. The Jewifh hiftorian
relates [c], " that the people defired of Ezra,
" that the laws of Mofes might be read to
" them. Accordingly he ftood in the midft
" of the multitude and read them. Now by
" hearing the laws read to them, they were
" inftructed to be righteous men for the pre-
" fent and for the future; but as for their paft
" offences, they were difpleafed at themfelves,
" confidering, that if they had kept the law,
" they had endured none of thofe miferies
" which they had experienced." Hence it is
evident, that they did not refer to their prophets to examine, how their calamities had
coincided with the predictions, but to the laws
of Mofes, to obferve the deviations of their
conduct from the injunctions of their vene-
rated legiflator. For prophecies, without any
derogation from their awful and fublime nature, cannot be faid to be ftandards of moral
conduct, by the application of which degrees
of guilt or righteoufnefs may be determined.

[c] Antiq. lib. xi. cap. 5. Whifton's tranflation; and
Ezra.

Tranfgreffions are greater or lefs according to their deviations from certain laws.

It is invidiouſly obſerved, that the Jews apoſtatized, " notwithſtanding the numerous " miracles recorded in their hiſtory;" as if prophecy would have prevented that defec- tion, from which afterwards, according to our author's fuppoſition, they were reclaimed through the fuperior influence of this more perfect evidence. But the Iſraelites were not led to repentance in former ages by the ac- compliſhment of the prophecies againſt the houſe of Jeroboam. The very perſon, who exterminated the houſe of Jeroboam accord- ing to the prophecy of Ahijah, committed the fame abominations as his predeceſſor; and the fame fentence, which was prophetically de- nounced againſt Jeroboam, was propheſied and fulfilled againſt his race alfo. Even Zimri, who executed the prophecy, tranfgreſſed in a fimilar manner, and received a fimilar con- demnation. The fons and fucceſſors of Joſiah, who had witneſſed the fulfilment of the pro- phecies in the perſon and actions of their fa- ther, were as corrupt and difobedient as any of their predeceſſors. We may therefore en- quire, whether it appears, upon an examina- tion of the hiſtory of the Jews, that they were

more reftrained from apoftafy by the means
of prophecy under their kings, than by the
means of miracles under their theocracy ?

There are ftrong exceptions to the obfervation, that miracles derive their authority from
preceding predictions. They fometimes enhance the credit of a prophecy at the time
that it is delivered, and impart affurance to
the perfon who is the object of it, that it fhall
be fulfilled. When Hezekiah was informed
by Ifaiah that he fhould recover from his
ficknefs, and that his life fhould be prolonged,
he required a fign which fhould confirm the
prophetic promife. He believed the prophecy
on the evidence of a miracle, the retrograda-
tion of the fhadow on the dial of Ahaz, which,
although intended for his own conviction, was
of fuch a nature as to be obferved at Babylon,
and was probably recorded in their aftrono-
mical regifters, and was otherwife well calculated, without fuch affiftance, to be remembered by individuals of other countries, for a
longer period than that to which the life of
Hezekiah was protracted. When alfo a prophet of the Lord unexpectedly appeared before Jeroboam, while he was ftanding at an
idolatrous altar, and performing abominable
rites, he, without regarding the authority of

Jeroboam, or the prefence of the children of Ifrael at this " feaft," which their king had " ordained,". " even in the month which he " had devifed of his own heart," abruptly addreffed his awful denunciation to the altar; on which the offenfive facrifices had been of-fered up, and foretold, that a time would come, when the bodies of the priefts of the high places fhould be burnt upon it, as a fa-crifice to avenge the crime of its prefent pol-lution. " And he gave a fign the fame day; " faying, Behold, the altar fhall be rent, and " the afhes that are upon it fhall be poured " out. When Jeroboam heard the faying of " the man of God, he ftretched forth his hand " from the altar," as a fignal of violence to the perfon of the prophet, and " his hand " dried up," " the altar alfo was rent, and the " afhes poured out from the altar, according " to the fign which the man of God had given " by the word of the Lord.". The event here predicted was not to take place till the time of Jofiah, a period of 350 years; but we can-not doubt that the impreffion of the truth of the prediction on the minds of the fpectators of thefe miracles was their real end and purpofe.

The author of " The Diffonance" has pur-fued ftrongly, but inaccurately, a parallel be-

tween miracles and prophecy. "To thofe of
" the prefent age," he obferves [d], " who have
" any doubt about the certainty of the Chrif-
" tian religion, and confequently of the truth
" and authenticity of thofe hiftories in which
" it is recorded, it cannot be of the leaft ufe
" to alledge the miraculous acts there, and
" there only, related, to have been performed
" by the firft teachers of that revelation, be-
" caufe thofe acts, making a very confiderable
" part of the narrative, the authority and cre-
" dibility of the hiftories muft be firft firmly
" eftablifhed before the miracles contained in
" them can reafonably be admitted as real
" facts." That the eftablifhment of the credibility of the hiftory fhould precede any reafoning from the miracles recorded in it, may
be allowed. We may alfo add, that the moral precepts, which are inculcated, derive their
obligatory fanction, as divine rules of conduct,
from the refult of the fame enquiry. We
may, and indeed muft think, that the morality
contained in the Gofpel is, when taken in a
fpeculative light, *worthy* a divine original;
but fome direct evidence of this is required to
enforce the duty of applying its maxims to

[d] Diffonance, p. 22, 23.

the regulation of our actions as Christians.
Its purity, its excellence, its fublimity, are
characteriftics of evangelical , morality; but
thefe qualities are not the fanctions by which
its precepts have been eftablifhed, nor the authorities upon which they have been received.
Our obligation to obey them is derived only
from the authenticity of the records which
contain them; records, by which we are affured that thefe rules of life were delivered by
a teacher, whofe miffion was fhewn indifpu-
tably to be from heaven. The genuinenefs
or authenticity of every hiftory muft be eftablifhed in the fame manner, whether the hiftory contains miracles, or not. This circumftance does not affect the fpecies of evidence;
nor compel us to admit any proof, with which
we fhould not otherwife be fatisfied; neither
does it make lefs evidence, nor a greater proportion, nor a different kind of it, indifpenfable for conviction. The reafon alfo does not
appear why it is more or lefs neceffary to
afcertain the authenticity of thefe books, becaufe the miraculous acts form " a very con-
" fiderable part of the narration," and becaufe
" they are there, and there only, related." If
external evidence were required to be of fuch
a nature as to extend to every portion of a

book, and to recite or to refer to each fact or opinion, taken feparately, then indeed the proportion of the number of miracles to the whole book might make more or lefs of that evidence neceffary for its authentication. But what form would fuch evidence then affume? It would become merely a copy of the writing in queftion. Nor fhould we obtain more af-furance, even if thefe miracles were all fepa-rately fpecified in any other book.' It would be ftill neceffary to examine that book by the fame canons of evidence, which we apply to the Gofpels. And of what defcription would that work be, which fhould contain all the miracles of our Saviour? We muft fuppofe that the miracles are all related in the fame manner as we find them in the evangelical hiftories, or otherwife they could not be iden-tified with thofe which they were defigned to confirm. If all the miracles were recorded, and nothing more, how could fuch docu-ments, even if they were contemporary works, corroborate the authenticity of the prefent Gofpels? The readers would juftly conclude, that the Gofpels were the perfect hiftory; and the other, the miracles detached from their connection with thefe very narratives. No advantage therefore is gained by recurring to other accounts, as if they would communicate authority to the Gofpels. The objection would have had fome appearance of reafon, if there had been but one Gofpel only; but, in the prefent circumftances, it is little lefs than abfurd to fay, that the miracles are " there, and " there only, related."

With refpect to prophecy, and its fuppofed fuperiority to miracles, as evidence, an attempt is made to deduce it from an imputed peculiarity in its nature, which, if true, would feem to prove, that it did, as a fpecies of evidence, exceed that of miracles. " The tefti- " mony of prophecy," it is faid, " does not " depend in the leaft upon the veracity or " credibility of the writer; but every man, " capable of underftanding the meaning of " the prediction, and comparing it with the " correfponding events, whereby it hath been, " or is completed, is a competent judge of the " degree of proof it affords." But this affertion of the infallibility of prophecy, as a teft, cannot be made with reference to the inftances of miracles and prophecy which the author himfelf has adduced as credible, on the " general teftimony," as he calls it, " of the " fpirit of prophecy." Where the interval between the prediction and the accomplifhment is very fhort, the credibility both of the miracle and the prophecy depends on the veracity of the writer, and the authenticity of the hiftory. In the other cafe, where prophecies allude to remote periods, are they to be confidered as infulated, and detached from the credibility of the reft of the book, in which they are inferted? We can fcarcely indeed admit, that they are independent of all connection with the other fubjects in it; but, even if we allow that this might be fo, yet we cannot feparate them from the age of the writer. If we do, it will be very difficult, perhaps impoffible, to determine, whether the prophecy preceded the alledged accomplifhment, or not: particularly, if they have no appropriate place in the writing to which we can affign their date, and no reference to collateral incidents. It is faid, that we have only to compare the prediction with the events to which it refers, in order to be convinced of the preeminence of prophecy over miracles. But the priority of the prophecy, which is the moft difficult part of the enquiry, is here affumed; and that priority can be determined by that external evidence only, of which it is declared to be independent. A prophecy, which is not fulfilled at the time predicted, is of no value; but how can we afcertain the fulfilment, if we cannot rely upon the veracity and credibility of hiftorical teftimony? The truth or falfehood of facts cannot be determined either by argument or prophecy, but by a fimple appeal to written evidence. If there be any reafon to doubt whether thefe predicted events actually came to pafs, to what other teftimony, befides that of hiftory, can we refort? Unbelievers have faid, on fo many occafions, that they do not require fpecification, that the hiftory of the accomplifhment was accommodated to the prophecy, and that they have no fatisfactory evidence of the divine origin of a prediction. But how fhall we ever be able to convince the profeffed infidel upon the principles of the author of "The Diffonance?"

It is further afferted, "that prophecy is "not only the moft fatisfactory, but alfo the "moft lafting fupernatural evidence of the "truth of any revelation." As the author of "the Divine Legation of Mofes[e]" has ex- preffed the fame remark partly in the fame, and partly in more forcible terms, and at greater length, I wifh to exhibit the pofition

---

[e] Book ix. c. 6. p. 275. 8vo.

which he affumes, of the fuperiority of prophecy over miracles, with the advantage of a
more expanded reprefentation. " But by the
" time this miraculous power began to fail,
" another was preparing to fupply its place,
" of ftill greater efficacy; I mean, that of
" prophecy. For the fovereign Mafter has
" been gracioufly pleafed to give to the later
" ages of the church *more than an equivalent*
" for what he had beftowed upon the earlier,
" in beginning to fhower down on his chofen
" fervants of the New Covenant the riches of
" prophecy, as the power of working miracles
" abated. So early was this preparation made
" for that *ftronger and more lafting fupport.*"
The epithet " lafting" may denote, either
fome intrinfic durability in the fupport itfelf,
as oppofed to that kind of fupport, whofe
ftrength and ftability diminifh from fome external caufes; or, as one that is not to be fuperfeded by fomething elfe; or, laftly, one
that is continued from one age to another.
" The evidence of miracles," according to the
fame writer, f " feems by its nature to leffen
" fomewhat by time; while that from pro-
" phecy gains ftrength by it, and grows more

---

f Divine Legat. b. ix. c. 6. p. 277.

" and more convictive, till the gradual and
" full completion of all its parts makes the
" fplendour of it irrefiftible." It is of importance to examine whether there is any
thing of this perifhable kind in the nature of
the evidence of miracles. Let us fuppofe that,
at a given period, a prophecy receives its completion ; and a miracle, unconnected with the
prophecy, is performed at the fame time. The
events, by which the prediction is fulfilled,
and the circumftances of the miracle, are both
recorded with the fame accuracy by contemporary writers. Ages pafs away before the
accomplifhment of another prophecy arrives.
During this interval, do the miracle exhibited,
and the prophecy fulfilled, continue to be refpectively of the fame authority and credibility, or do they not ? What caufe is there,
which fhall impair the credibility of the miracle, which fhall not equally affect the hiftory of the events, by which the prophecy is
fuppofed to be accomplifhed ? On the contrary, it is evident the foundation of the credibility both of miracles and of prophecy,
when recorded, is the fame ; that they both
equally derive their authority from their truth
and reality, and muft have, as written evidences, an equal durability and permanence.

Befides, what fhall we obtain, if we fuppofe predictions and their fulfilments to be
increafed to any number whatever; is this accumulation any thing more than an augmentation of the quantity of this kind of evidence?
As to the kind of evidence, it cannot acquire
any additional ftrength; and, indeed, though
the quantity of it may be augmented, it is but
an accumulation of the fame kind of materials, without connection or dependence. The
truth of each particular prediction is founded
upon the limitation of it to its own period,
and can neither be invalidated nor confirmed
by the truth or falfehood of thofe of higher
date, or different difpenfations. If a prophecy
be not fupported by external evidence, it is
nothing in itfelf; whereas the reality of a miracle may be examined by that evidence,
which in "The Diffonance" is preferred to
every other. We may enquire into the circumftances of its performance, its degree of
publicity, the apparent means employed, the
occafion, the completenefs of the effect produced, and the advancement of the intereft,
if any, of the agent. Thefe particulars belong
to the head of internal evidence, and the oral
delivery of a prophecy fcarcely admits of its
application.

Miracles are however thought to be fuperfeded by prophecy. " The fupernatural power
" of working miracles," it is faid, " was only
" intended to gain the new religion attention
" from the world, and to be a prefent tefti-
" mony of its divine origin and authority till
" the more lafting and more fatisfactory proof
" of completed prophecy could take place."
To affirm that any evidence poffeffes, on one
hand, fo much force, as to be fufficient to
prove, that the origin and authority of a new
religion are divine; and, on the other, to have
only a temporary duration; is inconfiftent and
unintelligible: for in whatever manner or degree we weaken the evidence, either as to its
foundation, its fupport, its extent, or its permanency, in the fame degree alfo its general
credibility is affected. Befides, we do not
perceive any fuch characteriftic difference in
thefe two fupernatural fpecies of teftimony,
miracles and prophecy, whatever there may
be in others, that miracles proved a religion
to be divine during the time that more lafting
and more fatisfactory evidence was preparing.
Completed prophecy could do no more than
prove a religion to be divine in its origin.
And this is fuppofed to have been previoufly
done by miracles. Can there be this ftrange

diverfity in the two, that one kind proves, for a time, the religion to be divine in its origin, while the other proves the fame to be divine for ever? The believers therefore of that new religion muft be divided into two claffes; thofe who receive it on the proof of miracles, and thofe who live when they can have the more lafting and more fatisfactory teftimony of prophecy: and yet both believe their religion to be divine in its origin. The introduction therefore of the new religion muft have been unfeafonable, if the beft proof of its divine authority were not ready at the time of its publication.

But the power of proving, even for a feafon, a new religion to be divine, cannot be afcribed to miracles, confiftently with the principles of " The Diffonance." The author does not attribute any credibility to miracles, not preceded by prophecy; and here miracles are fuppofed to have a reality when feparated from prophecy, and to anfwer a moft important purpofe. He has previoufly obferved, that the Jews were cautioned by Mofes, that they might be " deceived and deluded" by fuch evidence; and yet the fame evidence is in this paffage regarded as capable of proving, at leaft for a time, the origin of a new religion to be divine: and therefore is confidered by this writer as fatisfactory grounds of faith during that interval. The author alfo of the Divine Legation incurs a fimilar imputation of inconfiftency, when he afferts, that the evidence of prophecy " was not wanted while miracles " in a fort remained ;" and yet, in defcribing the preeminence of prophecy above miracles, he argues, that " this advantage is further " feen by its being lefs fubject to the miftakes " and fallacious impreffions of fenfe than mi- " racles are." Upon comparing thefe paffages we find, that in one a miracle is admitted to be a perfect proof, and in the other to be no proof whatever.

It was an argument of an acute metaphyfician, who was alfo the diftinguifhed hiftorian of our own country, that the teftimony. of facts became every day lefs credible by lapfe of time. But the exiftence of the hiftorical facts related of feveral eminent perfons of antiquity are at prefent more credible than they were ten centuries ago. The circumftances connected with their actions have been more accurately examined; they have been confirmed by the teftimony of ancient writers, fcarcely known, or perhaps difcovered, in thofe dark ages; by the accounts of modern

travellers; by the progrefs of geographical
fcience; by the adjuftment of chronology to
hiftory; and even by the evidence of ancient
memorials, brought to light in later ages.
Thefe concurring and auxiliary proofs have
removed difficulties in hiftory fo effectually,
that the facts of the ancient periods have now
a more fecure foundation of credibility than
many parts of our ᵍ own hiftory, the events
of which occurred at a much lefs confiderable
diftance of time. It may indeed be objected,
that there is only an accumulation of the fame
fpecies of evidence, and that time may affect
it in its largeft as well as fmalleft collections.
But it is difficult to conceive how time can
operate towards the invalidation of evidence
of this kind, otherwife than by the deftruction of the hiftorical memorials themfelves.
But this effect of time upon different kinds
of evidence would (if it did at all) equally
diminifh the credibility of a prophecy as well
as that of a miracle. The former is a matter of fact as well as the latter, and more
liable to have the credibility of its exiftence
injured by lapfe of time, as it muft always
precede, and often does precede, the fact of

ᵍ The hiftories of the families of the Lancaftrians and
Yorkifts. See Hume.

fulfilment, feveral centuries. The author of
" The Diffonance" inverts this order of things,
and the grounds of his conviction. He profeffes to believe facts in hiftory becaufe they
were predicted. Others believe the divine authority of prophecy becaufe the facts, which
are predicted, are hiftorically true. It is indeed abfurd to fuppofe, that prophecy can, at
the time of its delivery, be an evidence to the
truth of hiftory, as it muft be adduced as a
teftimony to what was not in exiftence at the
time it was pronounced. The prophet, according to the former fuppofition, muft have
forefeen the compofition of the hiftory, in
which fhould be recorded the accomplifhment
of his own predictions.

We may next enquire, whether any delufive miracles are related in fcripture to have
been performed by any agents, human or de-
moniacal. In " The Diffonance" we are informed, that " in the New Teftament our Sa-
" viour and his apoftles Paul and John have
" warned us, that the falfe and fabulous fu-
" perftition, which would for fo many cen-
" turies fupplant the true religion of the Gof-
" pel, would be embraced by the people, in
" confequence of their delufion, by figns and

" lying wonders, and all the deceivablenefs of
" unrighteoufnefs." The Apoftle does not fpeak
of falfe miracles ; and the miracles performed
by falfe prophets and deceivers, and even by
the man of fin himfelf, are no where faid to
have been illufory.   The trial confifted in refifting the efforts of an adverfary, who might
adduce true evidence for a pretended revelation,
and the delufion itfelf confifted in believing
that he came from God, not in believing falfe
evidence to be true.   It feems, that if in any
fingle inftance, well authenticated, the evidence of miracles had been rendered ambiguous by unreal phenomena, a revelation
would have been requifite, whenever a miracle was fubfequently performed, in order to
convince the mind that the fenfes had not
been deluded.   If we recur to the hypothefis
of " The Diffonance," that miracles in general, unlefs accompanied with prediĉtions,
may deceive the fpeĉtators, how are " lying
" wonders" to be diftinguifhed from any
others ?

The author of " The Diffonance" reproaches
the advocates of the truth of the Gofpel with
being unable to adduce any demonftrative
proof of its divine authority, and affirms, that

he has learnt from the [h] "only infallible au-
" thority the direct contrary." We are then
to confider whether completed prophecy has
in it the nature of demonftrative evidence.
" Demonftration," according to the definition
by Locke [i], " is the fhowing the agreement
" or difagreement of two ideas by the inter-
" vention of one or more proofs, which have
" a conftant, immutable, and vifible connec-
" tion one with another." It is evident from
this definition, that we are removed by the
author of " The Diffonance" into a very different fphere of objects, the relation of which
to each other is determined in a different
manner from that by which the reality of the
facts of a written hiftory is afcertained. We
are required to compare together a prophecy
and its accomplifhment, and to obferve their
difcrepancy, or agreement. But in this comparifon we are not to fhew the agreement of
two things by the intervention of a third, and
not to determine the equality, but the identity of both. This however is the laft procefs
of the enquiry. We muft previoufly know
that the prophecy is not a contemporary ab-

[h] Diffonance, Pref. p. vi.
[i] Effay on the Human Underftanding, book iv. ch. 15.
§. 1.

ftract of the hiftory. Befides, there is no
effential repugnance in their natures between
a falfe prophecy, and the alledged facts to
which it is faid to relate. In matters of quantity, the abfurdity or impoffibility at which
we arrive in our conclufions, fhew the errors
of our reafoning; but the obfcurity of prophecy does not confine the enquirer to one
conclufion, and exclude every other. The
difcovery of truth and falfehood may refult
from different modes of reafoning; but a difference in the effential properties of one fet
of fubjects prevents us from transferring a
mode of inveftigation, which is adapted to
determine their truth or falfehood, to others,
of which it is not the appropriate inftrument.

The author of " The Diffonance," the bold-
nefs of whofe affertions increafes with the
deficiency of his proofs, avers, that the orthodox religion, eftablifhed by Conftantine, is an
idolatrous fuperftition, an apoftafy from the
religion of Jefus Chrift, which it has fup-
planted; that it is the apoftafy predicted by
St. Paul and our Saviour, that it was occafioned by " turning away their ears from the
" truth, and liftening to fables, and believing
" falfehoods," " circumftances of the predic-

" tion, which, if taken together, cannot have
" been fulfilled, unlefs fables and falfehoods
" are at leaft intermixed with difregarded
" truth in thofe writings, to which the church
" of Conftantine hath in all ages appealed, as
" containing the grounds and foundation of
" every doctrine fhe hath taught[k]." The whole
of the argument then, as directed to the queftion of the alteration of the canon of Scripture, may be thus briefly reprefented. Miracles, unaccompanied with prophecy, are faid
to be fictitious; thofe books, which contain
miracles of this kind, may not be genuine, or
their authenticity may be fufpected in any
part. It is faid, that an apoftafy took place,
at an early period, from the pure religion of
Jefus Chrift; that the apoftates were, the
members of the church eftablifhed by Conftantine; that they were influenced by " fa-
" bles" and falfehoods; that thefe " fables"
muft have been contained in the prefent volume of the New Teftament; that we are to
feparate the falfe miracles from the true, and
the mythological interpolations from the genuine writings, and the remainder will be the
books of pure revelation, cleared from corrupt

[k] Diffonance, p. 26.

additions by the direction of prophetic intimations alone, without the affiftance of any external evidence.

Such then are the expedients, which it is neceffary to employ when we attempt to felect our own grounds of belief. The Almighty, we may be affured, has eftablifhed the connection between the proof and the thing to be believed, which cannot be broken with impunity. We cannot fay that we will believe on this kind of evidence, and on no other, or that we will reject one portion, and adopt the remainder, without believing, either upon lefs evidence than is afforded, or than ought to be required, or upon evidence, which, having no appropriate reference to the thing whofe exiftence or properties we admit, is equivalent to no evidence whatever. Even to affect habitually a faftidious fcepticifm in matters where the proof is fufficient and appropriate, is to trifle dangeroufly with the underftanding, and is an act not deftitute of criminality. The mind foon lofes its power of difcriminating between the various degrees and kinds of evidence which fhould authorize affent, till it is at laft characterized by a fort of credulous fatuity. It will not be eafy, and at length not poffible, to return at pleafure from

the defence of paradoxes, or the ftructure of
hypothefis, to the exercife of correct judgment; and the faculty, the ufe of which has
been long perverted, will be found at laft to
be irrecoverably impaired: and, according to
the language of revelation, which expreffes
not only the fentence of the Almighty upon
this abufe of the intellectual powers, but alfo
the general conclufion of a juft philofophy,
that voluntary deception is deftined to terminate in believing a lie.

SERMON III.

Pet. i. 16.

We have not followed cunningly devised fables.

WHETHER the Apostle intended to allude to the same species of falsehood, which St. Paul expresses by the same term, when he says, that some would turn " unto fables," it is not necessary to determine. There is indeed this difference, that what St. Paul describes as future, St. Peter speaks of as already existing and operating. The author of " The " Dissonance" is of opinion, that St. Paul refers, prophetically, to certain forged and spurious writings, and to corruptions of the Scriptures, which should appear, and which were to be instrumental in producing the apostasy, as he calls it, of the church of Constantine from the pure religion of Jesus Christ. He insists upon the probability, that the Scriptures were interpolated in the second and third centuries, when certain pseudo-evangelical books

F 2

were thought to have been fabricated. It is reprefented as a practice at this period " fo
" common amongft feveral, who called them-
" felves Chriftians, to produce entire pieces of
" their own, or others' forgery, under the
" name of any writer they pleafed, that, if
" what we call the fcriptures of the New Tef-
" tament were not fo tampered with, they
" are almoft the only writings upon the fame
" fubject, of thofe early times, which have
" efcaped free." It will therefore be necef-
fary to examine, whether the fame caufes, to which the compofition of fuch writings is to be afcribed, operated towards the corruption of the facred writings; whether fuch forged writings were ever fubftituted wholly, or in part, for the acknowledged records of Chriftianity; and, whether there is any ground to fuppofe, that they, who compofed, or they, who ufed thefe forged works, extended the impofition to the falfification of the genuine Scriptures.

" Irenæus," it is faid, " informs us, that
" the different fectarifts of thofe early ages
" had publifhed an innumerable multitude of
" apocryphal and fpurious fcriptures to afto-
" nifh the weak and ignorant." The mode of quoting and applying thefe words might

induce the reader to conclude, that the aſto-
niſhment of the weak and ignorant was the
ſole object of the ſectariſts of that age; that
they were ſatisfied with an inglorious triumph
of this kind; that the embarraſſment and perplexity of ignorance and imbecillity was the
ſole reward which they expected from their
laborious frauds. It is however evident, that
this could neither be the intention of the Father, nor is it indeed the import of his words.
He has ſimply deſcribed the effect of theſe
writings, and the kind of perſons whoſe minds
they influenced, without aſſigning any motives
to the authors. But were our adverſary more
correct in aſſigning motives for theſe corruptions, the corruptions would ſcarcely have
been extended to the Scriptures, merely for
the ſake of deluding ſuch guardians of their
integrity and purity as the weak and ignorant.

If he admits the authority of Tertullian to
be valid in one part of his narrative, when he
relates, that [a] an Aſiatic Prieſt had been detected in " aſcribing a work, entirely his own,
" to St. Paul," we may juſtly expect the declaration of the ſequel, that the offender was

---

[a] Lardner, vol. ii. p. 285.

depofed, and by thofe perfons who had the
fame veneration, as *he* profeffed, for the character of the Apoftle, and whofe worldly interefts and religious opinions were the fame.

That they, who had the temerity to forge,
would interpolate a writing, is perhaps a plaufible prefumption. But the authors of fuch
books would fcarcely extend their fraudulent
innovations to the Scriptures, becaufe alterations, favourable to their particular opinions,
could not always be reduced to the compafs
of a few fupplemental interpolations. When
a new fyftem of doctrine was to be framed,
the foundation muft have been broader and
deeper than the infertion of a fhort paffage,
or a fingle fentence. Thefe perfons therefore
compofed exprefs treatifes, in which they
might inculcate their tenets at large. It might
have been perhaps more eafy to miflead the
ancient Chriftians, *for a time,* by the production of a new volume, than by recent additions to the original collection of the facred
writings already in their hands. When an
evangelift or an apoftle had committed his
work to the cuftody of his converts, it had,
we may fuppofe, its due complement and full
perfection of parts. Nothing could fubfequently be added or fubftituted, or taken

away, without fome difhoneft purpofe. Whenever fuch an alteration took place, it might
have been known, becaufe it admitted of ready
proof; and muft have been known, becaufe
the Chriftian converts were qualified, merely
by habitual perufal, to detect the innovation.
They did not however authorize the inventions of men, who profeffed the fame fentiments with themfelves, and they were able
to difcriminate between fuppofititious and genuine writings.

It is faid, that there is an interpolation in
the Gofpel of St. Luke of fo late a date as the
third century, and that " we have the cleareft
" conviction of it;" " that Origen informs us,
" that feveral believers were offended with
" that part of St. Luke's Gofpel, wherein our
" Lord promifes the penitent thief upon the
" crofs, that he fhould that day be with him
" in paradife; that they declared, that the
" paffage was not in the older copies, but a
" late addition of fome interpolators." " It is
" clear," fays the author of The Diffonance[b],
" that as the doctrine of an intermediate ftate
" of purgatory and paradife gained ground in
" the orthodox church *after the fecond cen-*

[b] Diffonance, p. 29.

" *tury*, that particular paffage was interpo-
" lated to give the fanction of holy Scripture
" to the newly received doctrine." If this
interpolation were introduced before, or foon
after, the fecond century, Origen would fcarcely have related the furmifes of others, when
he could have afcertained, if not by his own
knowledge, certainly by teftimony contemporary with the interpolation, whether it were
a genuine part of the Gofpel, or not. If it
had exifted, continues the objector, in the
time of Tertullian, it could not have been
omitted " by him," when writing his treatife
upon the Soul, as it would " have fettled the
" point beyond difpute." If we confider the
tenour of Tertullian's difcourfe upon the Soul,
we may perhaps difcover a probable reafon
for the omiffion of a paffage apparently fo
well adapted to his fubject. When he refers
to the parable of the rich man and Lazarus,
his object is, not ᶜ " to confider exprefsly the
" intermediate ftate of the fouls of bad and
" good men after death," but to fhew the nature of the foul in general, and to derive from
thence a proof of its corporeality ᵈ. The pro-

ᶜ Diffonance, p. 29.
ᵈ See below the paffage of Irenæus for the meaning
of this term. It by no means implies mortality.

mife of our Saviour gave no direct information in what ftate the foul would then be, but
merely indicated to what place it fhould be
configned. It may then appear, that the citation of the paffage in queftion might, or
might not, be introduced into the treatife on
the Soul; that as the introduction of it would
not have ftrengthened, fo the omiffion could
not weaken, the argument; and the exiftence
of the paffage at the time of Tertullian can
fcarcely be difputed on the ground, that it
was not adduced, when inapplicable to the
reafoning of the writer. But this Father had
compofed another work, in which we might
have expected to find it, and probably fhould
have found it, if that treatife had been preferved. Indeed it is moft probable, that his
loft difcourfe " on Paradife [e]" originated in
the very paffage, whofe authenticity is queftioned. The authority therefore of Tertullian is not in favour of the hypothefis of interpolation.

· That Irenæus alfo fhould not " take the
" leaft notice of fo very remarkable a circum-
" ftance [f]," is to be afcribed to the fame rea-

[e] " Habes etiam de Paradifo a nobis libellum." Tertull. De Anim. §. 35. ad fin.
[f] Diffonance, p. 29.

fon as the filence of Tertullian. The courfe
of his argument did not lead to its confideration and infertion. " Our Lord," fays Irenæus, " has taught us moft fully in the para-
" ble of the rich man and Lazarus, that the
" foul does not only remain, (not paffing
" from body to body,) but alfo retains the
" figure of the body to which it is adapted,
" and that it recollects the works which it
" has done here, and now ceafes to perform."
In this parable " it is manifeftly declared, that
" the foul continues, and does not migrate
" from body to body, and preferves the re-
" femblance of the man, by which it is recog-
" nized; that it remembers thofe things which
" are in the world ; that Abraham poffeffed a
" prophetic power, and that to each nation
" is allotted a fuitable habitation, even before
" the judgment g." I am not further concerned [h] with thefe opinions, than to ftate,
that the principal object of this reafoning was
to prove, that the foul did not leave the original body, to which it was conjoined, in or-

---

g Irenæus cont. Hæref. lib. ii. c. 34.

[h] The controverfy on the nature of the foul originated
in a pamphlet written by H. Dodwell. His opponents
were, S. Clarke, Whitby, Norris of Bemerton, and Chif-
hull.

der to be united to another. Of what use
then would it have been to have alledged the
passage of St. Luke? The promise of an abode
in paradise did not imply the state and condition of the soul when it should be transferred thither. The mention therefore of this
place was omitted for the obvious reason,
that it was not suited to the purpose of the
writer.

With respect to the silence of Justin Martyr, it may not be easy to explain the reason
why he has not referred to this passage of St.
Luke, although [i] " he himself, Irenæus, and
" Tertullian, have quoted almost every other
" relating to the crucifixion." If the fact of
the crucifixion be taken as the subject with
which it is thought to be so intimately connected, that it could not be omitted, if it were
there related, the circumstance respecting the
penitent thief does not constitute a necessary
appendage to the principal transaction, and,
of course, the omission of it in the argument
of Justin does not bring any imputation upon
the genuineness of the passage.

When we recur to Origen's own account
of this part of St. Luke's Gospel, it is simply

[i] Dissonance, p. 29.

this: ᵏ" This saying of our Lord has so dif-
" turbed some persons, as appearing to them
" incongruous or dissonant, that they have
" ventured of themselves to suspect, that it
" was added to the Gospel by certain ˡ falsa-
" ries." Hence it is, at length, that we are
to derive " the clearest conviction" that it is
an interpolation, and that " some persons de-
" clared, that it was not in the older copies."

But the author of " The Dissonance" is not
satisfied with producing one suspected passage,
as a reason for extending his suspicions to
others, but at once affirms, that the testimony
of the witnesses ᵐ" cannot be depended upon
" respecting the writings of the several apo-
" stles and apostolic men, whose names they
" bear." He attempts to prove their incompetency generally by the following canon;
that, as there are " such very extraordinary,
" uselefs, ill-supported, improbable facts in
" the Gospels of Matthew and John," which
he supposes to have been the composition of

ᵏ Lardner's Credibility, vol. ii. p. 624. The version
of Lardner is slightly altered.

ˡ The word *falsaries* I find in Cockburn's Historical
Dissertation on the Books of the New Testament, and it
obviates the necessity of a great multiplication of words.

ᵐ Dissonance, p. 30—33.

perſons " infected with the groſſeſt ſuperſti-
" tious credulity," ſo no " ſuperſtitious and
" credulous perſon" can be admitted to be a
proper witneſs of the authenticity of any writings, in which ſuch facts are related. Let us
apply this rule to the writings of the martyr
Juſtin. That he employed an injudicious mode
of vindicating to the Romans the fact of our
Saviour's birth againſt the appearance of novelty, by producing analogies from their own
mythology, is, I think, the extreme point, to
which the accuſation can be extended ; but it
may be better to hear his own explanation of
the uſe which he made of the mythic ſyſtem.
" But be this known to you," ſays he [n], " that
" whatever things we declare, having learned
" them from Chriſt, and the prophets who
" preceded him, are alone true, and more an-
" cient than all writers ; and we do not think
" ourſelves worthy of regard becauſe we ſay
" the ſame things as thoſe writers, but be-
" cauſe we ſpeak what is true." Juſtin purſued his apology in this manner, becauſe it
was his opinion that the ſentiments of Plato
were to be traced in the writers of the Old
Teſtament, and that certain parts of the hea-

---

[n] Apol. i. p. 35. ed. Thirlb.

then mythology originated in the perverfion
of the language of the prophets refpecting our
Saviour, through the influence of evil dæmons. But that he fhould "illuftrate and
"plead for the toleration, by the Heathen
"Emperors, of the orthodox doctrine of the
"generation of the Word, becaufe of its re-
"femblance to the fabulous origin of their
"own deities, and juftify the doctrine of the
"incarnation by its fimilarity to the births of
"Æfculapius and Hercules, and the other il-
"luftrious god-men of Pagan mythology,"
and at the fame time "account for this fimi-
"larity between the orthodox doctrines and
"the fables of the poets, by afferting, that the
"poets delivered them through the infpira-
"tion of dæmons and evil geniufes, in order
"to prejudice the world againft the reception
"of thofe orthodox tenets, when the time
"fhould come for their promulgation," is to
attribute to the ancient Father inconfiftency,
aggravated by abfurdity. The only paffage,
to which the author of "The Diffonance"
may be fuppofed to refer, is the following, in
the firft Apology of the Father: "They, who
"teach the mythic compofitions of the poets,
"do not prefent to the youth who are in-
"ftructed any means of attaining to the truth;

and I prove that " they were uttered to de-
" ceive and feduce mankind through the agen-
" cy of evil dæmons." I conceive that it will
not be inferred from this paffage, that the belief in the influence of dæmons argues incapacity, or indeed the want of any quality,
which can detract from the competency of
Juftin's teftimony refpecting the authenticity
of the Gofpels.

The evidence of Irenæus alfo is thought to
be invalidated by a puerile defcription of the
ftate of the earth during the Millenium, a fubject where fancy and imagination might expa-
tiate without violating any other rules than
thofe of probability, and where the mifreprefentation of actual facts could not have any
place whatever.

The teftimony of Tertullian is weakened, it
is faid, becaufe, in his treatife on the Soul, he
relates concerning a perfon, with whom he
had been acquainted, fome extraordinary circumftances, which occurred after death. The
inference is, that we muft fufpect his teftimony refpecting the genuinenefs and authenticity of the Gofpels. There is not here, however, a fufficient indication of a credulous facility in receiving fuch accounts, and we are
not to infer that this was the propenfity of his

mind. The difqualification of the evidence of a witnefs muft principally proceed from fome moral incapacitation ; but fuperftition and credulity are not connected with any thing except paflive impofition. But in what manner is the imagination to be affected, or fuperftition and credulity to be operated upon, by fuch fimple facts as thefe ; that the Gofpels of Tertullian's age were thofe of the preceding times, and that fuch perfons, with fuch appellations, were generally reputed to be the authors ? This is what the Father believed and afferted, with ample means of information in his power to juftify his belief, and fubftantiate his affertions. But the credulity of Tertullian certainly did not appear even in the examination of *fuch* fubjects. He did not receive a forgery afcribed to St. Paul as an authentic writing of that apoftle ; and he knew how to vindicate the genuinenefs of the entire Gofpel of St. Luke againft the charge of corruption adduced by Marcion. The queftion then is, did he in the cafe of the Gofpels of St. Matthew and St. John fubmit his judgment to the authority of the credulous and fuperftitious, and the cunning, and exercife it only when he received that of St. Luke ? It feems, however, that Tertullian is to be confidered as a,

credulous, fuperftitious writer, and that his
evidence cannot be depended upon refpecting
the authenticity of the Gofpels of St. Matthew and St. John, which contain fuch facts
as he was always inclined to believe " very
" extraordinary, ill fupported, ufelefs, and im-
" probable." With refpect to the queftion of
authenticity, he could not be influenced by
fuperftition or credulity to afcribe the Gofpels
to one perfon rather than to another. Had
his credulity been as great as is reprefented,
the fpurious gofpels would have been more
acceptable to an intellect, in which the power
of diftinguifhing fiction from truth was fo
much impaired.

The preceding reafoning is followed by a
falfe but popular analogical illuftration. "When
" no court of juftice," it is faid, " will admit
" the teftimony of witneffes, who are them-
" felves notorioufly convicted of the fame
" crime of which the defendant is accufed,
" how can it be expected that any reafonable
" unprejudiced perfon fhould admit fimilar
" evidence to be of weight in a cafe of the
" greateft importance poffible, not to himfelf
" only, but to the whole human race ?" It
is here firft affumed, that the Gofpels contain
ill fupported and improbable facts, and then

G

it is afferted that thofe, who do *not* think
them improbable and ill fupported, are unworthy of credit on that account. , This au-
dacious propofition is fuppofed to be confirmed by the preceding analogy.   But let us
obferve the practical effect of the principles *
of "The Diffonance" in the very example
which is produced to illuftrate and confirm
this argument.   A witnefs lays his hand on
the Gofpels, and attefts the truth of his alle-
gations by profeffing, as a fanction of his own
veracity, a belief in the authority of thefe facred books.   If the judge maintained the doctrines of "The Diffonance," he muft, confiftently with fuch opinions, reject the evidence altogether, or reprefent the witnefs as
unworthy of attention on account of his credulous weaknefs in paying any regard to fuch
"fuperftitious, ill fupported, improbable" narratives.

Credulity and fuperftition often prevail in
minds which are not weak, and in moral dif-
pofitions which are characterized by rigorous
veracity.   But to reprefent the martyr Juftin
as an unfit witnefs of the authenticity of the
Scriptures, becaufe he believed in the agency
of dæmons, is to affign a caufe which has no
relation to the imputed effect.   Were fuch

reafoning admitted, it would invalidate all the
hiftories of our own country, which preceded
the laft century, and indeed thofe of Europe
to a ftill later period. The great Lord Bacon
was himfelf a believer in the influence of
°dæmons, and in the ufe of the ftudy of reformed Paftrology. By that fpecies, which he

° Cæterum fobria circa illos (Angelos fcil.) inquifitio,
quæ vel per rerum corporearum fcalam ad eorum naturam pernofcendam afcendat, vel in anima humana, veluti
in fpeculo, eam intueatur, neutiquam prohibetur. *Idem
de fpiritibus ftatuendum immundis, qui a ftatu fuo deci-
derunt. Confortium cum iis, atque ufus operæ eorum illi-
citus eft; multo magis qualifcunque cultus vel veneratio.*
At contemplatio et cognitio illorum naturæ, poteftatis,
illufionum, non folum ex locis fcripturæ facræ, fed ex ra-
tione, aut experientia, haud poftrema pars eft fapientiæ
fpiritualis. Sic certe Apoftolus, ftratagematum ejus non
ignari fumus. Ac non minus dæmonum naturam invefti-
gare in theologia naturali conceditur, quam venenorum
in phyfica, aut vitiorum in ethica. De Augment. Scient.
lib. ii. c. 2. p. 97.

P Adhibetur autem aftrologia fana; ad prædictiones
fidentius, ad electiones cautius, ad utraque autem intra
terminos debitos. Prædictiones fieri poffint, de cometis
futuris, qui (ut noftra fert conjectura) prænunciari poffunt: et de omni genere meteororum, de diluviis—bellis,
feditionibus, fectis, tranfmigrationibus populorum; denique de omnibus rerum vel naturalium vel civilium moti-
bus, aut innovationibus majoribus. De Augm. Scient.
lib. iii. c. 4. p. 103, 104.

It is curious to examine the conftituents of the aftrolo-

diftinguifhes as the aftrologia fana, he allows may be foretold, not only phyfical events, as meteors, deluges, and tempefts, but alfo wars, feditions, the rife of religious fects, and popular ᑫ emigrations.

gia fana. *Primo*, in aftrologiam fanam recipiatur doctrina de commixtionibus radiorum, conjunctionibus fcilicet, et oppofitionibus et reliquis fyzygiis, five afpectibus planeta-

tranfitum, et locationem fub iifdem fignis, etiam huic parti de commixtionibus radiorum affignamus.

Secundo, recipiantur acceffiones fingulorum planetarum propius ad perpendiculum aut receffiones ab ipfo, fecundum regionum climata.

Tertio, recipiantur apogæa et perigæa planetarum cum debita difquifitione, ad quæ pertineat planetæ vigor in fe ipfo, ad quæ vicinitas ad nos. *Quarto*, recipiantur (ut fummatim dicamus) omnia reliqua accidentia motus planetarum. *Quinto*, recipiantur, quæ naturas ftellarum, five erraticarum, five fixarum, in propria fua effentia et activitate, refecare et detegere ullo modo queant ; qualis magnitudo ; qualis color et afpectus ; qualis fcintillatio et vibratio luminis &c.

Pofremo, recipiantur etiam ex traditione naturæ et inclinationes planetarum particulares, atque etiam ftellarum fixarum ; quæ, quandoquidem magno confenfu tradantur, non leviter (præterquam ubi cum phyficis rationibus plane difcordant) rejiciendæ funt. *Atque ex talibus obfervationibus coagmentatur aftrologia fana*; et fecundum eas tantum, fchemata cæli et componere et interpretari oportet. De Augm. Scient. lib. iii. cap. 4. p. 102, 133.

ᑫ De Augment. Scient. lib. iii. c. 4.

But credulity and fuperftition are not the greateft defects in the teftimony of the ancient Chriftians. They difregarded " honour and " veracity (as it is faid) in whatever con- " cerned the caufe of their particular fyftem." " They have deftroyed (according to the af- " fertion of their enemies) every writing upon " the fubject of Chriftianity, which they could " not by fome means or other apply to the " fupport of their own fuperftition." The writings of " the many," alluded to in St. Luke's preface, are fuppofed to be fome of thofe which have been deftroyed ; and, from the multiplicity of thefe and other works, the pernicious " induftry" of the Fathers has been denominated by the author of " The Diffo- " nance," as, if it were true, it might juftly be denominated, " fingular." But we are not informed that there was any thing fingular in the mode of preferving the Gofpel of St. Luke which was contemporary. This Evan- gelift however merely intimates, that others had written upon the fame fubject before, and that his inducement to compofe another nar- rative was, a defire to communicate his own correct information to his own converts. He fent his hiftory into the world to be received or rejected on the fame grounds as the others, relating to the fame events, were to be received or rejected.

The names however of the authors of the various books are not preferved, although the author of " The Diffonance" has computed the number thus fuppreffed with a ʳ minutenefs and particularity, which has no foundation in the hiftory of the time. He muft therefore be regarded as attempting not to fupply by fpeculation the events of that period, but to forge annals to fupport an hypothefis. But in proportion as he aggravates the criminality of the early Fathers, by multiplying the number of gofpels originally written, in the fame proportion does he augment the difficulty of their project. If fuch books were received as the rule of faith, and confequently preferved in the different Chriftian churches that were founded at that time, the difficulty of deftroying them is ftill further increafed. Could they annihilate, do we fuppofe, all the Gofpels ufed in the Chriftian affemblies at the places fpecified in " The Diſ-" fonance," ˢ " at Jerufalem, in Samaria, Phœ-" nice, Syria, in every province of Afia Mi-

---

ʳ Evanfon's Letter to Dr. Prieftley's Young Man, p. 27.
ˢ Ibid.

" nor, and in many cities of Macedonia and
" Greece ?" We may however enquire, why
they permitted the fpurious and apocryphal
work of their own refpective periods to de-
fcend, even in fragments, to thefe times. Is
it not extraordinary, that this intention, purfued from the age of one Father to the age of
another, fhould have been a difcovery referved
for the prefent generation. Such writings,
and particularly thofe received by the early
Chriftian churches, if ever they had an exiftence, would have been in the careful cuftody
of thofe who ufed them; and they would have
maintained their credit on the ground of their
original reception. Surely we are juftified in
expecting fome evidence that fuch books were
written, if we are deprived of the opportunity
of examining their contents. The whole hypothefis however of "The Diffonance" refpecting the deftruction, or even the exiftence
of thofe books, refts entirely with the author
of that work; who produces no authority for
his affertions, and therefore the denial of the
truth of the fuppofition is at leaft as valid
againft it as the affumption of its reality can be
in its favour. The hypothefis is of large extent.
It involves various propofitions; that twenty
gofpels were compofed at the time of which

St. Luke fpeaks in his proem; that, at a diftance of half a century, fixteen more were
added to thefe; that the Chriftians, and particularly the Chriftian Fathers, were inftrumen-
tal at leaft in the deftruction of thefe writings;
that the books thus deftroyed contained facts
or doctrines contradictory to thofe adopted by
the Fathers. Of thefe pofitions he produces
no proof, not even the names of the authors,
on whofe imaginary teftimony he relies fo fe-
curely. The Greek and Roman hiftories, and
indeed every hiftory that was ever written,
might be invalidated by fuppofing in the fame
manner the exiftence of hiftorians, whofe
works and names are now loft, who might
have given different accounts of the tranfactions of thofe nations from any that are recorded by the writers, whofe hiftories we now
poffefs.

The number of gofpels, fuppofed once to
have exifted, is derived from the unfupported
conjecture, that each Chriftian church had an
original gofpel, compofed for its peculiar ufe.
Yet ᵗ Eufebius relates, and his authority will
avail where it has not been queftioned, and it
will not be queftioned merely becaufe he was

ᵗ Hift. Ecclef. lib. iii. c. 37.

an ecclefiaftic of rank, and an ecclefiaftical hiftorian, that in the fecond century great numbers of perfons[u], " difciples of the Apo-" ftles, travelled over the world, building up " churches where the Apoftles had before laid " the foundations, and preaching the faith of " Chrift in other places, which had never " heard of it before, carrying along with them " the written Gofpels." This teftimony, then, directly fubverts this pofition, (and the teftimony is without fufpicion, becaufe it was never defigned to be thus applied,) that, as the number of churches increafed, diftinct gofpels were written for their inftruction by perfons, who, as the author of " The Diffonance" expreffes their qualifications, had been " edu-" cated from their infancy in the religion of " Jefus Chrift, as taught by the Apoftles them-" felves." And further, Marcion, who had an opportunity of knowing what other works there were, which in authority might vie with that of the acknowledged Gofpels, was reduced to the neceffity of adapting the Gofpel of St. Luke to his own views and opinions.

Neither can we obtain any information refpecting thefe fuppofed writings from any evi-

---

[u] See Richardfon on the Canon of the New Teft.

dence refpecting their deftruction. When copies of writings were to be multiplied by
tranfcription, the number of copies would be
in proportion to the efteem in which the work
was held; and the defire of obtaining a copy
would of courfe be general, not merely as a
matter of curiofity or learning, but from a fear
of miftaking the rule of Chriftian conduct.
Any defect therefore, either in the importance
of the contents, or in the affurances refpecting
its authenticity, or the appearance of better
writings, would make the work itfelf to be
lefs regarded, and of courfe caufe copies to be
lefs fought after, and in time to be neglected,
and at length to be loft altogether. If this
reafoning will not account for the lofs of ancient works, as not probable in itfelf, in what
manner could the Fathers proceed to effect
the pofitive deftruction of any writings, which
derived their value from the inftruction and
education of their authors in the Chriftian religion, " as taught by the Apoftles ?"

It is to be remarked, that, although the accufation extends to a body of perfons, the
Fathers of the church, and their fucceffors,
yet not one is fpecified by name who is faid
by the author of " The Diffonance" to have
fuggefted, or to have attempted to execute,

this moſt extraordinary projeɛt. How then
ſhall we account for this ſubtle reſerve? Only
one reaſon for it can be produced; that we
know enough of the biography of the Fathers
to repel a charge ſo malevolent. But our information reſpeɛting the early periods of the
hiſtory of Chriſtianity is not ſo complete as to
enable us always to oppoſe licentious ſuppoſi-
tions with direɛt faɛts. We are obliged therefore to have recourſe to probability, where
proofs cannot be had; and this has already
occurred too often, and muſt occur again more
frequently, from the nature of this contro-
verſy. We may therefore enquire, in what
ſituation would thoſe churches have been left
which had been accuſtomed to uſe the writings that the Fathers had deſtroyed? Would
they adopt others, authorized by perſons who
were not diſciples of the Apoſtles, and ſilently
acquieſce in the loſs of works, which were
written by thoſe who were known to be ſo,
and when ſo few years had elapſed ſince they
had received them from ſincere depoſitaries of
the faith?

We may alſo enquire, of what nature were
thoſe books, which, by an ediɛt of Diocletian,
at the commencement of the fourth century,
were demanded of the Chriſtians by the impe-

rial inquifitors. The furrender of their facred
books was the object of this law, which was
enforced by fanguinary penalties. But whether the Roman emperors perfecuted the poffeffors of one fet of books, or the Fathers employed fubtlety to deftroy another collection,
neither the one nor the other were able to
effect their intention. The inquifitors could
not get into their power all the copies of thefe
writings, nor the perfons of all who ufed
them. Had this been the confequence of fuch
meafures, it might have happened that the
churches would have loft altogether, at this
time, their copies of the facred writings. The
decree of Diocletian was executed in Gaul, in
Africa, and in Paleftine ; but the traitors did
not, as far as we know, vilify the authority of
their books, even as a timid ftratagem to preferve them, nor did they intimate in this apoftafy any fufpicion of a fpurious original.
Why fhould the Chriftians deliver their books
with lefs reluctance to the officers of the Emperor, who could punifh oppofition with death,
than to the Fathers and their agents, who
could only offer in exchange fpurious works
for genuine, fince we may be affured that they
would not have been fatisfied without having
fome fubftitute for the books which they had

furrendered? How the ancient Fathers could allow one work to be tranfmitted, and fupprefs another, of apparently higher authority, muft be explained by fome extraordinary influence, which it is not recorded they ever obtained over the minds of Chriftians in general. It fhould alfo be confidered, that all the Fathers were not in public ftations, and thofe who were could have had only a very limited fphere of power. Befides, the foundation of the authority which their writings have at prefent is chiefly derived from their proximity to the times concerning which they write; a circumftance which, during their lives, could not be the fource of any extraordinary or particular influence, as they muft have only participated in it with others their contemporaries.

Nothing of this kind would have enabled them to tranfmit to pofterity a fet of fpurious evangelical hiftories, which might have been confuted by records, the authenticity of which might have been confirmed by perfons, who had the fame opportunities of examining them as the Fathers themfelves had.

To provide for the tranfmiffion of their own works would have required the formation of a moft fingular confederacy. They did not however fucceed in this; for moſt of the valuable compoſitions of the early times are loſt, notwithſtanding the intereſt which the orthodox evidently had, according to the hypotheſis of " The Diſſonance," in preſerving them from neglect or injury.

It is more than implied in another objection, that the Fathers inſidiouſly permitted " the works of a few other writers to be " tranſmitted, who were all of them not only " converts from Paganiſm, but men who had " been educated and well inſtructed in the " philoſophic fchools of the later Platoniſts " and Pythagoreans." The author of " The " Diſſonance" folicitouſly inſiſts upon the authority of a celebrated writer on eccleſiaſtical hiſtory for affirming, that " the Chriſtian " teachers, who had been inſtructed in the " fchools of fophiſts and rhetoricians, trans- " ferred the arts of their maſters to the Chriſ- " tian diſcipline, and adopted that mode of " contending with their adverſaries, in which " truth was not ſo much their aim as victory; " and they were confirmed in this practice by " the Platoniſts, who aſſerted, that a man did " no wrong who ſupported truth, when hard " preſſed, by deceit and lies. This vicious " eagerneſs not to vanquiſh their adverſaries

" by reafon and fair argument, but to over-
" throw and confound them, produced fo
" many books, falfely attributed to perfons of
" great eminence and renown, to oppofe to
" their antagonifts." Whatever abfurd opinions the latter Platonifts conjoined with the
profeffion of Chriftianity, or whatever unworthy methods they might employ in their controverfies, their teftimony is not affected where
no philofophical or theological fubtlety was to
be difcuffed, no interpretation of Scripture
propofed, and where particularly no difpute
exifted concerning the fubject of their evidence. In this cafe it is of no moment whether or not the witnefs were a philofopher
before he was a Chriftian. His philofophy
was an inftrument, which, if he had been difpofed to ufe it, he could not apply to the fimple fact of what books of the New Teftament
were received in his time. But the martyr
Juftin, although a philofopher, was not one of
the latter Platonifts; and what books he confidered as authentic is not determined by a
formal or authoritative enumeration, but his
teftimony is collected from incidental citations introduced, as various topics fuggefted
their application.

It has been afferted by the author of the

" Free Enquiry into the Miraculous Powers of
" the early Ages," that forged " books are
" applied to the defence of Chriftianity by the
" moft eminent Fathers of the fame ages, as
" true and genuine writings, and of equal au-
" thority with the Scriptures themfelves[x]."
This affertion has not indeed remained till this
time without fome examination; but it may
not be ufelefs to enquire, how it is fupported
in the inftance of one Father, whofe valuable
teftimony and extenfive learning have been
depreciated by this cenfure; I mean, Clement
of Alexandria.

The charge, which I propofe to repel on
the ground of exprefs enquiry, is this; that
Clement has quoted the Preaching of Peter
as authentic Scripture, and has affociated the
verfes of the Sibyll with the prophecies of the
Old Teftament. This Father has frequently
appealed to the firft Epiftle of Peter; and,
from a comparifon of his mode of citing the
genuine writings of the Apoftle himfelf with
that of the work, entitled, the Preaching of
Peter, it appears, that he did not confider the
latter as authentic Scripture. He cites the
firft Epiftle of Peter either without any in-

[x] Dr. Middleton, Introd. Difc. vol. i. p. 75.

troduction y, or with the fimple addition z of
his name, or with the preface, " this is chiefly
" to be had in mind, which was faid a holily,"
or by the Holy Spirit ; the " Teacher fays b,"
a name which in his work with this infcription he afcribes to the Lord ; " the Lord
" fays c;" " the admirable Peter fays d;" " Pe-
" ter in the Epiftle e;" " Peter in the Acts f."
On the other hand, in the various paffages,
where he cites the Preaching of Peter, the
extracts are not introduced with any terms
expreffing peculiar approbation, and much lefs
which afcribe to them any authority. The
form is univerfally either " the Preaching of
" Peter," or " Peter in the Preaching," unaccompanied with any of thofe emphatic additions, which he ufes in fpeaking of the canonical Epiftle. Befides, he is always cautious
to mark the citation from the Preaching ;
whereas he is not always folicitous to fhew
that his citations from the authentic writings
are to be found there particularly, but only

y Clem. Alexandrin. p. 40.   z Ib. p. 103.
a Ib. p. 244.   b Ib. p. 250.
c Ib. p. 261.   d Ib. p. 457.
e Ib. p. 473. 525.   f Ib. p. 646.

in fome part of the general collection of the
infpired writings [g].

With refpect to the infertion of paffages
from the Sibylline verfes, it cannot be alledged that Clement has ranked them in authority with the prophecies of the Old Teftament, although he mentions them together.
" Let the Sibyll firft fing to us the hymn of
" falvation:" and, after fome remarks on the
citation, he proceeds ; " But Jeremiah the
" prophet, full of all wifdom, or rather the
" Holy Spirit, fpeaking through Jeremiah,
" points out God to us." Wherever this Father traces a fimilarity of fentiment, he tran-
fcribes promifcuoufly from facred and profane
authors ; and out of fourteen paffages of the
Sibylline verfes, two only accompany citations
from Scripture : fo that we cannot deduce
from their combination in this manner with
Scripture any fuppofed equality in authority
which we may not, with as much propriety,
attribute to his other illuftrations of the fame
fubject, adduced at the fame time from Homer, Orpheus, and Xenophon.

[g] It does not feem " fo difficult" as Lardner thought
" to decide what authority Clement affigned to this
" book." Vol. ii. p. 239.

Another circumftance, fuppofed to counteract the teftimony of the Fathers relative to
the books of Scripture which were received
in their refpective ages, is difcovered [h] " in the
" pretenfions of the Fathers of the orthodox
" church of the latter half of the fecond cen-
" tury, and of the third, and of the members
" of the fame church after it was eftablifhed
" by Conftantine during feveral centuries, to
" the fupernatural power of working mira-
" cles." Gregory of Neo-Cæfarea, who lived
in the middle of the third century, obtained,
from a reputed power of performing miracles,
the appellation of Thaumaturgus. But if the
Fathers of the latter half of the fecond century, and of the third, had poffeffed the fame
power, the cognominal appellation would have
conferred little or no diftinction upon one
who only participated in a common gift. He
does not affirm, in the fragments of his own
writings, that he performed any miracles; and
his life was written by a perfon who lived a
century fubfequent to thefe times, and who
writes in a ftyle which renders the truth of
the whole narrative fufpicious. The Fathers
themfelves do not profefs ever to have had

[h] Diffonance, p. 37.

H 2

this power, although they relate its effects, as matters of history, when exercised by others. The life of Chryfoftom has been compofed in a fimilar manner. He avers in his own works, with much repetition, that miracles were no longer performed ; and yet his biographer fpecifies in detail miracles of various kinds, which the Father is faid to have wrought for the benefit of the fick.

It may be difficult to afcertain what period is comprifed in thofe " feveral centuries" before alluded to, which fucceeded the age of Conftantine. In the eighth century, in the time of Gregory I. " the miraculous powers" had ceafed in the church by his own reluctant acknowledgment. Even at the clofe of the fourth century Chryfoftom fays, " But be-" caufe miracles are not wrought now, do " not therefore conclude that none were " wrought at that time ; for then they were " ufeful, but now they are not ufeful:" and in another place he afferts, " God has now " ceafed to work miracles." I conceive however, that when this Father relates that " the " afbes of the holy martyrs repel dæmons," we are not to infer that there is any contradiction in his pofitions. The relics of martyrs, whether they are faid to have counteracted the influence of dæmons, or to have cured diſeaſes, were ſtill never conſidered as miracles, or as exceptions to the ceſſation of miracles, or as contributing to the diffuſion of Chriſtianity, as proofs of its truth. The ſame Father who records the property of repelling dæmons, ſuppoſed to be inherent in the relics, and even communicated to the receptacles of their aſhes, teſtifies alſo, that miracles were no longer needful; ſo that we cannot regard this power as any thing more than a kind of honorary and inferior energy, or an attribute derived from the veneration of the faithful, and which extended no farther than to augment the re-putation of the reſpective martyr.

It appears therefore that the Fathers did not pretend to the " ſupernatural power of " working miracles" at the periods which " The Diſſonance" aſſigns, nor indeed at any other whatever. The concluſion alſo, which we are required to draw, is; that the teſti-mony of thoſe, who pretended to miraculous powers, is not credible, not merely with re-ſpect to the exiſtence of ſuch powers at that time, and in thoſe perſons, but with reſpect to the authenticity of the books of the New Teſtament; a concluſion which, if correct,

would ftill fall fhort of its objeƈt, for other.
evidence would remain after the invalidation
of that of the Chriftian Fathers.

The authenticity of the books of the New
Teftament is thus impeached by a tenor of
argument fo dark and devious, that the inveftigation, with whatever profeffions it may be
accompanied, will convince us, that truth was
not the objeƈt of the enquiry, unlefs fallacy is
to be confidered as the moft approved guide
to certainty, and fophiftry the moft faithful
auxiliary of reafon. To cite the opinion of
one Father on a fubjeƈt of inferior importance,
and not conneƈted with faƈts, for the purpofe
of invalidating his teftimony upon every point
of great moment, and with the means of full
information ; to attribute to the Fathers in general the affumption of the power of working
miracles, that he may ground an indefinite
accufation of their moral incompetency as
witneffes ; to reprefent as faƈts what is not
recorded in any hiftory ; to advance as truth
what is only remotely probable ; are arts,
which can be employed by a difputant only
with the irrational expeƈtation, that perfons
in general would complacently receive, without fufpicion, as firmly eftablifhed truths, re-

fults, to which it can be objected, that they have been obtained by means, the ufe of which is effentially inconfiftent with perfonal veracity and integrity.

SERMON IV.

2 PET. i. 16.

We have not followed cunningly devifed fables.

DURING the interval between the afcenfion of our Lord and the publication of the
Gofpels in writing, the Chriftian difpenfation
remained among the converts in the form of
tradition. As it was at firft orally communicated to them, it was fubject to many of the
imperfections of oral communication. Something might have been added, or fuppreffed,
or. mifreprefented, or mifunderftood, according to the prejudices, or zeal, or weaknefs of
converts,. or the artifices of falfe teachers,
when the only ftandard to which they could
refer any variations, either in the doctrine or
the hiftory, was the recollection of one party,
oppofed to the alledged contrary recollection of
another. The Apoftles indeed received a promife,
that the Holy Ghoft fhould bring all· things,
which Jefus. Chrift had faid on earth, to their

remembrance; but we have no authority to fay, that this affiftance was continued to other converts. We do not expect that the providence of God, which does not act in vain, fhould neceffarily have interpofed in this manner after the knowledge of the Gofpel had been fo widely diffufed by its firft teachers, who alone were favoured with fupernatural ftrength of recollection. The extent of country, and the diverfity of people to whom the Gofpel had been communicated, enfured, in a great degree, truth and correctnefs, whenever it fhould be committed to writing. What the circumftances were which might fuggeft the neceffity of perpetuating the facts and doctrines of Chriftianity in written records at one time rather than at another, we are not informed. St. Luke was induced to compofe his Gofpel by the appearance of other accounts of the fame facts. The publication of other narratives by other teachers would make the converts of the Apoftles alfo expect, that the fyftem of their religion fhould be preferved in the fame permanent manner by fome of their original inftructors. It is an enquiry therefore more curious than neceffary, to determine precifely the refpective dates of the firft three Gofpels. For, whether we adopt

the dates which contract, or thofe which enlarge, the interval between the afcenfion of
our Lord and the appearance of the Gofpels
in writing, ftill Chriftianity had been preached
for a period of fufficient duration to enfure
the complete inftruction of the new difciples
in the nature of its doctrines, and the hiftory,
of its author. We muft fuppofe that the early
teachers of this religion were qualified for
their functions by the poffeffion of accurate
information on the topics peculiar to this religion. For we cannot imagine that, as far as
correct knowledge and fincerity of intention
were concerned, the qualifications for teaching could be in any refpect inferior to thofe
which would be required for writing a Gofpel. We are told indeed, by the beft teftimony, what were the qualifications of the
perfon who was admitted to participate in
the labours of the Apoftles. In fupplying
the place of the traitorous difciple, it was
judged neceffary that his fucceffor fhould have
a perfonal knowledge of our Saviour, his actions, and his teaching. " Wherefore of thefe
" men, which have companied with us all the
" time that the Lord Jefus went in and out
" among us, beginning from the baptifm of
" John, unto that fame day that he was taken

" up from us, muſt one be ordained to be a
" witneſs with us of his reſurrection ª." Theſe
qualifications are not to be reſtricted to the
knowledge, by which they might be able to
verify the identity of our Lord's perſon. They
were deſigned to include a perfect acquaint-
ance with the hiſtory of our Saviour's life,
and of the tranſactions which related to him
during his abode on earth, of his reſurrection
from death, of his aſcenſion into heaven, of
the doctrines which he communicated, and of
the precepts which he enjoined. A perfect
knowledge of all theſe important facts muſt
of itſelf have imparted high authority to the
preaching of the Apoſtles, and was intended
to have a due and correſponding influence on
their hearers. Their natural and uninſpired
teſtimony was not an oſtenſible inſtrument,
liable to be ſuperſeded by others of greater
utility and efficacy, on which their ſuccefs
principally and really depended. The requi-
ſites above deſcribed were conſidered as indiſpenſable, notwithſtanding the aſſiſtance which
the ſucceſſor of Judas would receive from the
Holy Spirit, in common with the other Apoſtles.

ª Acts i. 21, 22.

In another view it appears extraordinary, that thofe men, who were qualified as eye-witneffes for preaching the Gofpel, fhould afterwards find it expedient, through a confci-oufnefs of inadequate knowledge, to recur to documents of inferior authority as neceffary for perfecting their brief hiftories. Their previous preaching furnifhed their converts with a ftandard, by which the accuracy and. confiftency of the written Gofpel might be determined. They could not. preach doctrines and relate facts perfonally, and afterwards record others, inconfiftent with thefe, when the means of detection were obvious to all. The hifto-rical form given to the fubftance of their religion would enable the new difciples to recol-lect a greater portion of it, and with more correctnefs, than if it had confifted of a fyftem of abftract doctrines and unconnected precepts. The occafions, on which our Lord's precepts were delivered, have a certain natural and neceffary connection with the precepts themfelves, that imprints them more perma-nently on the memory. It is not neceffary to determine whether the members of the newly-eftablifhed churches received from heaven any peculiar aid, by which the naturally fugitive impreffions of oral teaching might re-

main perfect in the recollection till the information was committed to writing. Without
any intention of diminishing the meafure of
the promifed gifts of the Holy Spirit, we need
not infift upon the neceffity of their communication in this inftance, becaufe the natural,
although providential means, derived from a
more early publication of the Gofpels, were
probably interpofed before the evangelical traditions might require either renewal or correction. [b] Thofe writers, who affign dates to
the firft three Gofpels at a confiderable interval from the time of our Lord's afcenfion,
oblige us to fuppofe, either that the primitive
Chriftians could not be left to the fole direc-

[b] The human motives for committing the Gofpel to
writing are well affigned by a friend, whofe remarks I
have inferted in another part of this Difcourfe; the Rev.
R. Warner of Bath. " To me it appears, that the Gof-
" pels were written, not fo much to correct exifting er-
" rors, as to prevent future ones; to embody and perpe-
" tuate thofe facts and doctrines, the reality and truth of
" which the evangelical writers ' moft furely believed,'
" and what they would of courfe be anxious to put toge-
" ther and deliver in a written form, for the ufe of their
" hearers and profelytes, as early as they conveniently
" could, that in cafe of their own departure the Chriftian
" fyftem might remain with them perfect and complete.
" This has always weighed with me in adopting the hy-
" pothefis of the *earlieft* dates of the Gofpels."

tion of tradition for fo long a time without the danger of their lofing or impairing, through imperfect recollection, the effential doctrines of their religion, fo as to be unable to afcertain clearly the truth and the correctnefs of the written documents, when they were deli-vered to the Chriftian churches; or elfe, that fome fupernatural affiftance was afforded to ftrengthen their natural intellectual powers, both for receiving and retaining divine truth.

In a " Differtation concerning the Origin " and Compofition of the three firft canonical " Gofpels," it is faid, that the Apoftles had made communications of fome of the evangelical facts, of which they had been eye-witneffes. Their firft communications, as we know from c Irenæus, were oral, and confti-tuted the preaching by which they converted the nations to Chriftianity. Their written communications would naturally be addreffed to thofe, who had been their hearers; to thofe, who would preferve what was written on account of their recollection of the effect which had been produced on themfelves by what they had heard. It is not probable that the

---

c Non enim per literas traditam illam (veritatem fc.) fed per vivam vocem. Adv. Hæref. lib. iii. c. 2.

Apoſtles would make communications, whatever others might do, without directing them
to ſome uſeful or preciſe object. That object
was, the confirmation of their converts in the
Chriſtian faith, which required the written to
be no leſs ſatisfactory and complete than the
oral communication, and perhaps nearly the
ſame. Any hypotheſis therefore muſt fail,
which ſuppoſes, that the communications
made by the Apoſtles were ſo imperfect as
to form, " not a finiſhed hiſtory," but only
" materials for a hiſtory." On the contrary,
it appears probable that the written apoſtolical
communications were the preſent Goſpels,
and as perfect in form as was neceſſary for an
hiſtorical compoſition, intended for the explanation and proof of the truth of the Chriſtian
diſpenſation, and the foundation and teſt of
all future teaching. If there be any particular
advantage in point of argument in the re-
motenefs of the date of the facts upon which
I have reaſoned; I mean, the previous preaching of the Apoſtles ; it reaches, like the hypotheſis of the author to whom I am referring,
much higher [d] " than that proof, which is
" derived from ancient manuſcripts, from an-

[d] Letters, p. 15.

" cient verfions, and from the quotations of
" the Fathers."

The epiftles of St. Paul uniformly allude to
this preaching, and do not imply that the
Greek converts had at that time been inftructed by any other means. This is, we might
fuppofe, an irrefragable argument of the pre-
cedence, in point of time, of the epiftles of
St. Paul to any of the written Gofpels; and
the Acts of the Apoftles fhew, in conformity
with the language of St. Paul, that Chriftianity
was firft eftablifhed in other places, and by
other teachers, in the fame manner. If it be
allowable, in imitation of a learned ᵉtheolo-
gical writer, to examine a work no further
than the title for authority and proof, I might
likewife derive an equal fupport of my pofition, if fuch fupport were not fupplied from
better fources, from the apocryphal books of
the fecond century, called, " the Preaching of
" Peter," and " the Preaching of Paul."

ᵉ " I argued, that the *title* of thofe works, the Gofpel
" of the Twelve, and the Memoirs of the Apoftles, were
" derived from the *title* of the document which gave
" them birth. But though I argued from the *titles* of
" thofe works to the *title* of the document א, yet I never
" argued from the *contents* either of the Gofpel of the
" Twelve, or of the Memoirs of the Apoftles, to the *con-
" tents* of the document א." Marfh's Letters, p. 26, 27.

St. Paul, before he had any perfonal intercourfe with the Apoftles at Jerufalem, preached, by revelation from our Saviour himfelf,
the fame gofpel as they preached. They were
fatisfied that he had not preached a different
gofpel from their own, although he had not
participated with them in the advantage of
either oral or written communications. From
an attentive examination of this reafoning, I
conceive that it is not neceffary to fuppofe
the exiftence of any previous documents whatever, that may be confidered as the bafis of
the firft three Gofpels, becaufe thefe Gofpels
do not contain any thing which might not
have been there inferted by means of perfonal
knowledge, aided, but not fuperfeded, by the
common gift of infpiration.

If however we are to fuppofe, that fome
original document did exift, and that it was
incorporated with the Gofpels, it muft have
been compofed without any particular view
to publication, and not defigned for any fpecific objeƈt, (as it is faid to have been imper-
feƈt,) until others fhould be publifhed on the
fame fubjeƈt, which required the aid or explanation of fuch a fupplementary addition. Its
exiftence however, its original ufe, its fubfequent incorporation, and its final difappear-

ance, are equally unfupported by hiftory or probability.

When it was abforbed in the Gofpels, the original was foon loft, becaufe it was no longer neceffary; and [f] " few copies are fuppofed " to have ever exifted." That the Apoftles ever committed to writing any facts relative to the hiftory of our Saviour, which they did not defign for the inftruction of others, is not probable. The regard of the new converts for what the Apoftles had preached would intereft the former in the prefervation of every thing that the Apoftles had written.

The mode of multiplying copies by tranfcribers might, for any thing we know, have been a matter of very confiderable charge and coft to the poorer converts, and of courfe not likely to be undertaken unneceffarily; but, notwithftanding this obftacle, the multiplication of them is proved by the fubfequent progrefs of Chriftianity. We cannot pretend to enter upon a minute enquiry refpecting the fources of the means, which the early Chriftians poffeffed, of defraying the charge of copies of the Scriptures. It is certain that, wherever Chriftianity was eftablifhed, copies of the Scrip-

[f] Illuftration of the Hypothefis, p. 57.

I 2

tures, in sufficient numbers to prevent its sub-
version and decline, and to ensure its purity,
must have been procured in some way or another. We may not be able to compute the
expence, but we cannot suppose that Christianity long existed in any place where its records were scantily disperfed. If then this
expence of transcription were no obstacle to
the multiplication of copies at the first diffufion of the Gospel, we may conclude, that it
would be no obstacle afterwards ; for the difference between these two points of time was
too small to admit of such an augmentation of
expence as to prevent the difperfion of new
copies. Indeed, if it operated at all, it would
rather have a contrary effect. An increased
facility in executing this species of labour
would tend to diminish the expence. This
argument is still further weakened, if we consider the shortness of the writings which the
Apostles are supposed to have communicated ;
so that whether we refer to the compendious
brevity of these supposed apostolical works,
or the shortness of the period between *their*
publication, and that of the more complete
evangelical histories, we must be persuaded,
that the expence of copying cannot be assign-
ed as a reason why a small number of them

only fhould be publifhed and difperfed. If the document above alluded to had been of apoftolical authority, the zeal of the converts would moft probably in either cafe have increafed the number of copies, and caufed an anxious attention to the prefervation of them; whilft the neceffary retirement and privacy of the firft Chriftians afforded them fufficient leifure for this employment.

It is not neceffary to have recourfe to the farther fuppofition, that the copies were ⁵ loft at the time " Jerufalem was deftroyed, and " Judæa itfelf fubverted," if it were true that they were " already confidered by Chriftians " as ufelefs, and regarded with abhorrence by " the Jews." But the Jews would not have had more refpect for the Gofpels themfelves,

⁵ I cannot refufe myfelf the pleafure of tranfcribing from the oppofite page of my MS. the following remarks of a very able and eloquent writer, my friend, the Rev. R. Warner, of Bath : " The deftruction of Jerufalem does " not appear to be an event likely to have produced the " lofs of any thing highly efteemed by the Chriftians ; " it was not effected in a moment, but was the work of " years. Befides, the Chriftians, I apprehend, forewarned " of what was to happen, were fufficiently on their " guard to have fecured themfelves, as well as every " thing of importance to them."

than they had for the document, on which
the Gofpels were founded. The Chriftians
might indeed have loft their Gofpels " in the
" convulfions of that period," if they had not
been influenced by a particular regard to preferve them ; but the fmall number of copies
in exiftence, according to the hypothefis,
would have operated in awakening their folicitude, and invigorating their exertions, for
their prefervation. The copies of the Gofpels,
and the memorials of the preaching of the
Apoftles, were too widely diffufed to be annihilated at the deftruction of Jerufalem. All
the evangelifts, except St. John, were dead,
and their Gofpels were publifhed ; nor can it
be fuppofed that, even at Jerufalem, thofe
Chriftians, who had fuch warning to fly to the
mountains, would not remove the evidences
of their religion to the place of fafety, to
which they themfelves were inftructed to fly.
The document then, if any fuch ever exifted,
muft have been an object of care at this time.
A period of convulfion and national diftrefs
would have made the Chriftians attentive to
the prefervation of every authentic record of
their religion ; particularly when the danger, which extended to the minuteft object of
concern, and threatened the document itfelf,

might have deftroyed the fuller account that contained the document, which, if preferved, might have its ufe again.

The lofs of it however, it feems, is to be attributed to another [h] caufe; for we are informed, that the church was concerned only with " canonical Gofpels, but the document " was never taken into the canon." But ftill, if it had ever exifted, it would have participated in that regard and veneration which were due to the original authority and reception of the canonical Gofpels. For there is great probability that the Gofpels themfelves were received by the firft Chriftians, not merely becaufe fuch books were written by certain perfons, but likewife becaufe thefe books coincided with that preaching, by which they themfelves had been inftructed and converted. From this coincidence it is probable, that the written records of the Chriftian religion derived their claims to an acknowledgment of their authenticity, not from any decree of the Apoftles affembled at Jerufalem. The Apoftles had preached a certain doctrine, and propagated certain facts; and they were to take care that they did not write what was

[h] Illuftration of the Hypothefis, p. 57.

I 4

contradictory to either: and of this agreement their converts were to be the judges. The written Gofpels themfelves were, fubfequently, the guide to other teachers, and the teft in the hands of other converts; but they had originally been examined by a rule, which would fully eftablifh the confiftency of the authors, and would determine by this, among other proofs, the reality of the divine affiftance in their compofitions. Is it, in fhort, neceffary to reduce the meafure of infpiration, or to annihilate it altogether, in order the better to account for certain verbal agreements, or minute difcrepancies, in the narratives of the authors of the New Teftament? The infpiration was a promife which refted on the fame authority with the other promifes of the Scriptures; and one of its offices was, to do what the document, by the hypothefis, was not calculated to do, " to call *all* things to " their remembrance."

It is to be [i] lamented that the fubject of the origin of the three firft Gofpels has been pur-

---

[i] I allude to an able and ingenious pamphlet by the Rev. D. Veyfie, B. D. late fellow of Oriel College, Oxford. The examination of Mr. Marfh's Hypothefis was neceffary, and the expofure of its inadequacy is fuccefsful; but I confefs I fhould have been more fatisfied if

fued by another writer on a fimilar principle
of the exiftence of imaginary documents. It
is, I conceive, a miftake to affume that the exiftence of a given writing is a queftion to be
decided by a fuperiority of one hypothefis to
another. The queftion itfelf is a queftion of
facts, of which we have no information, connected with the operation of a fupernatural
power, the nature of which we do not underftand. Every hypothefis on this fubject muft,
probably from our ignorance, exclude infpiration in a greater or lefs degree; and it muft
therefore be defective, becaufe that affiftance
cannot be meafured under all the circumftances
of the compofition of the Gofpels. But were
we to declare that we neither can, nor wifh
to account for the verbal agreement in the
narratives of the Evangelifts, how would the
caufe of Chriftianity be difgraced by the
avowal of fuch an incurious difpofition, or by
fuch an expofure of irremediable ignorance?
How far would fuch a confeffion extend?
Merely to the acknowledgment, that we did

the above effay had concluded with proving, that hypothefis was inadmiffible in determining a queftion of fact.
Mr. Marfh's Hypothefis might be correctly denominated,
A Theory of a portion of the private lives of the Evangelifts and Apoftles.

not know under what circumſtances the Goſpels were written, and did not attempt to ſup-
ply by conjecture the defects, if any, of the
private hiſtory of the Apoſtles, nor to adapt a
theory of inſpiration to the nature and quantity of information which, we are to preſup-
poſe, previouſly exiſted in writing.

With regard to the preſervation of the records of the Chriſtian religion, it has been
ſaid, that both the wiſdom and goodneſs of
God required the interpoſition of his providence to preſerve [k] pure and uncorrupt " the
" genuine authentic records of that Goſpel,
" which he had thought fit, at the expence of
" ſo many miracles and prophecies, to publiſh
" to the world." To ſay nothing of the pre-
ſumption of adjudging the duties of divine
wiſdom and goodneſs, which with ſuch cold
effrontery here obtrudes itſelf, let it be recol-
lected, that, as ſoon as the Goſpels were committed to writing, and made public, the authenticity of theſe books was ſubject to the
ſame laws of evidence as any other written
document whatſoever. The Almighty did not
ſubſtitute other grounds of credibility for the
reception of the evangelical writings, in the

<hr>

k Diſſonance, Pref. p. xi.

place of thofe which are regarded as neceffary for the eftablifhment of the truth of any
hiftory that contains facts of an ordinary nature. And the diffufion of Chriftianity among
nations which had attained to different degrees
of improvement, and fubfifted under different
political forms, has not been attended with
any peculiar fluctuation in the purity of its
records that can be fuppofed to be connected
with the interefts oppofed to it, or the learned
difputes which arofe after its eftablifhment.
Yet it feems to be implied in the fuppofition of " The Diffonance," that whenever
the doctrines of Chriftianity, or its precepts,
or its facts, oppofed the theories of fome, as
well as the interefts of others, that an attempt was then made to pervert the writings
in which the precepts, facts, and doctrines
were contained; or that fome events were
continually occurring, the effects of which
upon the facred books it required the hand
of the Almighty to avert or to fruftrate.
One writer indeed has conjectured, [1] " that
" the canonical writings of the New Tefta-
" ment were concealed in the coffers of pri-
" vate churches, or perfons, till the time of

[1] Dodwell, Diff. in Iren. p. 66. Toland's tranflation.

"Trajan, or even perhaps of Hadrian, that
"they might not come to the knowledge of
"the catholic church." Had this been an
eftablifhed fact, we muft have received it on
the credit of the author, and have accounted
for it as we were able. But it is evident that
it is only a conjecture. It would otherwife
have protracted the period of tradition to an
extent, which would have required the conftant interpofition of a miraculous power to
preferve it in its original integrity. It would
alfo have fupported the invidious hypothefis of thofe, who think that the Chriftians
could not but have ufed every opportunity in
their power of adapting to their own purpofes
all the exifting copies of the New Teftament.
Thefe Chriftians are faid indeed to have withheld their copies from general infpection, under the apprehenfion of danger; but it does
not appear that they had recourfe to this project even in the perfecution of Diocletian: and
indeed it would be more difficult to vindicate
the purity of the books of the New Teftament, if it had happened that there was a
time when the Chriftians had at once in their
hands every copy of the books of the evangelical collection.

It is further ftated, upon the fame ground

of conjecture, that if [m] " by chance the books
" of the New Testament had been publicly
" circulated, they would have been over-
" whelmed by the multitude of apocryphal
" and [n] suppositititious books, so that the Scrip-
" tures could not have been distinguished from
" these without a new examination, and a
" new testimony." This argument rests upon
the assumption, that the apocryphal and sup-
posititious books were intended by their authors, or by those who used them, to super-
sede, or to be substituted in the place of, the
acknowledged writings of the New Testament. Ecclesiastical history does not confirm
any part of this suspicion. But if such had
been the design of the writers, it would still
have been necessary to examine what might
be the authority of the books which were then
received, and of those which were produced,
although at a subsequent period, in competi-

[m] Dodwell in Iren.

[n] Professor Less seems to have had similar doubts.
" Moreover, subsequent information is inadequate to esta-
" blish the authenticity of the scriptures of the New Tes-
" tament. It is too recent, and the foregoing centuries
" were too replete with spurious and forged works, to be
" capable of instructing us confidently what writings were
" actually composed by the disciples of Jesus in the first
" century." Kingdon's translation, p. 10, 11.

tion for the fame authority among Chriftians. The circumftance of mere priority of publication of the Gofpels could not have made fuch an enquiry fuperfluous at any time, but particularly at fo late a period as the reign of Hadrian °.

It is however of importance to infift upon the obfervation, that thofe, who ufed apocryphal books, did not on this account reject the genuine apoftolical writings. The P Marcoufians, who received the gofpel of the Infancy of Jefus Chrift, perverted the meaning, and mifapplied different paffages of the three firft Gofpels, in confirmation of their own opinions; but they did not falfify the words, nor infert fpurious additions. We may conclude, that thofe books of Scripture, which a particular fect interpreted in their own favour, with a view to deduce fome fupport to a particular fyftem, were received as authentic: but it is fingular, that they feemed to prefer the fanction of Scripture, when they might have appealed exclufively to their own apocryphal treatifes.

Some, however, of the older heretics, as

° Hadrian began to reign A. D. 117. or 119.
P Irenæus, p. 91—93.

q " the Ebionites and Marcionites, and fome
" other pretended Chriftians, rejected fome
" books of the New Teftament; but their au-
" thority," it is faid, " can be of no weight, as
" they could not fairly pafs for Chriftians."
This fummary condemnation of thefe witneffes will not excufe us from the farther labour of enquiring into the reafons on which
they are objected to. Whether they were
Chriftians or not is a queftion which has no
reference to the fubject. It does not affect
the antiquity of the period when thefe perfons
lived, nor their proximity to the apoftolical
times. Their teftimony, if favourable, would
perhaps have been regarded as important from
this very circumftance of proximity; and when
in oppofition, if it be not formidable, it is at
leaft worthy of examination. The Ebionites
however certainly received one Gofpel, that
of St. Matthew; the Marcionites, that of St.
Lake; and the Gnoftics, that of St. John.
The queftion then is, whether thofe perfons
are to be denominated Chriftians, who received one Gofpel only. But all the primitive
Chriftians were at firft, through neceffity in-

q Richardfon on the Canon of the New Teftament;
and Cockburn's Hiftorical Differtation on the books of
the New Teftament, p. 1.

deed, in the fame fituation; for they could
not probably know that others exifted, unlefs
the three firft Gofpels were compofed and
publifhed, and interchanged among the various Chriftian communities at the fame time.
Indeed there might have been a natural partiality for the Gofpel, written by the perfon
by whom the Chriftians of a certain tract of
country were converted. Befides, as all the
Apoftles preached the fame Gofpel, containing
nearly the fame facts, and promulgating the
fame doctrine, the reception of one Gofpel,
without mutilation, could not juftly expofe the
perfons to the lofs of the name and diftinction
of Chriftians; and it is indeed rather to be
confidered as one of the technical reproaches
of controverfy. 'It appears that the Carpocratians, Cerinthians, the followers of Prodi-
cus and Cerdon, received the fame books of
Scripture that other Chriftians received. He-
racleon the Valentinian compofed comments
on feveral parts of the New Teftament, and
probably, as it is fuppofed, on all the books.
Origen indeed, in his reply to Celfus, has faid,
that none but the Valentinians, the Marcion-

ʳ See Lardner under the refpective heads, Carpocratians, &c.

ites, and the difciples of Lucius, corrupted the Scriptures. But had any of the alterations of thefe heretics contaminated the generality of the copies of the Scriptures, it muft have been difcovered by the traces of their peculiar opinions in fuch variations.

· The author of " The Diffonance" fuppofes that the Scriptures were corrupted in the fecond and third centuries, becaufe at this time certain perfons wrote apocryphal books; and the tranfition was eafy from one fraud to the other. But admitting the principle, that the altered paffages would probably be accommodated to the peculiar tenets of the fectarifts, it is a fingular fact, that [s] " none of the " numerous manufcripts brought from Greece " favours any heretical dogma;" and that " no " criterion exifts for diftinguifhing the ortho-

[s] Wetftein, Prolegom. pp. 29. 33. " In tot codicibus " ex Græcia allatis ne una quidem hactenus reperta eft, " quæ hæretico dogmati faveat; ne jam dicam de codi- " cibus Græcis Latinorum imprimis de noftro Cantabri- " gienfi ejufque Luc. vi. 5. viros doctos aliter judicare. " Cum igitur omnes varietates partim negligentia, partim " ftudio emendandi adeoque fcriptorum facrorum honori " confulenti, originem debeant, nec κριτήριον relinquitur, " quo librarius orthodoxus ab hæretico diftinguatur, nec " rationi demonftrari poteft, in folos hæreticos cadere aut " negligentiam, aut ftudium emendandi."

K

" dox from the heretical tranfcriber.'" It may
be inferred, I conceive, from thefe facts, that
fome of the heretics corrupted their own private copies only; and the gofpel of this or
that herefiarch will denote only a copy of a
part of the Scriptures, altered in various modes
to favour the principles of their fyftem, and
not a new fabrication of their own. This
may explain the admiffion of only one Gofpel
among feveral of the fects, but this admiffion
does not imply a renunciation of the reft on
the ground of want of authority.

It is the opinion of an eminent writer on
the Canon of the New Teftament, that the
heretics, thofe efpecially who compofed an
apocryphal gofpel, could not receive, or [t]even
regard thofe, which were authentic and canonical. Bafilides is faid to have " compofed
" twenty-four books on the Gofpel: this is
" thought to imply his own gofpel, and not
" any of ours;" and it is confidered as " much
" the more probable opinion," " becaufe it
" cannot be imagined that herefiarch would
" fhew fo great refpect to ours." It is not
certain that Bafilides did fabricate an apocryphal gofpel, but it is more probable that he

[t] Jones, Canon of the New Teft. vol. i. p. 177.

commented upon the genuine books. However, whether he himſelf compoſed a goſpel or not, he received that of St. Matthew; [u] " and there is no proof that he rejected the " other three." [x] Leucius, or Lucanus, it is admitted, furniſhed a large proportion of the apocryphal works, which, neverthelefs, it is to be remarked, do not contradict the general facts of the canonical Scriptures. His followers, according to the [y] hypothetical declaration of Origen, are thought to have altered the received books of the New Teſtament; and it is to be preſumed that, if they received them even with their own alterations, they did not deviate from the injunctions and practice of their maſter : at leaſt it is evident, that they did not prefer his compoſitions altogether to the evangelical hiſtories. If this be correctly repreſented, and I am not ſenſible that it is inaccurate, we ſhall not aggravate the danger to which the faith of the early Chriſtians was expoſed, although " the ſpu- " rious writings of heretics were not rejected,

[u] Lardner, vol. ix. p. 305.
[x] Lardner under Leucius, and Jones on the Canon of the New Teſtament.
[y] Οἶμαι δὲ καὶ τοὺς ἀπὸ Ασκάνε. Lib. ii. p. 77. Edit. Cant.

" nor the faithful admonifhed to beware of
" them for the future."

It is indeed fuggefted, that the catholic
church fhould have taken thefe precautions
of determining the authenticity or fpurioufnefs of the books of the New Teftament. To
determine however what we are to underftand by the catholic church at this period, is
not eafy, fo as to be able to form any notion
of its concurrence in a general act. Befides,
it is here fuppofed that thefe fpurious writings
had been difperfed to nearly the fame extent
as the authentic Scriptures, if the effects of
their contents required the interpofition of the
catholic church. But how could the opinions
of all the churches have been collected for the
determination of this queftion? The church
acquired more real ftrength without fuch an
interpofition, than it could have obtained by
it. The fpurious works appeared not indeed
without the oppofition and cenfure of individuals, but they were not fupprefled or ftigmatized by the authority of the church. The
fentence of individuals will not be regarded
unlefs founded upon enquiry and examination: a body of perfons may decree praife or
cenfure, afluring others that they have indivi-
dually enquired and examined, and without

fpecifying the reafons of their conclufion. But
it is obvious that fuch determinations can have
no weight or title to regard.

It has been obferved, that the " writings
" of the ᶻ Apoftles were fo conjoined with the
" apocryphal, that it was not manifeft, by any
" mark or public cenfure of the church, which
" of the two fhould be preferred to the other."
It has appeared from previous obfervations,
that this mark or cenfure was unneceffary,
becaufe it was not the defign even of the authors of the apocryphal books to fubftitute
them in the place of the writings of the Apoftles. It is fatisfactory to know, that we do
not derive our prefent canon of Scripture from
the interpofition of the church, dictating what
books were genuine, and what books were
fpurious. The confent of the churches, both
as to what they received, and what they rejected, was the refult of independent enquiry,
and not the effect of a confederacy of fpiritual rulers, or the ftratagems of a party. The
liberty of judgment, whether flowing from
the ftate of the Chriftians at the time, or from
any religious forbearance, is indicated by the
numerous writings and fects of heretics ; and,

ᶻ Toland from Dodwell, p. 71; 72.

if we may ¡judge from the afperities of their
controverfial language, their adverfaries would
fcarcely have been fatisfied with oppofing the
uncertain and circuitous reftraint of argument
only, if, as a body, they had poffeffed either
power of their own, or could have engaged
that of the civil magiftrate on their behalf.
Thofe times muft be regarded as favourable
to Chriftianity, which, when its farther progrefs was to be effected by means of written
documents, obliged its profeffors to appeal to
the underftanding alone for the conviction of
their adverfaries.

The determination however of the queftion
relative to the canonical books has been refolved into authority of fome kind. It is the
opinion of an [a] eminent writer, that the Apoftles approved and authorized certain books
of the canon, and that " teftimonials were
" tranfmitted to the churches to prove them
" apoftolical."

It is [b] certainly a fingular circumftance, that
the form at leaft of fuch a warrant for the re-

[a] Richardfon, Canon of the New Teft. Vindicated,
p. 7—9.
[b] I had not read at this time the obfervations of Michaelis, vol. i. p. 88. " Another proof which has been
" given is much ftronger than the former; viz. that the

ception of the canonical books has not been any where preferved. Its importance was fuch, that it ought always to have accompanied the inftrument itfelf, which it fanctioned, particularly as fo momentous a confequence was involved in the exiftence of fuch a formulary; namely, that what was approved " by the Apoftles was, without controverfy; " dictated by the Holy Ghoft." If we apply this rule to the Gofpels of St. Mark and St. Luke, it is not neceffary to deduce their infpiration from any apoftolical recommendation. They had both preached the Gofpel; and, if one committed to writing what St. Peter delivered, and the other the preaching of St. Paul, it is probable that each of thefe written Gofpels was firft communicated to the converts of thefe Apoftles, and it was unneceffary to add the approbation as a corroborating authority, when the oral teaching muft ultimately try the approbation itfelf, as well as the genuinenefs of the written Gofpel. Befides,

" Apoftles themfelves have recommended thefe books as " canonical. If that be true, all doubt of their canonical " authority is removed. But which of the Apoftles has " given this recommendation or teftimony, and where is " it recorded? In their epiftles, at leaft in refpect to St. " Luke, no trace is to be found."

K 4

fuch a fanction might have been fo eafily imi-
tated, that it might have occafioned much
perplexity, at a very early period, in diftinguifhing the fpurious from the genuine apoftolical writings.   But the queftion of infpiration could not have been folely dependent
on the authenticity of a detached autograph.
The forgeries contained in the [c] decretals fhew
how inadequate fuch affurances would have
been to fecure credibility, when thefe affurances had been withheld for a confiderable
length of time after the fuppofed events had
taken place.   There can be no doubt, that,
had there been any hiftorical proof of fuch
approbation, we muft have admitted it ; but
an appeal to authority could fcarcely have
been made fecretly, when it would at firft
have been neceffary for the Chriftians to refer
to it frequently and publicly for the fatisfaction of new believers.

It is indeed faid, that [d] " we have no rea-
" fon to afcribe infpiration to the works of a
" prophet, except when he declares, as fuch,
" that what he writes is infpired, and that he
" in thofe inftances affumes that character.

[c] See Hume's Hift. of England, vol. ii. p. 229.
[d] Michaelis, vol. i. p. 88.

" But this neither St. Mark nor St. Luke have
" declared in any part of their writings."
But what fecurity for the validity of thefe
claims to infpiration fhould we find in men's
own affertions. e " How do we know that
" the books of Efdras, Tobit, Judith, were
" not divinely infpired, and that the books of
" Mofes, Jofhua, Judges, and others, were
" written by divine Infpiration, but from tra-
" dition ? We cannot learn it from the books
" themfelves, for the apocryphal Efdras, for
" inftance, tells us, that he was divinely in-
" fpired, which is more than the authors of
" the books of Jofhua, Judges, Ruth, or Kings
" tell us in any of thofe books." This criterion then is evidently ambiguous; and the
queftion may admit fome digreffive examination, in what manner we are to prove the
infpiration of thefe writers. It is admitted
that we could not deduce it from their own
affirmation. We could not infer it from their
being contemporaries or companions of the
Apoftles, for we do not reafon in this manner; f " a difciple accompanied an apoftle on

e " Tradition neceffary to explain and interpret the
" Holy Scriptures." By T. Brett, LL. D. 1718. p. 31.
f Michaelis, vol. i. p. 88.

" his journies, therefore his writings are in-
" spired." We are told, " that a disciple
" might possess the gift of miracles, be able
" to restore the sick, to speak languages which
" he had never learnt, and even be endowed
" with the spirit of prophecy, though his
" writings were not inspired." It may be
conceded, that there is no necessary connection in these circumstances. To advert again
to the argument from apostolical approbation;
nothing approaches so near to a proof of such
approbation having been given to St. Luke,
than his composition of the early history of
Christianity, contained in the Acts of the Apostles. But still the approbation itself is not
extant, however our reasonings from probability only would justify us in assuming such
an authority for the undertaking, and such a
sanction to it after its completion. I do not
indeed conceive how the inspiration of one
person could be so ascertained as to be a matter of testimony, which was to be received
upon the evidence of another inspired person.
Inspiration itself does not appear to have been
susceptible of that nice and clear examination,
which should be the ground of testimony; not
to omit, that this might occasion no unreason-
able suspicion of collusion between the parties.

In what manner then can we be fatisfied that they were infpired ? It is true indeed, that all who preached did not alfo write a Gofpel; but it is probable that they, who wrote a Gofpel, had previoufly preached it in fome " quar-" ters" of the Jews or Gentiles. The preaching of the Gofpel was neceffarily attended with the ability to perform miracles, which, while they teftified the divinity of the revelation, conftituted the evidence for the authority of the preacher, and the great public and cogent proof of his infpiration. Can any proof, except that by miracles, of infpiration, or, what is the fame thing, of knowledge being revealed, be addreffed to the fenfes or the underftanding ? The nature of the thing does not admit of any other proof. In what manner the faculties of the infpired perfon are affected, how his memory is affifted, that the fubject and language of his communication are fuggefted, and do not originate in himfelf, may be affirmed, and perhaps imperfectly defcribed; but what direct proof can we have that this is his real intellectual ftate ? It is evident that we cannot have any. We may apply this criterion to the enquiry, whether the genuine epiftle of Clemens Romanus,

and thofe of the other "apoftolic fathers, muft
" be received as genuine." We muft premife,
that the early Chriftians did not confider them
as part of the canon ; and we muft admire
their caution in not rafhly blending with the
known productions of infpiration, thofe, which
veneration for the fituation and characters of
their authors might have impelled them to introduce. In the epiftle of Clemens, for example, it may be remarked, that the quotations from the books of Scripture furnifh all
that is imperative in his exhortation. There
is nothing authoritative but what is derived
from the words of the Holy Spirit, fpeaking
in the writings of others ; whereas a writer,
who was himfelf infpired, would not appeal
fo frequently for the fupport of his injunctions, and ftill lefs for the injunctions themfelves, to extraneous authority. I do not prefume to affert, that this was one of the reafons which prevented the Chriftians from af-
figning to this epiftle the fame rank as to
thofe of St. Paul ; but it is a circumftance
which, even in our judgment, would indicate fome deficiency in the proof of infpiration.

We are willing however to be accufed of

credulity in admitting the infpiration of St. Mark and St. Luke. Any apparent incon-fiftency of theirs with the writings of St. Matthew and St. John, in feveral particulars, does not derogate from infpiration. It merely fhews our ignorance of the mode how thefe writings are to be reconciled. This is no fubterfuge. Any fuppofed inconfiftency in the narratives of the events of our Saviour's miniftry, where the fame acts were fo often repeated, within the compafs of a fmall tract of country, and at fuch a variety of places and feafons, may be refolved into a gratuitous affumption of identity in thofe incidents which were really different, or which occur-red at a different place, or at a different fea-fon, or at a different part of the fame road, . or city, or village. This however is an incon-fiftency of the loweft clafs. We have no re-pugnancies in the precepts, no failure of prophecy, no unreal miracles. We fhall not therefore abandon the infpiration of St. Mark and St. Luke upon the ground of diffonance from the other Evangelifts. The infidel might object to an excefs of harmonious uniformity, as an indication of collufive confederacy. But in accounting for differences on one hand,

and a verbal agreement on the other, between
the Evangelifts, it is fingular that infpiration
is equally excluded by the critic. We know
indeed that contradictions are inconfiftent
with infpiration; but are we certain that a
verbal agreement is incompatible with this
gift of the Spirit? We know what a contradiction is; but an hiftorical difcrepancy is
not to be confounded with variations which
affect the principles of morality or the veracity of the writer. There is therefore much
latitude for the reconciliation of the alledged
differences, without ufing the violent expedient of denying the infpiration in order to
take away the neceffity of attempting to har-
monize facts, which were never perhaps intended to be identified with others, or might
be fuppofed to be the fame facts without imputing to the authors contradiction or inconfiftency; or to thofe, who receive them as
true, credulity and fuperftition. But let credulity and fuperftition be imputed to us. We
can fcarcely boaft of much ftrength of underftanding, or of great Chriftian fortitude, even
if we fhould hold faft, againft fuch temptation, this part of our faith without waver-
ing; even if we fhould not be influenced to

reject a great portion of the records of Chriftianity by trite reproaches, difhoneft argument, unfounded pofitions, and perverted Scripture.

SERMON V.

---

2 Pet. i. 16.

We have not followed cunningly devised fables.

IN order to complete a part of the enquiry relative to the authenticity of the prefent canon of the New Teftament, we are in the next place to examine, whether " the fecond " and fucceeding centuries" were as favourable as is reprefented to the corruption of the facred writings; and whether the fabrication of books, which appeared at thofe periods under the names of apoftles, or apoftolical perfons, tended to confound the diftinction between authentic and fpurious records. The author of " The Diffonance" confiders it to be fufficient if he refers his imaginary interpolations and corruptions to the copyifts of thofe ages, and is fatisfied that by fuch an intimation he produces full authority for his critical fufpicions, and for the impeachment of the credibility of all which he prefumes to ftig-

matize. It is alledged, that, before the difcovery of ª " printing, it was very eafy for art-
" ful or fuperftitious copyifts, not only to in-
" terpolate authentic writings with fuch al-
" terations and additions as accorded with
" their own credulity or cunning, but even to
" produce entire works of their own or others'
" forgery, under the name of any writer they
" pleafed."   The facility, upon which the author infifts, of corrupting manufcripts before
the invention of printing, is affumed to be
much greater than I conceive it really was.
But this point will require farther elucidation.
It may be remarked, and, had the obfervation
been repeated as often as it was neceffary,
it would have recurred with tirefome frequency, that there is no hiftorical proof of the
other particulars.   We are expected to admit,
without teftimony, that the copyifts of the
facred writings were the perfons who were
authors of certain forgeries, of the exiftence
of which no trace is to be difcovered; and
that perfons engaged in this employment of
tranfcribing the facred volumes were more
likely to be the authors of fuch forgeries than
any other perfons.   But we are entirely igno-

ª Diffonance, p. 26, 27.

rant of the opinions of thefe copyifts, of the numbers that were employed, and of the mode of executing their tranfcripts; and therefore we cannot judge to what extent they were able to diffeminate the errors which they adopted or invented, and incorporated with the genuine apoftolical records. All that we know is, that fuch perfons had an opportunity of adapting their copies, by fraudulent alterations, to a certain fyftem of opinions; but there is no proof of fuch deviations from their originals. It is eafy indeed to afcribe to thefe copyifts any moral qualities which may fupport an hypothefis; but it is not according to nature, I conceive, to reprefent interpolated additions as originating in the credulity of the fuperftitious, whofe character it rather is to obferve fuch a rigid accuracy as would not admit any departure from the facred archetype. The fuperftitious copyift muft be excepted from the number of agents occupied in falfifying the genuine Scriptures, or in fabricating original fictions. But thefe credulous and fuperftitious agents are mere creatures of a fceptical imagination. They are to be regarded only as neceffary conftituents of a gratuitous hypothefis, and whofe exiftence is no more to be admitted than the vibrations of

the Hartleian theory, afcribed to [b] " a fub-
" ftance, which no man could ever prove to
" have vibrations, or to be capable of them."

It is more plaufible, perhaps, than juft, to
reprefent the invention of printing as a better
fecurity againft this fpecies of impofture, than
the multiplication of copies of compofitions by
means of tranfcripts. It does not however
appear from the hiftory of the times, that the
books of the facred writings could have been
more generally difperfed by means of the art
of the typographer, than they were by the
lefs expeditious labour of the pen of the copyift. The eftablifhment of Chriftianity might
be fuppofed to be fufficiently fecure on the
foundation of the authority of its firft teachers,
and upon tradition. But its further progrefs
could not be enfured without the opportunity
of recurring to the records of the religion, in
order to verify the inftruction which they received, or to fatisfy the doubts that would
naturally arife in minds more inquifitive and
more accuftomed to intellectual exertion. We
are further to confider, that the collation of
copies would not have been more facilitated
by the art of printing. This fpecies of labour,

[b] Reid's Effays, p. 94. edit. 4to.

although it was the more immediate concern of perfons who might be expected to be the guardians of the integrity and purity of the facred books, might have been fo eafy, that the mere impulfe of curiofity would have been a fufficient inducement to undertake it, even without any fufpicion of differences and contradictions. We muft alfo remember, that when no other mode of multiplying copies of writings was known but by means of manufcripts, the difcrimination of each nice particular was eafy and familiar to the contemporary reader. The argument however of the objector is reduced, towards the conclufion of the ftatement, to a form of affertion, mitigated and tempered, perhaps, on account of his own fufpicions of its invalidity. " This practice," he fays[c], " of interpolation and forgery was " actually fo common amongft feveral, who " called themfelves Chriftians, in the fecond " and fucceeding centuries, that, if what we " call the fcriptures of the New Teftament " were not fo tampered with, they are almoft " the only writings upon the fame fubject of " thofe early times which have efcaped free." With an adverfary, who avails himfelf of

[c] Diffonance, p. 27.

every minute circumftance which can be made
to favour his hypothefis, it cannot be thought
hypercritical or uncandid to obferve, that " if
" the practice was common amongft feveral
" only, who called themfelves Chriftians,"
their whole lives muft have been occupied in
this employment; and yet the names of thefe
falfaries have not been preferved, nor any particulars refpecting their frauds. Their bufinefs
muft be fuppofed to have confifted in corrupting the Scriptures, and in forging writings in
confonance to thofe corruptions. In examining this queftion of the corruption of the
Scriptures, it is not however intended to be
affirmed, that opportunities were not eafily
afforded of attempting any alterations in the
facred books; but we are to feparate the actions of individuals from thofe changes, which
are thought to have been effected by Chriftians in their collective capacity. Some of
the alterations of St. Luke's Gofpel by Marcion are refolvable into the variations of copies; yet he did accommodate the Scripture
to his own fentiments, but not without detection and cenfure. The imaginary falfaries
of " The Diffonance," however, although they
acted under the direction, and with the autho-

rity, of a fuppofed corrupt church, have not
yet been difcovered.

In confidering the queftion of the diffufion
of tranfcripts from various originals, we attribute perhaps more advantages to the invention
of printing than ought to be afcribed to it.
The mere mention of this fplendid acquifition
operates upon the mind in a confufed manner, and feems to imply a vifible and direct
fuperiority over the mode of communication
by means of the hand-writing of individuals.
It may perhaps appear, upon enquiry, that
this prefumed fuperiority is queftionable when
referred to this particular inftance, the difperfion of copies of the fcriptures of the New
Teftament.

With regard to the facility of multiplying
copies of thefe books, one confequence fhould
have enfued, which did not take place. Had
they been provided flowly, or at very confiderable charge, the promulgation of Chriftianity muft have been impeded by both thefe
caufes. But even if the whole of the prefent
collection had been copied by the fame individual, his zeal and induftry need not be fuppofed to exceed the zeal and induftry of later
ages, as exerted in the fimilar occupation of
copying the liturgical offices of the church.

The legal incapacities of the early Chriftians for civil offices, and their indifference to worldly advantages and purfuits, produced naturally a fpeculative and retired mode of life. This afforded much opportunity for fedentary employment, and the multiplication of copies of the facred Scriptures was probably the only active bufinefs in which they interefted themfelves.

We may remark, that in a printed book, whatever fubfequent infertion may be fufpected, its detection would be more difficult than in any manufcript. Every printed book retains and repeats errors of every kind, and prefents an uniformity of miftake in every copy : whereas in a manufcript one tranfcript checks the errors of another, becaufe we oppofe the negligence of one individual to the greater care of another ; or at leaft we have the contingency, that the fame error has not been committed by different perfons. In every different manufcript we can generally apply, or we can diftinguifh when we do apply, to the diligence of a different perfon ; whereas, in a printed book, the errors of the fame individual perplex every reader of the work, without any refource.

The very character of the letters of a ma-

nufcript is a criterion of its date, and a meafure of its value ; and fubfequent infertions
prefent the marks of a different period. Thefe
niceties, but all of them of great moment,
are loft, when the contents of a manufcript
are transferred to a printed book.

The fubftitution of printed books for manufcripts was not defirable at the period when
it is fuppofed that the art of printing would
have been a better fecurity againft impofition
than the art of the tranfcriber. There are
many nice particulars which would betray
anachronifmal errors. Indeed there is fcarcely
any thing, both from the materials employed,
and the formation of the letters, which does
not afford an appropriate indication of dates.
Thefe are incommunicable almoft by defcription, and could not have been transferred by
initiation into the copies deftined for general
ufe. We fhould not omit likewife to notice,
that where all learning was in the form of
manufcripts only, the difcrimination of age,
and the particulars neceffary to give authority
to any writing, muft have been familiar, and
have occafioned little or no trouble, and certainly none to have produced much uncertainty.

The invention of the art of printing would

in reality have been detrimental, had it been
introduced when, according to the fuppofition of fome perfons, it would have been
attended with greater utility. Although the
materials of manufcripts are fufficiently fra-
gile, and liable to decay and injury, yet,
when they have been copied, lefs care for
the prefervation of the originals has been
confidered as neceffary upon the fuppofition, that an inftrument of equivalent authority has been fubftituted. We cannot precifely afcertain the length of time before this
would take place; but we may be affured,
that this diminution of attention would, fooner
or later, be the effect of the introduction of
a new fpecies of cuftody, which would be regarded as fuperfeding any troublefome diligence that might have been previoufly required to protect them from the ordinary ca-
fualties of fituation or nature. Would it have
been defirable, we may afk, to have had fuch
an art as that of printing, at fuch a period,
which would have had fuch an effect as this?
The evidence for the Gofpel hiftory, when
in the form of a writing, would have been
greatly reduced in quantity, and would have
been made doubtful and even fufpicious in
kind.

The author of "The Diffonance" has objected, in a plaufible manner, to the authority
of that multiplicity of copies, which we fuppofe to have been derived from the fame original. He has again recourfe to his ufual
expedient, a fallacious analogy, to illuftrate
his argument. He compares the cafe to that
of a will, where one copy only can poffefs
full authority. But the comparifon of a copy
of a writing and of a will is defective. The
circumftances of a will originate in the perfon
whofe will it is faid to be; and if it cannot be
proved to be his, it is of no confequence
whofe it may be, or what are the circumftances, as they are all dependent upon the
determination, who was the individual. A
copy of a writing may have every mark of
genuinenefs as a hiftory, and every criterion
of probability; and we may be fatisfied of its
truth, although we fhould not be acquainted
with the name of its author. Internal evidence and analogy are admiffible in reafoning
on the genuinenefs of a narrative; whereas
they are excluded abfolutely by the nature
of a teftamentary inftrument. A hiftory admits teftimony relative to the circumftances
and facts; but a will does not admit any but
what is relative to the perfon who made it.

It feems as if the author of "The Diffonance" had at length difcovered a cafe, where the copy of a writing, after one remove from the original, was of no value as evidence, without confidering that the nature of the contents of each writing gives the fpecific difference to the evidence in queftion.

It is afferted in "The Diffonance," with refpect to the writings [d] "which are attri-" buted to any Chriftian writers within the "firft half of the fecond century, that of the "whole collection there is no fatisfactory "proof that any one compofition worth no-" tice is really the work of the writer whofe "name it bears, except the firft Epiftle of "Clemens the Roman; and even that this has "been evidently corrupted." The argument which is deduced from this obfervation ought to be well examined. Becaufe there are doubts refpecting the authenticity of fome ancient writings on certain fubjects connected with Chriftianity, therefore we can have no better proof refpecting the genuinenefs of other writings, of greater antiquity, and of different authority and importance. The queftion is artfully contrived to appear to depend upon

[d] Diffonance, p. 27.

the confideration of time, when it really relates to another particular. The argument indeed, if it were expected to have any weight,
fhould have fhewed, that the difficulty of determining the authenticity of thefe writings
was either contemporary with the writings
themfelves, or that there was no criterion by
which their real authority could be afcertained ; or, that although the evidence of the
authenticity of fuch writings was obfcure and
defective, yet they had been received as parts
of the ancient collection of Scripture, and
therefore that the records of Chriftianity itfelf, from being nearly contemporary writings,
were not capable of more fubftantial authentication than the Shepherd of Hermas, or the
epiftles of Clement. It is however fortunate
that this delufion has terminated even in fome
diftant age of the church. We may rather
perhaps be fatisfied, that, if there was any
reafon for doubt in compofitions of great antiquity and of fmall fize, fufficient teftimony
has remained to direct our judgment in af-
figning to them due authority, and a proper
place in a clafs fubordinate to the authentic
writings of apoftles and evangelifts. But there
is no teftimony of the early enlargement of
the canon by the infertion of works of du-

bious claims, and the fubfequent contraction
of it by the rejection of fuch writings, upon
the difcovery of their want of authority. We
know indeed that it did not originally confift
of fo many books; but it was never fubfequently diminifhed by the neceffity of obviat-
ing the precipitate admiffion of ambiguous
writings. The prefervation of the brief letter to
Philemon is a proof of the care of the Chriftian
affemblies in the cuftody of their documents;
and the exclufion of the Shepherd of Hermas
and the genuine epiftle of Clement from the
canon fhews alfo, that the canon was not formed without the exercife of judgment, and a
cautious examination of its future conftituent
portions. It ought to be proved by an adverfary who is never perplexed for the invention
of objections, that the Chriftian communions
did not poffefs, or, if they poffeffed, did not
ufe, the evidence which we have at this day;
that the practice of forgery and interpolation
had prevailed, fo as to render ufelefs the ordinary rules of determining the authenticity and
genuinenefs of any writing, and that what
they received they received in this ftate of
confufion and perplexity, and that the collection of the fcriptures of the New Teftament
was haftily and ignorantly feparated from a

mafs of writings contemporary in their publication, each of which had apparently an equal
claim to be a conftituent part of the projected
canon, and thofe certainly, that prefented
themfelves to notice with the commendatory
and authoritative diftinction of an apoftolical
name. The author of "The Diffonance" indeed
fays, e " that every competent impartial judge
" muft agree with the truly learned and candid
" Mofheim, that of the whole collection there
" is no fatisfactory proof that any piece worth
" notice is really the work of the writer whofe
" name it bears, except the firft epiftle of Cle-
" mens the Roman." But this difcovery was
not referved for the fagacity and erudition of
Mofheim, nor for the literary refearches of his
age. Eufebius was as well acquainted with
the different evidence for the authority of
both, and has fpoken of the two epiftles as
Mofheim himfelf would fpeak. " One un-
" doubted epiftle of his is circulated. The
" fame epiftle I have known to be publicly
" recited in many churches, both formerly
" and in our own times." Of the other epiftle
he fpeaks in this manner: " We are to learn
" that there is a fecond epiftle of Clement,

e Diffonance, p. 27.

" not fo notable as the former, and we know
" that the ancients did not ufe it." Neither
did he afcribe undue authority to the Shepherd of Hermas, or the epiftle of St. Barnabas.

It is further clear, that the ground on which
one book was received, and another rejected,
was not merely, that one was written by a
heretic, and the other by a perfon of. the catholic church. Eufebius, fpeaking in a well
known paffage of certain gofpels and acts,
fays, that " they were the inventions of he-
" retics, and are not fo much as to be ranked
" among fpurious books, but are to be rejected
" as wicked and abfurd." The production of
thefe paffages is fo far ufeful, that we perceive
that the fame criterion was applied to one
writing as to another, and that examination
preceded cenfure.

It might perhaps be fuppofed, that in the
early periods of the critical art the Chriftians
might receive books, which, after its introduction, and in its improved ftate, they, or at
leaft others, would have rejected. This is
however rather to anticipate, than to reply to
an objection which has been actually advanced. The fubject then of examination
would be either fuppofititious books, or cor-

ruptions of the Scriptures. It has however appeared, that the heretics, who ufed certain fpurious and apocryphal books in conjunction with the Scriptures, did not alledge any objection derogatory to the authenticity of the latter, although they appealed for the fupport of their peculiar fentiments to writings of no authority. Sacred criticifm might be faid to confift at that time of two branches only; the difcrimination of genuine and authentic from fpurious compofitions, and the collection, or rather perhaps the obfervation, of variations of the copies of the Scriptures, fuppofed to have been altered by heretical individuals, from thofe copies which were in general ufe. This fecond divifion was not neglected; and the comparifon of different copies among the early Chriftians, whether a matter of neceflity or curiofity, of common or of official vigilance, or the effect of a reafonable jealoufy of innovation, muft from thefe caufes have been frequently undertaken. The ftandard would firft be, the evangelical and apoftolical autographs, as long as they could be preferved entire; and afterwards, accurate tranfcripts from thefe, fo that an examination of this kind might to a certain degree be denominated critical. But when Tertullian, in his controverfial work againft

Marcion, affirms, that his Gospel was genuine, and that of Marcion adulterated; and
when Marcion is ^f represented as retorting the
imputation, and Tertullian asking, " Who shall
" decide between us ?'" we are anxious to
know what he regarded as sufficient to terminate such a doubt ; and we find that it was
the consideration of the priority of time, and
the writings in the possession of the churches
founded by the Apostles ; not the *decrees* of
churches, but the books which the most ancient churches followed as their source of religious instruction, and the law of their actions;
in short, it was virtually the comparison of the
copies of the Scriptures among the various
Christian communities, distinct from any exertion of power on their part to recommend, or
to constitute such a canon of Scripture, and no
other authority whatever.   It may perhaps be

---

f " Quis inter nos determinabit, nisi temporis ratio ei
præscribens auctoritatem, quod antiquius reperietur; et
ei præjudicans vitiationem, quod posterius revincetur ? ...
Videamus quod lac a Paulo Corinthii hauserint; ad quam
regulam Galatæ sint recorrecti ; quid legant Philippenses,
Thessalonicenses, Ephesii; quid etiam Romani de proximo
sonent, quibus Evangelium et Petrus et Paulus sanguine
quoque suo signatum reliquerunt.   Habemus et Joannis
alumnas ecclesias.   Tertull. adv. Marc. lib. iv. p. 504, 505.
edit. Lutet. 1634.

worthy of tranfient notice, that the paffage of
g Tertullian to which I refer has been lately employed by one of the Socinian improvers of the
verfion of the New Teftament to fhew the honefty of the Father in acknowledging, that the
queftion could not be determined whether his
Gofpel or Marcion's were the true one. But
the Father has not any title to the praife of honefty from this h modern upon the ground of
the confeffion, that fuch a queftion muft remain undecided ; for he appeals to antiquity
as the arbitrator, not in any remote part of
the fame treatife, but in the fame fentence,
and in words which furnifh the anfwer to his
own interrogation : " Quis inter nos deter-
" minabit, nifi temporis ratio ei præfcribens
" auctoritatem, quod antiquïus reperietur; et
" ei præjudicans vitiationem, quod pofterius
" revincetur."

g Tertull. adv. Marcion. t. i. p. 504. Lutet. 1634.

h I cannot have much refpect for the diffent of a perfon who adapts his authorities to his argument by omiffions. To do full juftice to the author of the letter in
the Monthly Repofitory of Theology, No. 44, I fhall
certainly ftate, that after *determinabit* he has put &c,
but he has alfo placed a note of interrogation after determinabit, *as if the fentence were finifhed.*

The author fays, thát " Epiphanius accufes Marcion
" of corrupting and mutilating his copy of Luke's Gof-

It is difficult, and indeed it is the prominent difficulty in the whole of this enquiry, to difco-

" pel; but Marcion himfelf maintains *his copy to be ge-*
" *nuine.*" Monthly Rep. p. 425. Dr. Marfh, in his notes
on Michaelis, fays, " But that Marcion ufed St. Luke's
" Gofpel at all, is a pofition which has been taken for
" granted, without the leaft proof. Marcion himfelf
" never pretended that it was the Gofpel of St. Luke,
" as Tertullian acknowledges, faying, ' Marcion Evan-
' gelio fuo nullum afcribit autorem.' Adv. Marc. lib. iv.
" c. 2." The whole paffage fhould be given : " Denique
" nobis fidem ex Apoftolis Joannes et Matthæus infinu-
" ant; ex Apoftolicis, Lucas et Marcus inftaurant, iifdem
" regulis exorfi, quantum ad unicum Deum attinet Crea-
" torem, et Chriftum ejus, natum ex virgine, fupplemen-
" tum Legis et Prophetarum. Viderit enim fi narratio-
" num difpofitio variavit, dummodo de capite fidei conve-
" niat, de quo cum Marcione non convenit. *Contra*
" Marcion, evangelio fcilicet fuo, nullum adfcribit aucto-
" rem; quafi non licuerit illi titulum quoque adfingere,
" cui nefas non fuit ipfum corpus evertere. Et poffem
" hic jam gradum figere, non agnofcendum contendens
" opus, quod non erigat frontem, quod nullam conftan-
" tiam præferat, nullam fidem repromittat de plenitudine
" tituli, et profeffione debita auctoris. Sed per omnia
" congredi malumus, nec diffimulamus quod ex noftro
" intelligi poteft. Nam ex iis commentatoribus quos
" habemus, *Lucam videtur Marcion elegiffe* quem cæ-
" ḋeret." Tertullian wifhed that he could have eftablifhed
the fact, that it was the gofpel of this or that writer, becaufe he had then his mode of arguing prepared for his
antagonift. " We," faith he, as Dr. Barrow has tranflated the paffage, " when we would difpatch againft he-

ver any facts whatever; and even those which
are collected do not preclude the necessity of

" retics for the faith of the Gospel, do commonly use
" these short ways, which do maintain both the order of
" times prescribing against the lateness of impostors, and
" the authority of the churches patronizing apostolical
" tradition *." Tertullian uses another word for Marcion's system; he calls it the Gospel of Marcion, and
says, that although such was the mode of proceeding
with heretics, yet in this case " sed alium jam hinc ini-
" mus gradum, ipsum (ut professi sumus) Evangelium
" Marcionis provocantes, sic quoque probaturi adultera-
" tum." The author of the letter avers boldly, " The
" fact then is clear. The disputed chapters were wanting
" in the copy of Marcion, a Christian writer of unim-
" peached integrity, in the beginning of the second cen-
" tury, who maintained, that his was the genuine un-
" adulterated Gospel of Luke; who probably had much
" better opportunities of information than those who
" came after him, and who could have no inducement
" to have rejected this narrative, had it been related by
" the Evangelist." Monthly Rep. p. 425. I should rather think that the opinion in the following passage
would be that inducement : " Marcion, ut carnem Christi
" negaret, negavit etiam nativitatem, aut ut nativitatem
" negaret, negavit et carnem, scilicet ne invicem sibi testi-
" monium redderent et responderent, nativitas et caro,
" quia nec nativitas sine carne, nec caro sine nativi-
" tate." It would seem that Marcion had objected to the
facts contained in these chapters, as Tertullian intimates :
" His, opinor, consiliis tot originalia instrumenta Christi

---

* Dr. Barrow on the Pope's Supremacy, p. 118.

M 3

hypothetical reafoning, either by relating immediately to the fubject, or by fupplying eafy
and indifputable inferences. Eufebius however has preferved an extract from an ancient
anonymous writer on the fubject of the alterations of copies of the Scriptures by fome early
heretics. It is a curious example of their
practice, and fhews that the evidence of ancient writers was not founded upon authority
exclufive of examination. [i] " They who abufe
" the fciences of the infidels for the fupport
" of their heretical fentiments, and with an
" impious fubtlety adulterate the fimple faith
" of the divine Scriptures ; of fuch men what
" need I fay, that they are far from the faith ?

" *delere* Marcion aufus eft, ne caro ejus probaretur."
After further expoftulation he fays, " defiderantes ratio-
" nem qua non putaveris natum effe Chriftum." Tertull.
de Carne Chrifti, cap. 1—3. The heretics were required
to fhew their originals, or the authority for the deviations in their books from thofe received in general ; but
Marcion certainly did not appeal even to any known
apoftolical writer. And the anonymous author againft
Artemo fays, that " they did not receive fuch books
" from thofe by whom they were firft taught the Chrif-
" tian doctrine ;" that " the copies had been written out
" with their own hands ;" and that they were not " able
" to produce the copies from whence they tranfcribed
" thefe things."
[i] Lardner's tranflation.

" for which reafon they have without fear laid
" their hands upon the divine Scriptures, fay-
" ing, that they have amended them. And
" that I do not charge them falfely any one
" may know that pleafeth. For if any one
" will be at the pains to procure a number of
" their copies, and compare them together, he
" will find that they difagree very much.
" For the copies of Afclepiades (or Afclepio-
" dotus) differ from thofe of Theodotus. And
" many of them may be met with, becaufe
" their difciples have diligently tranfcribed
" their feveral emendations, as they call them,
" but indeed corruptions. Again, the copies
" of Hermophilus agree not with thefe already
" mentioned. And thofe of Apollonides (or
" Apollonius) differ one from another: for
" any one, by comparing thofe firft put out
" with thefe, which were afterwards again
" perverted by him, may perceive a difference.
" How daring a crime this is, poffibly they
" themfelves are not ignorant: for either they
" do not believe the divine Scriptures to have
" been dictated by the Holy Spirit, and then
" they are infidels; or elfe they think them-
" felves wifer than the Holy Spirit, and what
" are they then but mad men? For they can-
" not deny this their daring crime, fince the

" copies have been writ out with their own
" hands; and they did not receive fuch books
" from thofe by whom they were firft taught
" the Chriftian doctrine: nor are they able
" to produce the copies, from whence they
" tranfcribed thefe things ᵏ." To this extract
it has been objected, " that it is probable that
" all the alterations or corruptions complained
" of concerned only the copies of the Old
" Teftament." But a paffage in a preceding
part of the citation, expreffed in fimilar language, will not permit us to avail ourfelves of
the advantage, if advantage it can be called,
of transferring thefe corruptions to other authentic books. " Moreover," fays the fame
author, " they have without fear corrupted
" the divine Scriptures, and have rejected the
" rule or canon of the ancient faith, and have
" been ignorant of Chrift ˡ."

ᵏ Eufeb. Hift. Ecclef. lib. v. verf. fin.
ˡ To this paffage I may add others from Lardner himfelf, which fhew that the Scriptures of the New, and not
the Old Teftament, were the fubject of this citation.

1. " The defign of the firft paffage of this work is to
" fhew the novelty of that herefy, that our Saviour was
" a mere man; whereas the perfons againft whom the
" author writes afferted its antiquity." We may now
obferve how the fubfequent paffages relate to this topic,
and confequently to thofe books which contain it.

It is not perhaps à correct affertion of the

2. "For they fay, that all the ancients, and even the A-
" poftles themfelves, received and taught the fame things
" which they now hold; and that the truth of the Gof-
" pel was preferved till the time of Victor : but by his
" fucceffor (or, from the time of his fucceffor) Zephyrine
" the truth has been corrupted." The words " of the
" Gofpel" are inferted by Lardner.   I do not mean that
the fenfe of the paffage does not juftify fuch an infertion;
but it evinces how he himfelf underftood the tendency of
the quotation.

3. " And poffibly what they fay might have been cre-
" dited, if, firft of all, the divine Scriptures did not contra-
" dict them; and then alfo, fecondly, the writings of bre-
" thren more ancient than Victor, which they publifhed in
" defence of the truth againft the Gentiles, and againft the
" herefies of their time."   " The brethren mentioned by
" name," proceeds Lardner, " are Juftin, Miltiades, Ta-
" tian, Clement, Irenæus, Melito, with a general appeal
" to many more not named, and to ancient hymns, com-
" pofed by the faithful in honour of Chrift."   Lardner
has not given the full import of the fentence.   " Who
" is unacquainted with the books of Irenæus, and Me-
" lito, and the reft, which declare the Chrift to be God
" and man? How many pfalms and hymns, compofed
" long fince by faithful brethren, celebrate and afcribe
" divinity to the Chrift the Word of God!" This is what
was faid " in honour of Chrift."

4. " There was one Natalis, a confeffor, not long ago,
" but in our times.   This perfon was deceived by Afcle-
" piodatus, and another, Theodotus, a banker, both dif-
" ciples of the firft, who had been-excommunicated by
" Victor for this opinion, or rather madnefs."   It was

very learned author of the Canon of the New

before alledged by the heretics, that the " truth of the
" Gofpel," or their own opinion, was preferved till the
" time of Victor." To which it is replied, that " what
" they fay might have been credited, if, firft of all, the
" divine Scriptures did not contradict them; and then
" alfo, fecondly, the writings of brethren more ancient
" than Victor, which they publifhed in defence of the
" truth againft the Gentiles, and againft the herefies of
" their time." I muft confider all thefe portions of the
extract, which I have feparated into thefe divifions in
order to examine them minutely; and I fee no reafon
why they are not to be confidered as forming, not fo
much the introduction, as a part of the citation itfelf,
which is faid to refer to the Old Teftament. If fo, there
is a great confufion in the references; for in the above
paffage " writings more ancient than Victor" would not
be affociated with " the divine Scriptures" in the preceding fentence, unlefs the periods of both approximated to
each other.

5. " They did not receive fuch books from thofe by
" whom they were firft taught the Chriftian doctrine."
I muft firft obferve, that the words " Chriftian doctrine"
are an addition of Lardner. I think therefore that I am
authorized by thefe paffages to conclude, that the fubjects of them were, the Chriftian doctrine and the Chriftian fcriptures. The termination of the extract relates,
it may be fuppofed, in part to the Old Teftament. " Nay,
" fome of them have not thought it worth the while to
" corrupt the Scriptures, but, plainly rejecting the law
" and the prophets, by means of a lawlefs and impious
" doctrine, [taken up] under pretence of grace, they
" have fallen into the loweft pit of deftruction." I can-

Teftament, that certain heretics agreed " in

not acquiefce in Lardner's inference, " that they are
" therefore the fcriptures of the Old Teftament that he
" had been fpeaking of all along, when he complained
" of the alterations of 'the divine Scriptures." Thefe
perfons feem to have rejected all the fcriptures both of
the Old and New Teftament, and were fatisfied that
grace was fufficient without either.

6. " And fince thefe alterations were made, or at-
" tempted to be made, in a verfion only, (fome Greek
" verfion of the Old Teftament, probably that of the
" Seventy,) the damage is the lefs." I do not perceive
what is gained by transferring the injury to the Greek
verfion of the Seventy, even if that were the fubject of
the citation. But the alterations evidently related to a
doctrine, the antiquity of which is not carried higher
by the difputants themfelves than the time of the Apoftles. " For they fay, that all the ancients, and even the
" Apoftles themfelves, received and taught the fame
" things which they now hold."

7. " It is reafonable to make fome abatements in the
" charges of this writer. He blames thefe perfons, againft
" whom he writes, for th ngs in which there is no fault.
" He cenfures them for ftudying geometry, and for ad-
" miring Ariftotle and Theophraftus." This is not candid. He explains it by faying, that they did not enquire
" what the divine Scriptures fay," but " carefully" ftudied " what figure of fyllogifm may be found out *to*
" *fupport their impious fyftem.* And if any one object
" to them a text of divine Scripture, they confider whe-
" ther a conjunctive or disjunctive form of fyllogifm can
" be made of it. He does not cenfure the ftudy of geometry in the abftract : he exprefsly fpecifies, that, " *leav-*

" receiving and efteeming. a fpurious work

" ing the holy fcriptures of God, they ftudy geometry,
" as being of the earth, and fpeaking of the earth, and
" ignorant of him that cometh from above."

8. " Poffibly they only joined together thefe two ftu-
" dies." That is not improbable, I allow; but how were
they conjoined? He fpeaks of them as perfons " who
" abufe the fciences of the infidels for the fupport of their
" heretical fentiment, and with an impious fubtlety adul-
" terate the fimple faith of the divine Scriptures."

9. " He infinuates too, that fome of them adored Ga-
" len, which is very improbable." The improbability
here is againft the refpectable author: Galen was a dia-
lectician of great eminence. Lardner could fcarcely be
ignorant of this note of Valefius on this paffage: " Ga-
" lenus enim *de figuris fyllogifmorum et de tota philofo-*
" *phia* libros confcripferat, ut ex librorum ejus indice
" cognofcimus.—Nec vero ex hoc tantum fcriptore, ve-
" rum etiam ex aliis quamplurimis idem colligere licet,
" qui Galenum Ariftoteli ac Theophrafto, ipfique adeo
" Platoni æquare non dubitarunt." And then follows
a paffage in confirmation of this fact from Alexander
Aphrodifienfis. I may perhaps be allowed to ufe the
authority of this extract from Eufebius to explain the
reafon why Ariftotle, Theophraftus, and a work of Galen, Περὶ Φιλοσόφȣ Ἰδέας, are found together in the fplendid collection of thefe writers printed by Aldus. They
are thus affociated, and perhaps not cafually, in the mag-
nificent copies on vellum and paper.

I cannot but remark, that Lardner has tranflated the
paffage from Eufebius as if he underftood it as the generality of readers would underftand its tendency, and has
reafoned from it in oppofition to the words which he

" above all other fcriptures^m." The Encra-
tites are faid to have ufed *principally* thofe
writings entitled the Acts of Andrew and
John, the Apoftolici to have depended *chiefly*
upon them, and the Manichees to have ufed
them ; but it does not follow that they rejected the Scriptures, becaufe they received
books of this kind : it rather feems that the
authority of each was diftinct and independent. The Scriptures ftill maintained, even
in the eftimation of the heretics themfelves, an
ufe and an importance, which certainly were
not deftroyed, nor even impaired, by being
affociated with fictitious compofitions. We
may be allowed to conclude likewife, that
thefe forgeries were ufed without any intention to vilify the genuine Scriptures, and without any attempt to corrupt them, however
contrary to the Scriptures thofe doctrines
might be, which the heretics introduced into

has, juftifiably indeed, added to his verfion, but which re-
ftrict all, except the conclufion of the citation, to the fubject of the doctrine of the New Teftament refpecting our
Saviour's nature, and the alteration of the copies of the
New Teftament; and even the laft part refpects the abufe
of a doctrine peculiar to the Gofpel of Chrift. Is this
one of the early intimations of the abufe of the doctrine
of grace ?

^m Jones, vol. i. p. 148.

such writings. This distinction is precisely and satisfactorily observed in the account of the practices of the Sabellians by Epiphanius; and probably the other heretical sects acted in the same manner. [n] " They make use of " all the Scriptures both of the Old and New " Testament; but principally of some certain " passages, which they pick out according to " their own corrupt and preposterous senti- " ments. But the whole of their errors, and " the main strength of their heterodoxy, they " have from some apocryphal books, but prin- " cipally from that which is called the Gospel " of the Egyptians."

The next instance, from which we may deduce a probable argument respecting the state of the Scriptures, is the life of Pythagoras by Jamblichus, who has been supposed to write this character with a view to put it in competition with that of our Saviour. I am not ignorant that this intention is disputed by an able and learned writer, but perhaps without sufficient reason. In representing Pythagoras as equal in every respect to our Saviour, the author found it necessary, in the adaptation of this fictitious resemblance, not merely to make

[n] Jones, Canon of the New Test. vol. i. p. 200.

him a rival teacher of morality, but to affign
to him a divine defcent. He is defcribed to
have had God as his father, and to have been
himfelf a god in the form of man for the fake
of men, left they might be overpowered by
the greatnefs of his majefty, and thus be de-
terred from becoming his difciples. The author of " The Diffonance" has afferted, as
I have remarked in a preceding Lecture, that
St. Matthew and St. Luke formed their genealogies of our Saviour on the model of the
ancient mythology. But in this account of
the origin of Pythagoras we may obferve a
ftriking and characteriftic variation. It is not
adjufted to the principles, if they may be fo
called, of the Pagan theogony. In this the
parent deities had previoufly paffed through
the ftate of humanity. In the comparifon of
Pythagoras with our Saviour, the former is
faid to be a god, and the fon of God, with
the form of man. The beneficence to men
followed from his power as a god, but was
not the caufe of a fubfequent deification. If
however it be a correct obfervation of ° Lardner, who is learned and judicious, but not always unprejudiced, when he affirms of the

* Vol. viii. p. 283. orig. ed. in 17 vol.

authors of the different lives of Pythagoras,
" that they have faid nothing new of him ;
" nothing, but what had been often faid of
" him before the appearance of the Chriftian
" religion in the world ;" then the latter Platonifts had no inducement to alter the Gofpels in this important particular, the divinity
of our Lord, or to accommodate the older accounts of Pythagoras to the evangelical ftandard of perfection.

We have reafon then to conclude, that
Chriftianity, upon its firft publication in writing, would not have been expofed to any peculiar danger even from the previous appearance of fpurious and apocryphal books. There
was a greater peril, which arofe from falfified
copies of the genuine Scriptures. But ftill
there was the fame mode, not indeed of avoid-
ing, but of paffing through both thefe kinds
of trial. We certainly cannot refolve the reception of the records of Chriftianity into the
degrading advantage of having preoccupied
the attention of mankind, but muft deduce
their fuperior difperfion, in oppofition to what
was either intrinfecally bafe, or partially vi-
tiated, as the refult of extenfive and equal inveftigation.

SERMON VI.

———◆———

2 PET. i. 16.

We have not followed cunningly devised fables.

PURSUING the inveſtigation reſpecting the authenticity of the writings of the New Teſtament, I am next to conſider in what manner the genealogy, and the two firſt chapters of St. Matthew's Goſpel, were received in the early ages. The ſubject has been frequently diſcuſſed by theological writers, but ſomething may ſtill remain for ſubſequent enquiry. All the facts reſpecting this ſubject may not have been collected, and the concluſions, which the well known facts ſuggeſt, may differ according to the peculiar object of the writer, and the extent of his previous examination of the queſtion.

The genealogy of Chriſt in the beginning of this Goſpel has been rejected by ſome on account of an alledged deficiency both in the internal and external evidence of its authen-

N

ticity. The author of ᵃ " The Diſſonance'" is
ſatisfied with boldly aſſerting " its irrecon-
" cileable contradiction to that introduced into
" St. Luke's Goſpel." ᵇ Others affirm, that
ſome of the ancient ſects of Chriſtians received
a copy of St. Matthew's Goſpel " which had
" not the genealogy." If this be intended to
imply, that ſuch was the original ſtate of the
volume, it is a falſification of its hiſtory. We
know that one of theſe ſects removed it from
its ancient and proper place by ſiniſter means,
as by eraſure, or exciſion; and then we are to
be informed, that the genuine copy did not
contain the genealogy. It is extraordinary
that it ſhould be taken away without aſſigning
any reaſon relative to its want of authenticity.
The perſons who removed or expunged it
were intereſted in the expoſure of ſuch an im-
poſition as the inſertion of what was repugnant to their peculiar opinions; and, inſtead
of rejecting it under the pretext of diſappro-
bation of the doctrines which it favoured,

<hr>

ᵃ Page 149.

ᵇ Williams's Free Enquiry into the authenticity of the
firſt and ſecond Chapters of St. Matthew's Goſpel, p. 33;
and Dr. Prieſtley's Hiſtory of Early Opinions, vol. iii.
p. 213.

ᶜ Free Enquiry, p. 54.

fhould have ftigmatized it as a forgery, and have juftified their rejection of it in this manner. Had their pretenfions been well founded, they might have proved from their own proximity to the time, when all the copies of the Gofpel might be faid to be recent, that they derived their tenets from the unadulterated and acknowledged language of Scripture; and they ought to have appealed for the proof of this to the numerous copies of the New Teftament, difperfed among the faithful in various parts of the Chriftian world. But they do not alledge reafons of this kind. They do not fay, that the genealogy was a novel and ftrange addition to this Gofpel. They affign a fpeculative reafon, the oppofition of their own opinions to the written word, when they ought to have produced direct evidence from the confent of the greater part of the tranfcripts that the obnoxious portion was an interpolation; and they fhould have determined and fpecified the time of its infertion. Both common fenfe and vulgar honefty concurred in dictating this mode of conduct; thefe fuperfeded the authority of criticifm, and impofed upon them the neceffity of collating copies, as an office of candour and integrity, and not an effort of learning

and ingenuity. They did not collate, becaufe
fuch a reference and comparifon would have
been deftructive of the opinions which they
wifhed to fupport, becaufe it would have appeared that the genealogy was contained in
all the authentic copies. Tatian indeed is
faid to have omitted in his Diateffaron " the
" genealogies, and every thing that fhewed
" the Lord to have been born of the feed of
" David according to the flefh." Hence it
has been argued [d], that Tatian " would not ufe
" any copies of the Gofpels but what were
" known to be authentic;" and therefore the
authentic copies did not contain the genealogy. But, allowing more force to this argument of the author of the Free Enquiry than
it deferves, it cannot be applied to a work
which profeffed to be a compendium only,
and therefore may reafonably be fuppofed to
omit whatever was not comprehended within
the plan of the abbreviator. If indeed Tatian
had propofed to give tranfcripts of each of the
former Gofpels, inftead of an epitome of them
all, then the argument would have had fome
weight; but even as it is circumftanced at
prefent, thefe fuppofed authentic copies of the

[d] Free Enquiry, p. 54.

Gofpels were not only without the genealogies, but likewife " every thing that fhewed
" the Lord to have been born of the feed of
" David according to the flefh." It is however not only not reafonable, but it is in contradiction to fact, to extend the deficiency of
Tatian's Diateffaron to the originals from
which he compiled that fummary. Theodoret
difcovered in fome Chriftian churches no lefs
than two hundred copies of this work of Tatian, which he took away, and fubftituted in
their place entire copies of the Gofpels. The
facility with which he fupplied the Chriftian
affemblies with fo many entire and complete
tranfcripts of the Gofpels proves, that the heretics might alter by mutilation or infertion
their own copies of the books of Scripture,
without any impeachment of the integrity of
thofe which were in the hands of others. In
thofe churches which had received the Diateffaron of Tatian, enquiries would be made
refpecting the portions which had been omitted in that work, and now appeared in thofe
volumes, which Theodoret had authoritatively
fubftituted. Tatian's book however had been
ufed, e " not only by thofe of his own fect,

---

e Lardner, vol. ii. p. 138.

" but alfo by them who follow the apoftolical
" doctrine, not perceiving the fraud of the
" compofition, but fimply ufing it as a com-
" pendious work." This is no confirmation
of the opinion of thofe who affert, that the
Unitarian was the apoftolical doctrine. Thefe
perfons, it feems, did not difcover the omiffion
of any material parts. Shall we then fay,
that the birth of our Lord according to the
flefh might, or might not, be inferted without
affecting the proofs of the Unitarian faith?
It is evident, that, from the time of Tatian in
the fecond century, to that of Theodoret in
the fifth, the knowledge of this deficiency in
the Diateffaron had not been fo generally promulgated, as we may conceive it would have
been, if the majority of the members of the
apoftolical church had been Unitarians. It
fhould alfo appear to be a remarkable incident,
that one of the fathers of the church, who
are fo frequently accufed of corrupting the
facred volume through their zeal for orthodoxy, fhould furnifh other copies of the Gofpels, which contained thofe paffages, that, in
the interpretation of the Cerinthians, " proved
" the human defcent of our Lord from the
" feed of David according to the flefh," and
which for this reafon would have difpofed

Theodoret to have recommended the ufe of the Diateffaron of Tatian. But the argument refpecting Tatian's ufe of none but authentic copies is equivocal, and may be applied to affect the credit of Tatian himfelf, at leaft as much as it does that of the genealogies. We have no reafon to think that Tatian would be very fcrupulous refpecting the authenticity of thofe copies of St. Matthew's Gofpel which he confulted, when he publifhed many opinions and doctrines repugnant to the principles contained in all the Gofpels. He that condemned marriage as a diabolical inftitution would not be much interefted in the prefervation of the purity of a record, which gave to it a religious fanction. We are preffed however with meaner difficulties than thefe, which, if they do not increafe the number or the force of the arguments of our adverfaries, ftrongly characterize the fpirit of their oppofition. They infift, that there is " full proof " that the genealogy was queftioned in very " early ages." It was the practice of feveral copyifts to place the genealogy at fome diftance from the commencement of the Gofpel; and hence it is concluded, that it did not conftitute a part of the Gofpel itfelf. We cannot believe that doubts refpecting its authenticity

would produce only a peculiarity in the arrangement of the introductory paffages. Are
we to collect an opinion fo important from
the mechanical procefs of meafuring the myftic
interval between one fentence and another? Are
thefe the ufual indications of critical difappro-
bation? But to what other caufe than imperfect enquiry can we afcribe the following affertion of the learned f tranflator of Michaelis,
who informs us, that " the writers of Latin
" manufcripts, who wrote the genealogy apart
" from the reft of the Gofpel, were actuated
" not by critical, but theological motives.
" They found difficulty in reconciling the ge-
" nealogy in Matth. i. with that of Luke iii.
" and therefore wifhed to get rid of it." It
is not pretended that the tranfcriber has intimated that there was any fignificant peculiarity in the collocation of the genealogy. When
one g copyift has explicitly apprized the reader,
that he " omitted the ftory of the adulterous
" woman in the Gofpel of St. John, as being
" wanting in moft copies, and not mentioned
" by the holy fathers Chryfoftom, Cyril, Theo-
" dorus, and others," we are juftified in ex-

f Vol. iii. part ii. p. 139.
g See Wetftein in loc. It is the Reuchlin MS.

pecting fome explanation of this critical invention, the interpofition of a certain interval
between the genealogy and the commencement of the narrative; and we ought to be
informed, that it is fymbolical of fufpected
authenticity, or expreffive of " the theological
" motives" of the tranfcribers. We cannot
admit that any mode of placing the genealogy
is equivalent to " getting rid of it." It is
fuppofed [h], " that the plain inconfiftencies be-
" tween this genealogy and the Old Tefta-
" ment hiftory might eafily be perceived, and
" fufpicions concerning its authenticity be
" foon fpread abroad." But in what manner
were thefe fufpicions made known? Was the
mode of difpofing the genealogy among the
means employed for this purpofe? Was it the
only evidence of fuch fufpicions? If fuch fufpicions were ever entertained, there were two
unambiguous ways of communicating them
to the affemblies of Chriftians; either an explicit declaration of the fact, or the abfolute omiffion in the generality of copies of
what was fufpected. It feems however as
if the genealogy exifted as a document independent and unattached. Epiphanius re-

h Free Enquiry, p. 36.

lates [i], that a Jew difcovered in a cell of one
of the treafuries at Tiberias, among other volumes, " the Hebrew ftemmata according to
" St. Matthew." In whatever way we interpret thefe words of Epiphanius, whether they
fignify the portion of the Hebrew Gofpel
which had been cut away by fome of the heretics; or whether they denote the whole
Gofpel, by expreffing a part, ftill the reference
to the writing is preferved, from which it derived its appellation and authority. It is admitted by the editors of " the improved ver-
" fion," as it is called, " of the New Tefta-
" ment, that the genealogy was in the copies
" at leaft of Cerinthus and Carpocrates." It
is fomewhat extraordinary that this conceffion
fhould be made in favour of the prefent Greek
Gofpel, when Cerinthus and Carpocrates certainly ufed the Gofpel according to the Hebrews, which was written in the Syro-Chal-

i Jones has noticed this paffage of Epiphanius, but
tranflated φυτὸν, *Gofpel.* Οὐ μὴν ἀλλὰ καὶ τὸ κατὰ Ματθαῖον
Ἑβραϊκόν φυτόν. Epiphan. adv. Hær. p. 130. ed. Petav.
The author of the Free Enquiry has fpoken of it in the
fame manner: " Epiphanius fays, that a Jew named Jo-
" feph found in a cell at Tiberias the Hebrew Gofpel
" afcribed to St. Matthew." He refers to Mofheim de
Reb. Chriftian. p. 207, whence he had the reference to
Epiphanius.

daic dialect. This Gospel, which had its double appellation from the Jewish party who
received it, and from the Evangelist Matthew,
whose narrative it professed to follow, was
used by the Nazarenes, Cerinthians, and Ebionites; but it underwent some change in the
hands of the latter sect. The Nazarenes do
not seem to have altered their copy in any
known respect; and Epiphanius calls it "most
" entire." The Ebionites had introduced un-
authorized additions, and had mutilated the
commencement of it; and the same Father
terms this "not wholly entire." It is thought,
however, that Epiphanius does not consist-
ently apply the epithet "most entire" to the
Gospel of the Nazarenes, and at the same time
express his ignorance, "whether they had
" taken away the genealogy from Abraham
" to Christ." k " With what propriety," it is
asked, " could he say that it was most entire,
" if he suspected that any genuine part of it
" was taken away?" But he did not suspect;
his want of information precluded suspicion.
He speaks in the same dubious language of
the opinions of the Nazarenes concerning the
nature of Christ: " I cannot affirm," he says,

k Free Enquiry, p. 74.

" whether, carried away by the impiety of
" Cerinthus and Merinthus, they confider him
" as a mere man ; or, as the truth is, that he
" was begotten of Mary by the Holy Ghoft."
It may perhaps be doubted whether a late
learned Prelate, in his reply to the writer of
" the Hiftory of the Corruptions of Chrif-
" tianity," has not impaired the general credibility of the evidence of the ancient Father
by the extent of his cenfure. [1]" The confef-
" fion of Epiphanius amounts," he thinks,
" to that of a bafe accufer, who had not the
" liberality to abfolve in explicit terms, when
" he found himfelf unable to convict." If
this were a juft character of the evidence of
the hiftorian in this inftance, it would be im-
proper to appeal to it in any queftion relative
to the tenets of particular fects. It appears
however, upon a careful comparifon of the
two paffages, that one doubt depended upon
another; that the rejection of the genealogy
would have afcertained their opinion concerning Chrift, or the knowledge of this opinion
would have determined the fact of the rejection of the genealogy. His language is certainly not reconcileable with the fuppofition,

[1] Horfley's Tracts, p. 144.

that he had feen the Hebrew Gofpel of the
Nazarenes; but no other reafon is affigned
for his having feen it, than that he ᵐ was a
native of Paleftine. This argument will only
fhew, that he could not be ignorant of the
contents of a certain book, becaufe he was a
native of the country where the perfons lived
who ufed it, and where the particular place
was fituated in which it was preferved. The
morality of the Father will not be impeached
by the mere authority of the objectors, whofe
furmifes cannot be admitted without proof.
Cerinthus and Carpocrates appealed to the genealogy as authority for their refpective opinions; and the Cerinthians ufed the Gofpel
according to Matthew on account of ⁿ " the
" carnal genealogy," as it is expreffed by Epiphanius. The Ebionites rejected the genealogy. It has been before obferved º, that the
editors of the improved verfion of the New
Teftament admit the authenticity of the ge-

ᵐ Free Enquiry, p. 84. " It is not credible that he
" was unacquainted with the Nazarene Gofpel," and the
reafon of this opinion is fubjoined in a note, " as he was
" a native of Paleftine."

ⁿ Διὰ τὴν ἐνσάρκον γενεαλόγιαν are the words of Epiphanius.

º Page 186.

nealogy in the Greek Gospel on the authority
of its insertion in the Hebrew Gospel of the
Nazarenes, which, it has been conjectured,
was the original of St. Matthew. It is not
my intention to consider the question, whether the Greek of St. Matthew is a version
from the Hebrew, not only because it has
been so often discussed before, but because it
must be nearly a mere conjectural enquiry
from the paucity of historical facts. But such
facts as remain are in favour of Greek originals, and Syro-Chaldaic versions. After the
destruction of Jerusalem, the Jews retired to
Tiberias; where they established synagogues
and schools, and preserved their writings. In
a cell of one of the treasuries at Tiberias, Hebrew versions, as they are called, were found
of those books of the New Testament which
are allowed to have been originally written in
the Greek language. It may also be remarked,
that whatever force there may be in the ob-
servation of the author of the History of the
early Opinions concerning Christ, respecting a
Hebrew version of the Gospel of St. John, it
is in favour of the orthodox faith. P " Though
" this Gospel," says he, " was written in

P History of Early Opinions, vol. iii. p. 161.

" Greek, there were not wanting among the
" Jewilh Chriftians men of learning, who
" would not have failed to give an account.
" of it to their more ignorant countrymen,
" or to tranflate it for their ufe, if it had been
" thought neceffary." Whether the verfion
were undertaken becaufe it was " thought
" neceffary," we are not informed; but only
that the books of the New Teftament, to
which I before alluded as exifting in Hebrew
verfions, were, the Acts of the Apoftles, and
this very Gofpel of St. John. We are not
told by Epiphanius, who has recorded the
fact, whether this Gofpel were fpurious, or
mutilated, or entire; but he defcribes it as a
tranflation from the Greek: and we may fuppofe, that it had at leaft as good a title to be
called the Gofpel of St. John, as the Gofpel of
St. Matthew, ufed by the Nazarenes, had to
be denominated after that Evangelift. It is
argued, however, that the mutilation or corruption of St. Matthew's Gofpel could not be
effected at all, becaufe it could not be effected
without difcovery; and that it would have
created new divifions among the heretical brethren, q " of which we have not the leaft foot-

q Free Enquiry, p. 72.

" fteps in all antiquity." But this is affuming, that the ftate of the books of Scripture determined the exiftence of fects, and particularly of thofe, which owed their origin to their different opinions concerning the nature of Chrift. But there is reafon to think that thefe opinions were adopted independently of the language of fcripture, and applied as the ftandard of its reception, without any view to the confideration of its fcriptural authority. The fear of difcovery did not operate in preventing the Ebionites from mutilating their Gofpel without referve, and from effecting, without any recorded endeavour to conceal it, the excifion of its commencement. Marcion indeed feems to have been reftrained by fome motive from afcribing his Gofpel to an Evangelift, after he had adapted it to his own fentiments; and Tertullian reproaches him with this filence, as an attempt to veil his fraud from the world : but ftill the fear of detection only produced the endeavour to conceal what he had done, but did not influence him fo ftrongly as to caufe him to abftain from his purpofe. We may alfo enquire, who were the heretics that were to be ftill further divided by altering this Gofpel, which was common to them all ? Thofe certainly, who maintained doctrines which thofe parts

of the Gospel, that were either to be retained
or taken away, confirmed or oppoſed. Theſe
then muſt have been the Nazarenes, the Ebionites, Cerinthians, and Carpocratians. The
Nazarenes had not perhaps altered the Goſpel
in any reſpect. Cerinthus and the Cerinthians
uſed it becauſe it contained the genealogy,
and ſhewed the human deſcent of our Saviour;
Carpocrates adopted it for the ſame reaſon,
but the Ebionites rejected it. It is clear then
that the ſects were already ſeparated ; that
their difference of opinion influenced their notion of the ſtandard of their Goſpel, and that
the preſervation merely, of the integrity of the
Scripture would not have diminiſhed the number of contending parties, becauſe their differences did not originate from this ſource.
Another expedient has been ſuggeſted, which,
if there were any foundation for the apprehenſion of multiplying diviſions among the
heretics, by the eraſure of the genealogy, or
of the two firſt chapters of St. Matthew's
Goſpel, would not have obviated the expected
conſequence. r " There was another way, by
" which Cerinthus and the other heretics
" might get clear of this difficulty, without

---

r Free Enquiry, p. 75.

O

" expunging two whole chapters ; they might
" have rejected St. Matthew's Gofpel alto-
" gether, and acknowledged St. Mark's as
" alone authentic." It is not eafy to underftand how the rejection of the entire Gofpel
would have promoted unanimity, when the
extinction of two chapters would have occafioned a new feparation among the fects. But
whatever advantage might have accrued to
the fects in preferring St. Mark's Gofpel,
which required no adaptation to their purpofe, at leaft of the fame violent kind, yet we
muft allow the ancient fects to have underftood their own reafons for feparation from
each other better than we can in the prefent
age. There muft ftill have been fomething in
St. Matthew's Gofpel, even when mutilated
by themfelves, which they preferred to that
of St. Mark, which did not accord fo well
with their own peculiar objects and fentiments. Our opponents are not unwilling to
admit that Cerinthus and Carpocrates were
not ˢ " afraid of thefe two chapters, as unfa-
" vourable to their peculiar opinions." Here
then we might hope to conclude the argument with this acknowledgment : but it does

---

ˢ Free Enquiry, p. 72.

not terminate at this point. The age of Cerinthus, it is alledged, is to be referred to a
later period than is ufually affigned, becaufe
the two chapters in queftion are not diftinctly,
alluded to before the fecond century. But it
muft be obferved, that the paffages, to which
thefe references are made by the Fathers, who
flourifhed in the fecond century, occur in the
Greek copy which we now have; and they
did not cite, as Cerinthus and Carpocrates
did, a Hebrew Gofpel. It fhould alfo be remembered, that, in this controverfy refpecting the genealogy and the two firft chapters of St. Matthew, the parties appeal indifcriminately to the copy ufed by Cerinthus
and the Ebionites, which was the Gofpel according to the Hebrews; and the Greek
copy, which thofe Fathers ufed, who could
not ufe any other, on account of their ignorance of the Syro-Chaldaic language. The
want of references to thefe chapters in the
writings of the apoftolical Fathers is to be accounted for on the fuppofition, that there was
not a proper occafion to introduce them. Their
debates with Jewifh unbelievers were not of
a kind, probably, to require an appeal to this
part of the Gofpel. The preceptive and hor-
tatory portions of Scripture were more adapt-

ed to their paſtoral addreſſes than proofs of
controverted ſubjects.   But the martyr Juſtin
has made ſuch frequent appeals to theſe chapters, that the author of the Hiſtory of the
Early Opinions ſays, '" that it is almoſt cer-
" tain that the ſtory of the miraculous con-
" ception was in the received Goſpels of Mat-
" thew and Luke in the time of Juſtin Mar-
" tyr.'"   We are not however to employ this
evidence, becauſe it is doubted whether theſe
facts were in all the copies of the Goſpel in
that age.   We do not indeed pretend to know
what was in all the copies of that age, nor
what particular copy each ancient Father
might have uſed ; but the hiſtorical evidence
which we now poſſeſs relates to a period prior
to the times of Juſtin : and we are told that
from the Hebrew Goſpel of St. Matthew one
ſet of heretics eraſed the two firſt chapters,
and another ſet retained them.   Whether the
Greek copies underwent, at that time, the
ſame alteration, or were adopted entire, it is
impoſſible now to aſcertain.   It is important,
however, to know upon what grounds the
ſects mutilated the books which they received.
They do not ſpeak of copies which did not

t Theological Repoſitory, p. 268.

originally contain what they expunged, but
condemn the paffages from their contrariety
to their own tenets. But there is another
mode of reafoning, which would annihilate all
hiftorical teftimony, and not that of Juftin
only. ᵘ " The argument of general reception
" we ufe in favour of Chriftianity, and with
" great juftice; becaufe this made its way
" amidft the greateft oppofition, and the moft
" dreadful perfecution. But this cannot be
" faid with refpect to any particular fyftem of
" opinions contained, or fuppofed to be con-
" tained, in the New Teftament. Thefe there-
" fore may have not only found their way,
" but may have become very prevalent, among
" Chriftians, without having gone through a
" proper difcuffion. And as this may have
" been the cafe in Juftin's age, as well as in
" any other, no conclufion can be drawn.
" from his mere declaration, that any parti-
" cular doctrine which he advances is to be
" regarded as part of the original Gofpel of
" Jefus Chrift." There is a peculiarity in the
facts of the Gofpel, of which this adverfary
has availed himfelf, and that will admit of a
double interpretation. The facts related in

ᵘ Pope on the Miraculous Conception, p. 205.

the Gofpel are not merely hiftorical anecdotes, but are to be confidered as objects both of hif-. torical and religious belief. When therefore it is faid that any particular doctrine, which an ancient Father advances, is not to be re- garded, from the authority of his mere decla- ration, as part of the original Gofpel of Jefus Chrift, we have no hefitation in affenting to this pofition. But when the particular doc- trine is alfo a fact, as the miraculous concep- tion, and the declaration of the Father is a reference to the hiftory, of which the miracu- lous conception is one of the events, the tefti- mony of the Father is of the greateft weight, when conjoined with the agreement of the co- pies of the hiftory with his citations or allufions. But it is faid, firft, that thefe doctrines had not, at the time of Juftin, been properly dif- cuffed. And again, another adverfary affirms, that the chapters containing the doctrines are not noticed till the fecond century; which, whilft it allows time for the difcuffion, fup- pofed to have been fo neceffary by the other opponent, detracts on the other fide from their antiquity. But the fact is otherwife. The early divifions in the church were founded on difference of opinion relating to the nature of Chrift; and it was in confequence of opinions,

formed upon the difcuffion of parties feparating 'from one another upon fuch enquiries;
that the Hebrew Gofpel was mutilated and
corrupted.   It is in confequence of the perverfion of the prophecy of Ifaiah by the Jew
Trypho that Juftin Martyr adduces the paffages relating to the miraculous conception ;
and we may conclude that this conference,
whether real or fictitious, related to topics
which formed the moft interefting fubjects of
difcuffion in that age.   It would alfo follow
from the preceding hypothefis, what cannot
be proved, that Juftin could not ufe any tranfcripts of the Gofpel but thofe which had
been made within the period of his own life.

.. The internal evidence of thefe chapters has
been fo frequently impugned by the fame objections, and defended by fuch well known
arguments, that it is neceffary to felect fuch
of the former as will admit of fome novelty
in the reply. The author of " The Diffonance"
afferts, " that they contain many wonderful
" circumftances, repugnant to the other fcrip-
" tures, and to common fenfe, and unfup-
" ported by any other hiftory, facred or pro-
" fane."   Some of thefe circumftances, as the
arrival of the Magi at Jerufalem, guided by
fome celeftial phenomenon, the declaration of

the object of their journey, the alarm of Herod, and the folicitude of the whole Jewifh
capital, form a natural combination of incidents, not impoffible indeed to be forged, but
agreeable to every teft of moral certainty; as,
if falfe, the impofition would be fo eafily detected, from the publicity with which the
facts are faid to have been tranfacted, and the
numerous opportunities of minute examination to which they were fubjected. We cannot draw from this, or any other confideration deduced from the narrative itfelf, a pofitive conclufion that the events were real, but
we do not fee any defects in this argument
which diminifh its probability. The pretended
repugnancy of the facts to Scripture is faid to
confift in the felection of a defcription of perfons to announce the Meffiah, whofe art had
been ridiculed by the ancient prophets, and
who, when they appeared among the Jews,
were to be put to death. Not fatisfied, however, with this mode of oppofition, our adverfary proceeds in the fpirit of infidelity to reduce it to a mere cafe of judicial aftrology.
There may be perhaps cafual refemblance
enough to afford a pretence for the perverted
analogy of the fcorner, but there muft exift
an effential difference in the nature of thefe

inftances, which fhall leave no doubt refpecting the folly and the impiety of the comparifon.   In the firft place, the fimilarity arifes
from the literal interpretation of the word
ftar, which does not neceffarily denote a heavenly body of that kind.   It was not Sirius,
nor Arcturus, that was fo indicated, nor any
of the planets, but a luminous appearance in
the fkies, fufficiently diftinct to guide their
fteps; refembling in its purpofe, though not
perhaps exactly in its appearance, the pillar
of light that directed the Ifraelites, when they
were conducted by the prophet of the Lord
from Egyptian bondage and idolatry, to liberty, and the worfhip of the true God.   Admitting that genethliology were a branch of
aftrological knowledge cultivated in the time
of our Saviour, and that there were judicial
aftrologers coeval with the Jewifh prophets,
and the fubjects of the denunciations of the
Almighty, it is ftill a queftion whether this
ftar, as it is termed, would have fupplied any
data whatever for the procefs of the aftro-
loger.   His art is founded upon the appear-
ances, and arbitrary arrangements and fictitious qualities, of the known ftars and con-
ftellations; but the Magi were called away
before they could have time to afcertain the

nature of this new light, its course and aspect,
or whether, in short, it could be used at all
(from its ˣdoubtful permanency) in any of
their computations.   But it is useless to pro-
tract the discussion of these matters according
to the principles of the art.   The author of
" The Diffonance" speaks of the Almighty as
ʸ" permitting Pagan diviners to discover the
" nativity of the promised Messiah by their
" skill in astrology."   He has here confounded
the calculation with the prediction of the nativity.   In the calculation of a nativity, the birth
of the particular individual is assumed, and the
computation of the astrologer commences
from this period.   He does not in this case predict the time of the nativity of the individual,
but foretells, from the known circumstances
of this fact, the future events of his life.   The

ˣ I had reasoned this as well as I was able, without
an opportunity of recurring to any authority.   I am now
happy in being able to refer to Picus of Mirandula in
confirmation of what I had advanced.   " *Et ecce stella*,
" &c.   Quod nemo, nisi insaniens, existimabit de cœli
" sideribus configurationibusque esse intelligendum.   Erat
" igitur illa *factitia*, et *temporaria*, non *perpetua* stella et
" *naturalis*, condita ad id officii a Creatore, per quam
" significari natum regem Judæorum."   In Astrol. lib. iv.
c. 15. tom. i. p. 370. edit. Basil.
ʸ Diffonance, p. 155.

celebrated Cardan computed, as it is expreffed, according to the technical jargon of the art, his own nativity, which he did without any violation of the rules of this abfurd fyftem, but which muft have been an obvious impoffi- bility if this phrafe, according to its accep- tation by the author of " The Diffonance," never denoted any thing but a prediction of a birth. Thefe things may appear to be un- becoming the dignity of this place, and un- worthy of the attention of a learned affembly; but an objector may perhaps triumph more in retaining poffeffion of a fource of ridicule, than in defending himfelf againft the moft fubtle and recondite argument.

The next objection, which furnifhes mate- rials for a continued difcuffion, relates to the alledged ignorance of St. Matthew refpecting the geography of Paleftine, evinced in the con- clufion of the fecond of the difputed chapters. When St. Matthew relates, that multitudes of people followed Jefus from Decapolis, it is faid to be an error indicating great ignorance, becaufe, according to the author of " The " Diffonance," it is *evident*, that the Decapolis " was not any country or continued diftrict, " as the pretended Matthew and Mark repre- " fent it, but merely the general appellation

" of the detached infulated cities, lying all,
" except Scythopolis, beyond, or eaft of the
" river Jordan, which in later times were
" taken from the jurifdiction of the original
" tetrarchies, and made fubject to Syria."
Pliny, however, fpeaks of the [a] Decapolitan
region as adjoining on one fide to Syria; and
in another paffage he defcribes it as being
fituated inland from Anti-Libanus. Here he
ufes the formal and precife language of a geographer; but, even in fpeaking of the fame
tract, he familiarly calls it the Decapolis of
Syria, and [b] commends the excellence of one
of its peculiar productions, which would
fcarcely allow of the appropriation of it to
one of thefe detached cities. Auguftus united
[c] *two*, and not three towns of the Decapolis
to Syria; and it is argued, that, as no other
diftribution of Paleftine took place till the
twelfth year of Claudius, the term Decapolis,

[a] Jungitur ei latere Syriæ Decapolitana regio a nu-
mero oppidorum, *in quo non omnes eadem olfervant*. Plin.
Nat. Hift. lib. v. c. 18.

[b] Decapoli Syriæ perquam parvæ (olivæ fcil.) carne
tamen commendantur; quam ob caufam Italicis tranf-
marinæ præferuntur in cibis, quum oleo vincantur. Plin.
Nat. Hift. lib. xv. c. 3.

[c] Gaza was not one; Gadara and Hippos were the
others.

in whatever fenfe we take it, could not have
had exiftence when St. Matthew is faid to have
written his Gofpel. If this annexation of thefe
cities to Syria were the foundation of the diftinction of the Decapolis, the name could not
have been given till the whole decad were included within the province. But Pliny exprefsly fays, that the tetrarchies furrounded
fome, and were intermixed with others of the
conftituent cities. We may therefore be permitted to conjecture, without refining upon
flight intimations, that as the Decapolitan region retained its defignation, notwithftanding
its d interfection by the divifion of the country
into tetrarchies, that the Decapolis was a more
ancient diftribution and appellation than the
tetrarchies themfelves, and related to a period
when the ten cities were conjoined by fome
bond of union, the memory of which remained, but its exact nature was not expreffed
in the denomination of Decapolis. We may
alfo appeal to a e Palmyrene infcription for the

d " *Intercurfant, cinguntque has urbes tetrarchiæ, re-*
" *gnorum inftar, fingulæ,* et in regna contribuuntur."
Plin. Nat. Hift. lib. v. c. 18. And in another paffage;
" Poft eum introrfus *Decapolitana regio, prædictæque cum*
" *ea tetrarchiæ.*" Lib. v. c. 20.
    e Nec alia eft Abila, quæ Decapoli attribuitur in in-

duration of the name, to whatever age the antiquarian enquirer may affign this monument. It is neceffary alfo to remark, that the teftimony of Pliny is not the teftimony of writers of his own times only, but alfo of more ancient hiftorians and geographers, who had either themfelves feen the countries which they defcribed, or followed the accounts of thofe who had travelled in that part of the world. Our opponent, however, produces a fupplementary objection. He afferts, that the author of the Gofpel fpeaks of it as a country f " which did not lie eaftward of Jordan, be-
" caufe he exprefsly diftinguifhes it from the
" country beyond Jordan." But he cannot think of any diftinctions which may reconcile an apparent contradiction. The multitudes who affembled to hear our Saviour came from every quarter ; and the Evangelift, by fpecify-ing the Decapolis, included but a part of the country beyond Jordan. The g Jewifh biftorian has diftinguifhed the tetrarchy of Gaulo-

fcriptione veteri, quæ extat n. 3. inter monumenta Palmyrena, quæ cum fcholiis Edvardi Bernardi et Thomæ Smith prodierunt ubi legitur ΑΓΑΘΑΝΓΕΛΟΣ ΑΒΙΑΗ: ΝΟΣ ΔΕΚΑΠΟΛΕΟΣ. Reland. Pal. p. 525.

f Diffonance, p. 165.

g Jofeph. Antiq. lib. xvii. c. 13. et de Bell. lib. iii. c. 2.

nitis from the country beyond Jordan, not
becaufe they were fituated on different fides
of that river, but becaufe the former did not
comprehend the latter. We may here paufe,
and obferve on what foundation the whole
argument has been raifed. It depends merely
upon the date, which has been arbitrarily afcribed to the publication of St. Matthew's
Gofpel. If we admit that the argument has
been fuccefsful, it will only invalidate the probable affumption of fome writers on the canon of the New Teftament. It will not affect
the veracity of any hiftorian whatever. And
why fhould not fome latitude be allowed in
determining a point of much obfcurity, which
again refts upon fuch circumftances as thefe ;
at what precife year a written Gofpel became
neceffary, was then undertaken, and at laft
completed and divulged ?

SERMON VII.

2 Pet. i. 16.

We have not followed cunningly devised fables.

THE eſtabliſhment of the church of Conſtantine is ſaid by the author of " The Diſſo-
" nance" to be ſignified by " the apoſtaſy from
" the truths of the Goſpel, predicted in dif-
" ferent ſcriptures of the New Teſtament."
The queſtion will not be miſrepreſented, if
we underſtand the eſtabliſhment of the church
of Conſtantine to be equivalent, in the meaning of our opponent, to the eſtabliſhment of
Chriſtianity as the religion of the ſtate. The
import of the accuſation is, that this religion
was derived from corrupted copies of the
books of Scripture. The incarnation of our
Saviour is deſcribed as a fundamental doctrine
of this church, and the tendency of the adoption of corrupted books was to authorize and
diffuſe this interpolated tenet. It may be remarked, that the corruption of the books of

P

Scripture, to which this apoſtaſy is attributed, is ſaid in " The Diſſonance" to have been effected in the latter part of the ſecond century. From this period, then, downwards to the age of Conſtantine, the obnoxious opinions muſt have been ſpreading among thoſe who uſed the adulterated volumes ; that is, for the ſpace of more than a century and a half : and yet the failure of the true faith is not ſuppoſed to have become general, till it can be invidiouſly repreſented, that it then correſponded with the terms of the predictions, when it had acquired the ſanction of the civil magiſtrate.

It does not appear that the ſtate of the books of the Chriſtians was ever examined by Conſtantine, or that he decreed that certain books, and no others, ſhould be received as the ſtandard of the Chriſtian faith throughout the Roman empire. We can only alledge, that the eccleſiaſtical annals do not furniſh a direct reply to the poſition, that the corruptions of the books, which had been admitted or ſuggeſted before, were eſtabliſhed, as far as the influence of political power extended, under the adminiſtration of Conſtantine. We muſt therefore attempt by ſome circuitous enquiry to diſcover facts, which may invalidate

objections that originate folely in the filence
of hiftory; and which, it fhould be remarked,
is filent only, and not defective. The edict
of Milan, whether we adopt the words of the
ª hiftorian of the Decline and Fall of the Roman Empire, in fpeaking of its tendency, or
extract a portion of the edict itfelf, granted
fuch abfolute permiffion to perfons of every
religious denomination to follow their own
tenets, that they could not be reftricted to
any particular fource, or to the ufe of certain
books, from which they were expected to derive them. " The indulgence which we have
" granted in matters of religion," fay Conftantine and Licinius in their edict, " is ample
" and unconditional; and that you might per-
" ceive, at the fame time, that the open and
" free exercife of their refpective religions is
" granted to all others, as well as to the Chrif-
" tians." It was alfo provided, that no man
fhould be denied leave " of attaching himfelf
" to the rites of the Chriftians, or to whatever
" other religion his mind directed him to."
That Licinius did not adhere to the terms of
this declaration, is not denied; but his col-

ª Gibbon, vol. iii. p. 244, 245. edit. 8vo. De Mort.
Perfec. tranflated by Sir D. Dalrymple, p. 114.

league, when he poffeffed the empire undivided, was fo far from revoking it, that the
b hiftorian of the Decline and Fall of the Roman Empire has been induced to confider
fome of its provifions as having the fame authority with " the maxims of the civil law."
But Conftantine afterwards violated, rather
than retracted, the privileges which this edict
conferred. Heretics were diftinguifhed from
other believers, and not merely excluded from
a participation with the orthodox in their civil
diftinctions. By the confeffion of Eufebius,
the places of their religious affemblies were
deftroyed, and perfons were confidered as heretics when they were difcovered to have in
their poffeffion certain books. From thefe
circumftances we may infer what was the
operation of the edict of Milan in thofe parts
of the empire more immediately fubject to the
government of Conftantine. The mere eftablifhment of Chriftianity by the ftate, without

---

b " The edict of Milan (de Mort. Perf. c. 48.) acknow-
" ledges, by reciting that there exifted a fpecies of landed
" property ' ad jus corporis eorum, id eft, ecclefiarum,
' non hominum fingulorum pertinentia.' Such a folemn
" declaration of the fupreme magiftrate muft have been
" received in all the tribunals as a maxim of civil law."
Gibbon, vol. iii. p. 306. edit. 8vo.

a toleration of all the fubdivifions of its fects, would not have been favourable to the interefts of religion at that time. This toleration indeed might in part be attributed to the indifference of Licinius towards all modes of religion; and to Conftantine alfo, who was not yet qualified by information, or induced by intereft or perfuafion, to diftinguifh one form of opinion among Chriftians from another. It is indeed curious to contemplate the ftrength which the different bodies of the heretical Chriftians had acquired at the time of the publication of the edict. They had their refpective buildings for the celebration of public worfhip. Their oppofition does not feem to have been obvioufly connected with political intrigues; but we find that they excited, by their variety and numbers, the jealoufy of thofe, who were dignified with the ecclefiaftical honours of the empire. All the fects, however, were not indifcriminately expofed to the perfecution of the magiftrate. The opinions of the Novatians were examined and tolerated. But this fect received, we may prefume, the fame books of Scripture as their founder adopted in the third century; and it is admitted that Novatian did not reject the facred canon received in his own times, and

that he does not mention any fpurious apocryphal Chriftian writings.

The manners of the ecclefiaftics might be
in fome degree corrupted by the exuberance
of profperity, and the purfuits of ambition,
which opened upon them in the reign of Conftantine; but in what manner the interefts of
the ftate could be promoted by the adoption
of the fuppofed old corruptions of the records
of their religion, it is difficult to conceive.
According to the hypothefis of " The Diffo-
" nance" we are to fuppofe, that certain books
of the New Teftament were either forged or
corrupted in the fecond century; and that, in
this ftate, a collection of them was received
and eftablifhed when Chriftianity became the
religion of a powerful and extenfive empire.
But what are the grounds of this bold conjecture? Conftantine himfelf did not determine, nor authorize others to determine, what
books were to be regarded as authentic, and
what to be rejected as fpurious. This queftion
was not difcuffed during his reign. Whatever
was afcertained refpecting this fubject had
been previoufly examined by the council of
Laodicea. Not that any other authority is to
be attributed to the decifion of this affembly,
than what may be derived from its antiquity,

and the nature of the enquiry in which that
affembly was engaged. It had likewife fome
advantage in being only a provincial council;
a circumftance which, if it fubtracts from the
univerfality of the opinion which they pronounced, increafes the validity of that opinion
by the probability that it was exempt from
the influence of fecular rulers.

We are required, however, to fuppofe, that
in the latter part of the fecond century all the
copies were corrupted, and the forged books
generally difperfed; and that in the time of
Conftantine the Chriftians had availed themfelves of thefe corruptions. But would not
the Arian controverfy have brought to light
fuch a deception as this? Or, without recurring to antiquity, can it be imagined that the
author of the Decline and Fall of the Roman
Empire overlooked, in his extenfive refearches
into this reign, a fact of fuch importance,
which accorded fo well with his purpofe of
degrading the character of Conftantine, and
impugning Chriftianity as an impofture? The
wifhed-for difcovery, however, muft eafily
have been made at the time of the Arian controverfy, if the impofition had then exifted;
and it is not a little fufpicious, that the author
of " The Diffonance" fhould have effected a

difcovery, without any intimation or affiftance
from ancient authors, after an interval of fourteen hundred years, and that he fhould have
fuggefted corruptions and interpolations, which
did not occur to the difputants, nor are recorded by the hiftorians, of that diftant period.
Nor can we avoid admiring the good fortune,
as well as the acutenefs, of the inventors and
fabricators of thefe writings, who could at
fo early a time infert paffages, or compofe
books, that fhould afterwards be fo exactly
accommodated to the future interefts of Chriftians, the eftablifhment of whofe religious fyftem, as the religion of the ftate, could not be
traced in any events of their own age. If we
fuppofe that the copies of the interpolated and
of the forged writings were the fame throughout both the eaftern and the weftern empire,
to what are we to afcribe this conformity?
Was it fo ancient as to have acquired no additional authority from the favour and protection of the Emperor? If it were the refult
of fome act of political power, it muft, from
the extent of its operation, have been noticed,
if not preferved, among the memorials of the
empire. But we have no record of fuch tranfactions; and we are juftified in concluding,
that no fuch ever exifted.

If this mode of reply fhould be regarded as unfatisfactory, it muft be confidered, that it is the only mode which can be employed. When objections relate to periods of time, of which no hiftorical monuments whatever remain, it is eafy to invent fome anfwer, deduced from probability, which may fatisfy common enquiry, and be applicable to ordinary doubts. But when objections relate to periods of time, of which hiftories are preferved, and the hiftorians do not fpeak of events, which are ftated in the objections to have occurred, we can only fhew, that the objectors affume more than the annals of hiftory furnifh, and argue upon fuppofititious and prefumptive data.

We are next to confider the effects of the alledged corruptions upon the Gofpel in general. The author of "The Diffonance" affirms, that the prefent Gofpel c" is totally " unlike the Gofpel originally preached by " Jefus and his Apoftles." This boldly afferted diverfity he attempts to eftablifh by an hypothetical comparifon of the prefent and former intelligibility of the intent and purpofes of the Gofpel, and of the evidences of

c Diffonance, Pref. p. v.

its truth. He ſtates it to be indiſpenſable,
that [d] " ſatisfactory proofs of the truth and
" divine authority of the Goſpel, and a com-
" plete knowledge of its intents and doctrines,
" ſhould be really attainable to the ordinary
" faculties of the human mind, and eaſy to be
" comprehended by children, and the moſt
" illiterate of the people." In the firſt place,
the ordinary faculties of the human mind are
incorrectly oppoſed " to children, and the
" moſt illiterate of the people;" whoſe faculties are the ordinary faculties of the ſpecies.
The ſtate of intellectual powers not yet ma-
tured, or left uncultivated, cannot be taken
for the ſtandard of the intelligibility or ſatiſ-
factory nature of " proofs of the truth and
" divine authority of the Goſpel, or of its in-
" tent and purpoſe," or of any other book or
ſyſtem whatſoever. Here however are three
diſtinct objects to be conſidered ; the Goſpel
which was preached, its intent and purpoſe,
and the proofs of its truth and divine authority. The Goſpel which our Saviour preached
conſiſted, in its moral part, of purity of thought
and intentions, and univerſal benevolence; in
its religious ſyſtem, it inculcated the reſur-

[d] Diſſonance, Pref. p. v.

rection from the dead, a ftate of future re-
wards and punifhments, an atonement for fin,
through the blood of the divine Teacher of
thefe doctrines.   Its intent and purpofe was
reprefented by the Jews to be, to deftroy the
law of Mofes, inftead of being the fulfilment
of one difpenfation, and the introduction of
another.   The proofs of its truth and divine
authority were, miracles, and the completion
of prophecy.   In what then, we may afk, did
the fuperior advantage of the unlearned perfon in the days of our Saviour confift, with
regard to the facility of underftanding the
Gofpel, with its intent and its proofs ? He underftood the language in which it was principally communicated, which now perhaps
conftitutes a part of the literary refearch of
modern ages.   The Gofpel itfelf was intelligible to the poor, or the reply to the Baptift's
enquiry, " the poor have the Gofpel preached
" to them," was delufive.   The proofs of its
truth and divine authority were intelligible to
all.   The fick were healed inftantaneoufly,
the fight of the blind was reftored, and devils
were caft out.   But thefe were not " fatif-
" factory proofs" to all.   The fick, indeed,
were healed, but it was upon the fabbath-
day ; the power of fight was communicated

to a man who was born blind, but it was
fufpected that he had not been blind from his
birth; devils were caft out, but it was churl-
ifhly alledged that it was by the power of
Beelzebub, the prince of the devils. The fact
is, fomething elfe is intimated to be wanting
to produce conviction befides plenary and
intelligible evidence; befides being contemporaries of our Saviour, hearers of his wifdom,
and witneffes of his power. Proofs may be
fufficient, although not fatisfactory in the
event of their influence; although they do
not produce conviction; becaufe it may be
objected at any time, that facts were deficient,
as proofs: either that the miracles were not
performed at all, or not at a convenient feafon, or not by the inherent power of the vifible agent; for wherever a doubt can be fuggefted, or a difpute is intended, objections to
the beft received truths may be invented; ingenious, perhaps, but not fubftantial; plaufible,
but vifionary; learned, but irrational and in-
conclufive. With regard to the full compre-
henfion of the intent of the Gofpel, a degree
of prejudice prevailed at its firft publication,
which is no reproach to the revelation itfelf.
It required repeated affurances from our Lord
himfelf to fatisfy his followers, that he did not

come to deftroy, but to fulfil the law of Mofes; and the fame prejudices fubfifted to a
diftant period. The circumftance, therefore,
of living at the time did not in this refpect
tend to clear, but rather to obfcure, this particular defign of the Gofpel.

It is not however doubted, that there exifted a fource of more complete information than could be poffeffed in fucceeding
times, and had no reference to the intellectual
qualifications of thofe, to whom it was afforded : this was, the advantage of a perfonal
communication, and in hearing the doctrines
promulgated, and in being eye-witneffes of
thofe tranfactions in which our Lord and his
Apoftles were concerned. Yet this is likewife
independent of the peculiar intelligibility of
the revelation itfelf, and its proofs.

We are further informed, that [e] " the truth
" of the Gofpel, and the authenticity of the
" Scriptures which teach it, reft folely upon
" the plurality of the voices of corrupt and
" erring men, of no authority from heaven,
" and fupported only by the power of earthly
" magiftrates." But, upon a review of the

[e] Diffonance, Pref. p. v.

records of the early centuries, it does not appear that the civil magiftrate interpofed to adapt the teftimony of the authenticity of the Scriptures to any objeét of his own; but the Chriftians received fome as genuine, and rejeéted others as fpurious, upon the proper evidence and examination, without arrogating to themfelves any exclufive authority to determine for others, and certainly without the fanétion of the civil magiftrate. For it is well known, that the canon of the New Teftament was formed and eftablifhed, not merely before the civil magiftrate proteéted Chriftianity, but during his oppofition and hoftility. No agreement of a plurality of voices, either pure or corrupt, in a council, fo early as the fourth century, determined that the canon of Scripture fhould confift of fuch books, and no others. If we feek for this majority of fuffrages in the proceedings of the council of Laodicea, or that of Nice, the refult will be in contradiétion to the affertions of the author of " The Diffonance." If our accounts on this fubjeét are true, we do not difcover that any difference of opinion divided the affembly at Laodicea; fo that, for any thing we know, they were unanimous in their decifions. Their

conduct, as far as it is to be collected from hiftory, was candid and unexceptionable. They.
examined what books were received by the
churches in former times, and, as the conclufion of that enquiry, determined which were,
or were not, the canonical books. But their
catalogue is to be regarded rather as an affurance that the enquiry was duly and carefully
conducted, than as an authoritative fanction
of a collection of facred books. And fomething of weight on this topic ought in reafon
to be afcribed to the opinion of the council of
Laodicea, becaufe they might poffefs fources
of information which are not now in exiftence. If we refer to the meafures of the
council of Nice, at which Conftantine himfelf
is faid to have prefided, the queftion refpecting the canon of Scripture was not difcuffed.
It is faid to have been attended by an incredible number of ecclefiaftics of inferior rank,
as well as bifhops. Much indeed has been
feverely, and in general ᶠ forcibly alledged,
againft the decifions of thefe conventions; but
it is fcarcely to be fuppofed, that, in fuch a
multitude of various orders of men, no perfon
could be found, whom the affectation of fin-

ᶠ I allude to Jortin's Remarks on Ecclefiaftical Hiftory.

gularity, the pride of diftinction, or the per-
verfenefs of jealoufy, might not have led to
diffent from the majority of their affociates?
But where are we informed of the amount of
the numbers on each fide, which determined
the authenticity of the evangelical writings?
The independent conftitution of the primitive
churches had a tendency to leave to the dif-
cretion of each fociety of Chriftians refpectively the reception of fuch books of Scripture
as they had reafon to think were genuine,
uninfluenced by the fuperiority of any one
church or fociety in particular. The temporary exclufion of the Apocalypfe from the
canon evinced caution in the determination of
the ancient churches, and proved that they
did not rafhly admit the books, which had
been already placed in the number of thofe
that were genuine, and that they waited till
farther enquiry juftified their reception of this
book under that character, like the reft.

We cannot indeed difcover any mode of
corrupting the facred Scriptures, or of eftablifhing the authority of fuch as are fuppofed
to have been corrupted, that neceffarily re-
fulted from the eftablifhment of Chriftianity
as the imperial rule of faith. We are not informed what reafons induced Conftantine to

adopt the faith of the majority, nor whether any intrigue was employed to attach him to that party; and no political reafon can be affigned why he might not have apoftatized after his converfion. We muft therefore fuppofe, that the ordinary motives of conviction operated upon *his* mind as they had done on perfons of inferior rank, and as they ftill operate upon mankind in general. What determined one man to be a heretic, and another to profefs orthodoxy, at that time, was probably the fame caufe which has always produced diverfity of opinion, and will continue to produce it, under all modes of government whatfoever.

It is remarked by ᵍ Mofheim, in anfwer to thofe who would refer the profeffion of Chriftianity by Conftantine to motives of ambition, that upon attentive reflection, and after a diligent examination of the hiftory of that period, he could not perceive that the profeffion of the Chriftian faith either did or could promote the attainment of his wifh to reign without a colleague; an object which, he does not deny, he ardently purfued. His government

ᵍ Mofheim de Reb. Chrift. ante Conft. Magn. p. 969, 970.

Q

was profperous before he was a Chriftian, and not a difciple of any religious fyftem whatever.

The [h] heretics of that age were feverely treated, and the various edicts againft their followers fhew that they were numerous and powerful bodies of men, and able in their turn to impofe confiderable reftraint upon the more favoured profeffors of orthodoxy; and their proceedings continued to excite the jealoufy of the prince, and ultimately provoked his coercion. They would affuredly at this time have reproached the orthodox, if there had been any foundation for it, with having fubftituted a forged and interpolated canon of Scripture inftead of the genuine writings, when the fufferings, which the fupreme authority inflicted, confifted of the demolition of their places of public worfhip, and the plunder and deftruction of their books. But we do not hear of any complaints of this kind; nor does it appear, that the public reading of the Scriptures was under any reftraint, or that any methods were ufed to prevent the diffufion of the knowledge and information which they contain. This muft have taken place, we may

[h] See Bingham.

conclude, had the ruling party been confcious that they had by fraud and impofition obtained the fanction of the civil authority for the reception and acknowledgment of forged Scriptures. The very exiftence of the heretics fuppofes, that there was in their poffeffion a ftandard of fcriptures of the New Teftament, by which the deviations of the orthodox, if any, might have been afcertained.

One of the effects of the corruption of the Gofpel is faid to be, the alteration of its original character of perfpicuity. [i] " Its moft " important, becaufe its fundamental doc- " trines, are to be interpreted only by the fa- " gacity of the learned refpecting the mean- " ing of a few controverted words or fentences " of Greek or Hebrew." For this confe- quence neither the church of Conftantine, nor any other church, is refponfible; nor do we know how the difficulty would be leffened, if the Gofpel had been preferved in any other language than the Greek. The fagacity of the learned would ftill have been neceffary, and perhaps lefs fuccefsful, becaufe it muft have been ftudied under much greater difadvantages. The Gofpel indeed, if it had been the

[i] Diffonance, Pref. p. v.

intention of Providence, might, and it would,
have been written in fome other of the tongues,
the knowledge of which was imparted to the
Apoftles on the day of Pentecoft. But this
circumftance would not have obviated objections deduced from the language in which it
was compofed. The language in which it is
written correfponds with the publicity of our
Saviour's actions. They were not performed
in fome obfcure and remote diftrict, nor is the
language of the Gofpel the ancient dialect of
fome barbarous or illiterate tribe of Afia. It
fubjected the facred hiftory and doctrine to
the examination of the whole civilized world.
We can have the Gofpel only in two ways;
with or without writing. Would the fuppofition enhance the credibility of what we of
the prefent day are to receive as the rule of
our faith, were we to fuppofe, that the Gofpel
might have been communicated and tranfmitted orally from the firft apoftolical teacher,
who underftood the language of the converts
by fpecial revelation? As the language in
which the Gofpel is written was the beft underftood, the moft widely diffufed, and prevailed longer in the world than any other,
therefore we have better fecurity for the
prefent refemblance of the Gofpel to its

prototype, than we otherwise could have had.

Another pofition of our opponent is, that to underftand the doctrines of the Gofpel requires critical learning and fagacity ; but this may be applied with more force to any other ancient language. The objection, however, comprizes feveral particulars ; as, what are to be confidered as the fundamental doctrines of Chriftianity, and in what fentences of Greek or Hebrew are they contained ? We are not favoured, however, with any direction to difcover what thofe fundamental doctrines may be which are characterized or alluded to by the author of " The Diffonance," no otherwife than that they are " contained in a few " words or fentences of Greek or Hebrew." Is it meant that we fhould collect briefly, that the fundamental were the intelligible doctrines ? Thefe doctrines, however, were preached intelligibly to the bulk of mankind by Jefus and his Apoftles. But it will not detract from the authority or authenticity of any part of the New Teftament to fuppofe, that thofe paffages, which are now interpreted by the affiftance of the critical fagacity of the learned, were the fame, that were eafily underftood by the generality of the hearers who

were at the time addreffed by our Saviour and
his Apoftles. If thefe paffages were not the
fame, ftill more fagacity and more critical
knowledge would be neceffary to eftablifh the
difference, or the interpolation. That the contemporaries of the Apoftles and Jefus Chrift
underftood many allufions, many parts of the
hiftory, the metaphorical language, and other
circumftances, more perfectly than we can
underftand them at prefent, is no more than
what muft be faid of the readers of the works
of all ancient authors : but if the Gofpel were
to be committed to writing at all, it muft neceffarily follow, that whatever language was
ufed, it would equally require the ftudy of the
learned to deliver correctly the plainer parts,
for the inftruction of Chriftians in general, as
to fupport a difcuffion of the more difficult
or lefs obvious ones with adverfaries. Want
of intelligibility, however, cannot be alledged
candidly againft the fundamental doctrines of
the Gofpels, when it is faid folely to confift in
the language. The language is not a fource
of unintelligibility, when that language conftitutes a part of the education of every liberal
fcholar. It is not a myftic language, confined
to the priefts of our religion ; it is not the
hieroglyphic lore of the hierophant. If the

fubject indeed has difficulties which perplex the underftanding, and which, without fome labour, and perhaps after every exertion of the underftanding, are not apparently fufceptible of explication, the mere words and phrafeology, as belonging to the extinct dialect of another country, cannot be adduced as a fair criterion of priftine intelligibility.

The four Gofpels were received by the church of Conftantine, according to the author of " The Diffonance," k " upon the au-
" thority of thofe profeffed Chriftians of the
" fecond and third centuries, whom they have
" thought fit to denominate orthodox ; and
" who, rejecting all thofe numerous evange-
" lical hiftories, which, Luke informs us, were
" written in his time, admitted and preferved
" thefe four alone, and attributed them to the
" authors, under whofe names they now ap-
" pear." It is here affumed, without evidence, that the hiftories, to which St. Luke alludes, were contradictory to his own. It is then argued, that the Chriftians of the fecond and third centuries rejected thefe evangelical hiftories becaufe they were in oppofition to the accounts in the other Gofpels. But who has

k Diffonance, p. 19.

related any of thefe circumftances, the facts
of the hiftories of which St. Luke fpeaks, the
names of the authors, the names of the profeffed Chriftians who adopted or rejected them,
in what manner the rejection was agreed upon
and declared, or who has preferved the minuteft fragment of any one of thefe " nu-
" merous evangelical hiftories?"   The author
of " The Diffonance" has himfelf fet the example of interpolation in his own perfon by
audacioufly prefuming to fupply the alledged
defects of hiftory by fubftituting his own unfounded conjectures and affumptions in the
place of the records of truth.   But it is not
eafy to conceive how thefe Chriftians could
admit and preferve four Gofpels only, without
expofing themfelves, not merely to the notice,
but to the refentment of thofe perfons, whofe
facred books were anterior to that of St. Luke.
It is difficult to imagine that a mere ftratagem
of party, in favour of four fpurious narratives,
could at once annihilate the credit, or even
deftroy the exiftence, of all the other more
ancient and more authentic accounts of the
fame fubject; and it is ftill more difficult to
imagine by what means the contents of thefe
loft writings have been fo well afcertained, as
to juftify the affirmation, that they contra-

dicted the accounts contained in the Gofpels
which we now receive. But as the general
prefervation of any particular writing is not
eafily accomplifhed by intereft or favour, fo
neither is the annihilation of oppofite accounts
of facts to be effected completely by any
means whatever. The procefs is not altogether mechanical. The inftruments are not
merely fire and violence, or a combination of
a party, or a tribunal of inquifitors. Public
opinion is of much too intellectual a nature
to be tangible by any of thefe human con-
trivances. How could the Chriftians controul
and direct, to their own ends, fuch a fubtle
and delicate, but extenfive engine as this, in
the fecond and third centuries ? Both the orthodox and the heretics refpectively preferved
copies of their own books, in oppofition to
the fame fpecies of political force ; the former
in the reign of Diocletian, and the latter under that of Conftantine.

The author of " The Diffonance," however,
does not wholly attribute the reception of
what he confiders a fabulous and fpurious
Gofpel to the influence of a great worldly ruler. He is perfuaded, that it has been admitted, according to a prediction of St. Paul,
that men would believe " a ftrong delufion,"

becaufe they took " pleafure in unrighteouf-
" nefs." He has " no doubt" " that the doc-
" trine of Chrift's death being a full fatis-
" faction to the divine juftice for all the fins
" and unrighteoufnefs of men, which is found-
" ed principally upon this fabulous and fpu-
" rious Gofpel called Matthew's, *is particu-*
" *larly alluded to by the Chriftian prophet in*
" *this prediction;* and that this has always
" been the grand inducement with the mem-
" bers of the orthodox church of Conftantine,
" next to compulfion and temporal allure-
" ments of the civil magiftrate, to attach them
" to its fabulous, idolatrous fuperftition." The
true hiftory is fuppofed to be that in which are
omitted the words " for the remiffion of fins,"
which St. Matthew has recorded in his account of the inftitution of the laft fupper. As
it has not been my object to difcufs the doctrines contained in the feveral books, the authenticity of which this writer has endea-
voured to invalidate, I fhall here only obferve,
that the rejection of the words, " for the re-
" miffion of fins," will not be fufficient for
the purpofe of the objector. For although he
wifhes to reduce the inftitution of the laft fupper to a mere memorial of the former exiftence of fuch a perfon as our Saviour, yet he

retains as genuine other words, which cannot be referred to the notion of a merely comme-morative rite. St. Luke, whofe narrative is afferted by the objector to be more correct than that of St. Matthew, relates, that our Saviour's words were, " This cup is the New " Teftament in my blood, which is fhed for " you." We cannot fo far fimplify the mean-ing of this expreffion as to fuppofe, that its whole force is employed to fignify, that our Saviour fhed his blood merely to imprefs the memory of his death upon the recollection of his difciples. As the final caufe of the death of Chrift, this explanation will not fatisfy any enquirer. The great object of the appearance of our Saviour in the flefh, after the promulga-tion of the Gofpel, was his death; and a very inadequate reafon of his death is to be found in the purpofe of the perpetuation of his own memory. If the rite fimply commemorated the fact, and did not denote its nature and de-fign, the words " my blood, which was fhed " for you," would exprefs, that the memory of his mere appearance would not have been preferved without this fhedding of his blood.

It is remarkable, that this doctrine of atone-ment is faid to have been received by the mem-bers of the church of Conftantine, upon its

own intrinfic tendency, next to the compulfion
and temporal allurements " of the civil magif-
" trate." Among fo many powerful motives it
is not eafy to difcriminate the feparate operation of each, and to affign to it the appropriate effect. A doctrine, which is reprefented
as being fo favourable to the vicious and im-
moral propenfities of our corrupt nature, could
not fail of alluring numerous profelytes. This
indeed would defervedly claim a place among
the fecondary caufes in the propagation of
Chriftianity. Temporal allurements and political compulfion were unneceffary, and could
not be compared in influence with the agency
of the other caufe. But the doctrine is reprefented as acting only in fubordination to
compulfion and allurement. This indeed is
an inftance of metaphyfical accuracy, which
does not perhaps yet belong to the fcience.
The mind is here fuppofed to be under the
influence of various caufes, and the order is
afcertained in which the energy of each is
exercifed. This furely furnifhes a moft extraordinary picture of the ftate of the Chriftian
community at that period. They are fuppofed
to have been actuated by feveral interefted
confiderations in receiving one of the fundamental doctrines of their religion; by the dread

of force, by the allurement of temporal com-
penfation, and by the abfolute atonement for
the fins of the wicked by the death of Chrift.
For what period are we to fuppofe that thefe
principles of conduct continued to operate on
the minds of men ? The delufion is fuppofed
to have been ftrong, yet it might have been
diffipated. It required only the interpofition
of fome innovating enthufiaft, or exafperated
heretic, to expofe to the multitude the inftrument of the deception, the forgery of the book
from which the doctrine of the atonement
was firft divulged. This could have been attempted at any time; for we can fee no moral
or political obftacle to prevent the difclofure
of fuch an impofture, if fuch an impofture had
exifted. The fame fpirit, which reformed the
weftern churches in fubfequent ages, would
have burft forth and have undeceived that of
Conftantine. But the church of Conftantine
did not prevent any of its members from applying the fame teft for the general authenticity of the books of the New Teftament that
the author of " The Diffonance" has employed. The Gofpel of St. Luke was as open to
their examination, as it has been fince to his.
They might have affumed it as the ftandard
of the truth of the other narratives, or, from

the frequent perufal of it, they might have obferved that difcrepancy with the other Gofpels, which might have led to a fimilar conclufion of want of accuracy in the reft. But of fuch proceedings there is not the flighteft intimation any where. It is indeed acknowledged by the objector, that his own ftandard is not without imperfections. The interpolators, he thinks, have altered fome portions; fo that the rule, by which we are to afcertain the correfpondence or variation of the thing to be examined, is itfelf correct only to a certain degree. The interpolations indeed are faid to be " not difficult to be diftinguifhed " by an accurate attentive reader;" but the characteriftic of a rule is not, that it has deviations eafily difcernible, and that it is ftraight in general; but this, that it fhall be capable of fhewing the equality or inequality in every part of that to which it is applied. By this acknowledgment, we are juftified in rejecting an appeal to fuch an imperfect and inadequate teft of truth or falfehood.

In commendation, however, of the Gofpel of St. Luke, and as a reafon for preferring it to that of St. Matthew, it is faid, that " St. " Luke wrote his hiftories in the language in " which we have received them ;" but that

St. Matthew wrote his Gofpel in Hebrew or
Syro-Chaldaic, and we have received it in
Greek. Without adverting to the obfcurity
refpecting the nature and exiftence of the
Syro-Chaldaic original of St. Matthew's Gofpel, it is affumed, that the Greek is a tranflation, and that [1] " a critical attention to the
" language of the writing itfelf, compared
" with that of Luke's hiftories, fhews that it
" is not a tranflation from any uniform ori-
" ginal;" that " it was written long after
" Luke's fecond hiftory;" that it was of later
date than the " hiftory of Jofephus;" that
the author " was not an Apoftle;" that " his
" ignorance of the geography of Paleftine, and
" of the cuftoms of the Hebrew people," fhew
" he was not a Jew; and that he did not un-
" derftand the prophecies of the Jewifh Scrip-
" ture." Of thefe particulars we fhall here confider two only. That there is a difference in
the ftyle of St. Luke from that of the other
Evangelifts, has been too often remarked to
leave a doubt, that the critics have not been
miftaken. But to affirm that this difference
of ftyle fhall denote the difference, in thefe
inftances, of the age of the refpective writers

[1] Diffonance, p. 41.

with great, or indeed with any approxima-
tion to exactnefs, is to affign to it the property of a criterion, which it does not poffefs.
When we fpeak of the pure writers of antiquity, then we may appeal to this ftandard;
but when we are confidering the compofitions
of authors in a language not indigenous, a difference not only in the general education of
the perfons, but merely the difference of place
where they acquired the language in which
they wrote, was fufficient to produce a variation in their ftyle, which might be miftaken
for the characteriftics of different ages in which
the writers are faid to have lived.

We are next to remark, that the very omiffions of St. Luke are affumed as decifive of the
propriety and authenticity of what is inferted
in St. Matthew. This is an unwarranted application of the ftandard of the truth of hiftory. It is ufed likewife by this management
to determine, not merely what portions are
omitted, but to afcertain the reafon why they
have been omitted by the other writer. Such
is the exemplification of the licentious and irregular ufe of a rule, affumed under the pretence, and indeed with an oftentation, of accuracy; and fuch are the confequences of
abandoning the ufual kinds of evidence, and

inventing modes of inveftigation, which could
not perhaps, even to the author, feem to promife refults of greater certainty.   A queftion
however occurs in this place, with what degree of innocence can this be done ? The enquiry after truth is laudable: and we are not
affirming that there is guilt in fearching for
it, where others have not preceded us ; but in
fearching for it by means which are known
not to be adapted for its difcovery.   The profeffion of the love of truth has been repeated
by polemics till it produces wearinefs and reafonable diftruft, becaufe it has too often proceeded from the lips of thofe who have previoufly perverted the neceffary evidence, or
who have directed others to fearch for it in
fources, which they knew would be explored
in vain.

SERMON VIII.

Acts xxi. 37.

And as Paul was to be led into the caſtle, he ſaid unto the chief captain, May I ſpeak unto thee? who ſaid, Canſt thou ſpeak Greek?

[a] IN conſidering the queſtion of the authenticity and genuineneſs of the evangelical writings, the language in which they are written claims our attention, not merely as a ſubject of curious reſearch, but alſo as it comprehends the enquiry, whether any of them, in the form

[a] The reader is deſired to obſerve, that the " Herculanenſia" were not publiſhed when this diſcourſe was finiſhed ; and no facts have ſince been inſerted from that work. The whole aſſiſtance which I have received in the compoſition of this diſcourſe has been derived from the " Appendix" to " Obſervations on the Words of the " Centurion uttered at the Crucifixion of our Lord, by a " Layman ; Oxford printed, 1809 :" and I have acknowledged it, as the occaſions occur. For the reſt of the facts, their diſcovery, their diſpoſition, and their application, I am to receive, without participation, cenſure or praiſe.

in which we have received them, are verfions
from another tongue; and whether the firft
introduction of Latin terms can be fo afcertained as to form an argument to prove a fpurious original, when they are found in writings of a particular date. The author of "The
" Diffonance" has declared, that " this fingle
" circumftance of the language," the mixture
of Latin words, induces him to " fufpect every
" paffage and writing, wherein it is found, to
" be either an interpolation or fiction of no
" earlier date than the middle of the fecond
" century; and, if corroborated by other cir-
" cumftances of inconfiftency or great im-
" probability, to afford a full conviction of
" their fpurioufnefs, and want of apoftolic au-
" thenticity b." The moft complete mode of
refuting this objection feemed to be, that of
giving an hiftorical fketch of the diffufion of
the knowledge of the Greek language among
various nations in general, or among fuch as
were connected with the Romans by fubju-
gation or alliance; although a fhorter, yet fufficient anfwer, might be found in the confideration, that in the books of the Evangelifts,
and the apoftle Paul, we have inftances of the

---

b Diffonance, p. 53.

current colloquial. phrafeology of the country, which we cannot expect fhould be exemplified or repeated in authors, whofe bufinefs it was to record other events, in which other fub-jects, and perfons of a different and higher clafs, were concerned.

It is fome prefumption in favour of the au-thenticity of a revelation, when it is commu--nicated in the language which is moft general, and beft underftood, in thofe places where it is the object and bufinefs of the agents to dif-fufe a knowledge of that revelation. To pro-mulgate it originally through the means of a tranflation would be a fufpicious introduction of a new religious fyftem. A verfion removes the original too far from general examination, and interpofes a veil, which obftructs and li-mits the enquiry to which a recent revelation fhould be unrefervedly expofed. We muft contend for the prefence of every circum-ftance which could facilitate inveftigation, and extend to all, the knowledge of the fubject re-vealed, and which would leave the judgment undifturbed with any fufpicion of a fraudulent interpretation of the original.

It is faid to be afcertained by fufficient tef-timony, that the Gofpel of St. Matthew was originally compofed in the Hebrew language of that period. As we have no remains of this work in that language, it is argued, that ^c " the eaftern Jews, and the many thoufands " of Jewifh Chriftians who fled to Pella, and " alfo the Nazarenes," would require a Gofpel in their own language, becaufe they did not underftand Greek^d. If this reafoning be admitted to prove a neceffity for the compofition of a Gofpel in the Syro-Chaldaic or Hebrew language, it ought likewife to be admitted to prove, that fuch a Gofpel would have been neceffarily preferved among the members of fo confiderable a community. The queftion is not, whether any infpired writing is loft; nor do we infift upon the infpiration as a pledge of the interference of the Almighty to preferve it. We rather enquire, whether a book ever exifted which was purpofely defigned for fo large a number of converts, and which, if it exifted, muft have been loft by the intervention of fuch caufes only as, we might prefume, would have affected the condition of the people in fuch a manner, as would have

^c Michaelis, vol. iii. part i. p. 115.

^d Michaelis, vol. iii. part i. p. 143. " Dr. Mafch indeed " has brought nine arguments to prove, that the Jews, " even at Jerufalem, univerfally underftood Greek; but " they really are of no value whatever."

attracted the attention of the hiftorian. But
we learn alfo from hiftorical evidence, that
the Greek Gofpel of St. Matthew was early
known, fo that the period, during which the
ufe of the Hebrew Gofpel fubfifted, if it ever
fubfifted exclufively of the other, muft have
been fo fhort, as almoft to have made it unneceffary to compofe fuch a work. We might afk,
how a Greek tranflation became neceffary at
all, but particularly fo foon after the publication of the Hebrew original. Who were the
perfons that required St. Matthew's Gofpel
to be publifhed in the Greek language, rather
than the Gofpels of St. Mark and St. Luke?
Againft thefe hypothetical arguments the teftimony of Papias will perhaps be adduced as
decifive. This teftimony it is not my intention to weaken by any attempt to depreciate
the underftanding and abilities of the witnefs,
becaufe a very fmall portion of either was fufficient to qualify him for this very fimple
effort. He fays, that "each perfon interpret-
"ed the Hebrew Gofpel of St. Matthew as
"he was able." Thefe words feem to defcribe the ftate of the knowledge of the Hebrew language at that time; but in what
place, and among what perfons, is not fpecified. If however St. Matthew wrote, as it is

related upon as good authority, for Jews, who underſtood Hebrew only, what neceſſity was there for the interpretation of which Papias ſpeaks? There certainly are difficulties in the evidence of Papias; but we are not juſtified, in explaining away, or in rejecting that evidence. He had not ſeen the book itſelf, although he was an ancient writer; nor was he informed, although he was particularly aſſiduous in collecting information on ſubjects of this nature, in what place it was to be found. And yet his [e] diſtance from the time of the appearance of the Hebrew Goſpel needed not to have precluded him from knowing theſe circumſtances from the ſame perſons who related the others. The ſimple explanation of the words of Papias certainly juſtifies the reader in concluding, that the Hebrew language was not well underſtood by the perſons who uſed the Hebrew copy of St. Matthew's Goſpel; and thoſe perſons could not be, on the other hand, Jews, who underſtood the Greek language only. It is not uſual to repreſent as a remarkable occurrence, that a certain body of people were able to comprehend the meaning of a book which was written in their native language;

---

[e] He was a diſciple of St. John.

but it certainly is a curious fact, that they underftood it fo imperfectly as the expreffion implies. But whatever theory the teftimony of Papias may contradict, we muft never-thelefs retain it. The Jews of Jerufalem, it has been afferted, did not underftand Greek. But thefe perfons might, from their fituation and connections, have been fuppofed to be almoft neceffarily acquainted with the Greek language; and this not as a part of a learned, or even an ordinary education, but from the neceffity there was for its employ-ment in the ufual intercourfe of life, and from their connection with Greeks and even with Romans. The annual refort of Jews to the me-tropolis from the countries where the Greek tongue was the vernacular language, was alone fufficient to induce, if not to oblige them, to attain in early age this additional medium of communication. The text indeed fhews, that f " when St. Paul fpake in pub-" lic before the Jews in Jerufalem, he ad-" dreffed them in Hebrew." But he ufed the Hebrew with an obvious intention, and for the fame reafon that he ufed Greek in ad-dreffing the captain of the band, who was

f Michaelis, vol. iv. p. 215.

furprifed at it, and immediately enquired,
" Art not thou that Egyptian, which before
" thefe days madeft an uproar, and leddeft
" out into the wildernefs four thoufand men
" that were murderers?" It is affumed that
St. Paul was, at this time, known to the body
of the people; but it is evident, from the
words of a fubfequent paffage, that they were
acquainted with him only as he had been reprefented by the Afiatic Jews, as " the man
" that teacheth all men every where againft
" the people, and the law, and the temple;"
and that " he had brought Greeks into the
" temple, and had polluted that holy place."
St. Paul had conciliated the courtefy of the
Roman officer by fpeaking Greek, and obtained permiffion to addrefs the people, whofe
violence he thought he could reftrain till he
had explained the hiftory of his life, and the
particular actions of which he was accufed.
Nothing therefore could more fuddenly excite
their curiofity, and prefent a motive for attention, than the contraft of their accufation with
the language of his defence; which, otherwife, might have been loft in clamour at its
commencement, and he might not have had
the opportunity of faying, " I am verily a
" man which am a Jew." St. Paul therefore

fpoke in Hebrew to obviate this part of the accufation, and to fhew that he was a Jew, and not a Greek, and had no inducement to pollute the temple by introducing into it Greeks, or other ftrangers.

There can be no other reafon for an anxious and minute inveftigation of the fact, whether any book, or part of Scripture, be a tranflation, but that it is connected with the enquiry, whether or not, on that account, it can be regarded as divinely infpired. This very addrefs of St. Paul was in the Hebrew tongue; but it is tranfmitted to us in Greek only. Now we muft have it either from St. Paul himfelf, or from St. Luke. In the firft cafe, there muft have been two originals; and in the other, we are not ignorant who was the tranflator. In confidering the queftion of the infpiration of a tranflated work, it feems neceffary that the tranflator fhould be known, and that an original fhould be found to have exifted, or to have been ufed among thofe perfons where it was firft publifhed. It is not intended to deny the claim of infpiration to any work merely becaufe it is a verfion. If it is correct to explain, according to this notion, the interpretation of tongues, this was no lefs a fpiritual gift to the apoftolical teachers

than the power of speaking the tongues which
were interpreted; and then the only queſtion
that remains is, whether an oral had better
pretenſions to inſpiration than a written verſion. This power of interpretation would
not merely facilitate, but enſure the correct-
neſs of ſuch a verſion. We might after all
expect, that the ſame tradition, by which the
Goſpel itſelf is aſcribed to St. Matthew, would
alſo inform us who was the tranſlator. But
it is not neceſſary to purſue theſe conjectures.
It may be more uſeful to trace an outline of
the hiſtory of the diffuſion of the Greek language among the inhabitants of thoſe countries who reſorted to Jeruſalem, and witneſſed
the ſudden communication of their reſpective
dialects or languages to the uninſtructed Galileans. It may perhaps in this view be regarded as an illuſtrative comment upon this
part of the Acts of the Apoſtles.

We may firſt examine, to what degree the
Greek language was cultivated, not merely
" in Egypt, and in the parts of Libya about
" Cyrene," but in the northern region of
Africa in general. One of the moſt remark-
able effects of the ſettlement of the Greeks in
Africa, after the conqueſts of Alexander, was
the verſion of the ſacred books of the Jews.

We may deduce ufeful conclufions from either
fide of the difputed hiftory of this verfion. If
the fecond Ptolemy applied to the Jewifh San-
hedrim for tranflators; then the Jews of Jerufalem underftood the language of Greece more
than two centuries and a half before the age
of our Saviour. And what caufes, we might
afk, had operated fo as to make them lofe
what they had once poffeffed in fo eminent a
manner ? If, again, it were the work of the
Alexandrine Jews, we fee at what a remote
period the people of that nation, and in this
country, were qualified to ufe the Greek language for every purpofe. If we continue our
progrefs fouthwards, we difcover, not far from
the coaft of the Erythrean fea, the fovereign
of a confiderable tract fkilled in the language
of Greece; not perhaps the remains of the
literature of the age of the Ptolemies, but
the effects of the commerce of the adjacent
fea. The comparatively recent infcription at
Axum marks the public ufe of the fame language; and its continuance probably in the
fame diftrict to the beginning of the fourth
century. If we return to the northern fhores,
we are reminded, that although the Carthaginians, who were jealous of expofing their government or their commerce to the enquiry

of foreigners, had with this view interdicted the acquisition of the Greek learning; yet they did not enforce the law. Hannibal was acquainted with it not only as a soldier, but is said to have composed several historical works in that language, and was attended in his expeditions by a native of Lacedæmon. Indeed their frequent wars in Sicily would have obliged their commanders to neglect the edict made at Carthage, if they meant to qualify themselves to conduct their military affairs with success. The Greeks of Lacedæmon, of Corinth, and of Italy, were required to assist their ᵍ oppressed countrymen in the Sicilian colonies, which were subject to the Carthaginians. What would the law above alluded to avail against the probable effects of a hostile or a pacific intercourse of their armies with the Greek inhabitants of their foreign possessions? At a later period the younger Micipsa invited to his court learned Greeks, passed his time in their society, and studied their philosophy. Nor should we omit the name of Juba, who, during his residence at Rome, acquired so much knowledge of the Greek learning, and indeed of general literature, that he

ᵍ Diodor. Sic. p. 449. ed. Wessel.

did not obtain more diftinction[h] from his empire of Mauritania as a fovereign, than from his liberal erudition as a fcholar.

. If we pafs from " the parts of Libya" to " the dwellers in Afia," it will not be neceffary to prove formally, that the Greek colonies in Afia Minor preferved the language of the mother country, or that Phrygia and Pamphylia, which muft have had fo much intercourfe with them, were not ignorant of it. It is exprefsly related of the celebrated [i] Prince of Pontus, that he ftudied the Greek philofophy ; and, in the age of Tiberius, the [k] Cappadocian geographer did not exclude his countrymen, we may fuppofe, from the perufal of his writings, by his ufe of the Greek language. On the conqueft of the more eaftern parts of Afia by Alexander, the poetry of Homer was commonly recited ; (or, if I may be permitted to ufe the ftronger expreffions of [l] Plutarch, Ὅμηρος ἦν ἀνάγνωσμα·) and the youth of Perfia, Sufiana, and Gedrofia, rehearfed in public the tragedies of Sophocles and Euripides [m]. But,

---

[h] Plin. Nat. Hift.

[i] Appian. de B. Mithrid. p. 815. ed. Schweigh.

[k] Strabo.

·[l] De Fort. et Virt. Alex. p. 385. ed. Steph.

[m] Plut. ibid.

prior to the time of the conquests of Alexander, the Greek language was not merely
known, but used in the east for public purposes and occasions. The inscription on the
tomb of Cyrus at Paffagardæ was written
both in the Greek and Persian tongues. But
Darius had settled a colony of Greeks from
Miletus near the extremity of the Persian
gulph. The generals of Alexander might
make the use of the Greek language more popular, and more neceffary through their refpective fovereignties; and the foundation of
Seleucia on the Tigris fpread the language
among " the dwellers in Mefopotamia." We
are not to conclude that all the knowledge of
this language in thefe parts of the world is to
be afcribed to the influence of the Macedo-
nian conquefts. We are informed, upon the
authority of Ariftotle himfelf, cited by [n] Jofephus, that he met with a learned Jew of Cœle-

[n] Jofeph. cont. Apion. lib. i. p. 1347.
" There I met a Jew by birth from Cœle-Syria. Thefe
" are defcendants of the philofophers of India; and are
" called among the Indian philofophers Calani, but among
" the Syrians Jews, from the name of their country,
" which is termed Judæa. But the name of their city
" is very uncouth, for they call it Jerufalem. This man
" then, who had travelled much, and was going down
" from the countries of Upper Afia to the maritime

Syria who had cultivated the philofophy of
the Greeks with fo much ardour, that he was,
as he is defcribed, º" an Hellenic, not in his
" language only, but in his foul alfo." The
cities on the Euxine fea were Greek colonies,
founded long before the age of Alexander.

" coafts, was a Greek, not only in his dialeƈt, but in his
" foul alfo. And during our ftay in Afia Minor, hap-
" pening to arrive where we were, he joined us, and fome
·" other fcholars, in order to make trial of our wifdom ;
" and, when we had converfed on many topics of litera-
" ture, *he communicated rather more information than he*
" *received.* Thefe circumftances Ariftotle mentioned to
" Clearchus," [his pupil, and inferior to none of the Peri-
patetics,] " and moreover detailed the great and wonderful
" temperance of the Jew in his diet and fobriety." This
reference I owe to " The Infpeƈtor," a work written by
a moft learned and excellent man, and my own and my
father's friend, the Rev. Dr. Hales of Killifandra, formerly of Trinity College, Dublin. The Eftablifhed Church
has been greatly indebted of late to the erudition and
ability of Irifh fcholars. I wifh they would increafe the
effeƈt of their exertions by more candour in their treatment of each other as authors.

  º Plutarch, Vit. Craffi. I am indebted for this important reference to the " Appendix" to " Obfervations
" on the Words of the Centurion uttered at the Cruci-
" fixion of our Lord." " In confirmation of this we
" learn from Plutarch, that it was well underftood at
" the courts both of Parthia and of Armenia. Orodes
" the Parthian, and Artuafdes the Armenian monarch,
" were both of them fkilled in the Greek language and

If we furvey the nations adjacent to Mefopotamia, we find that, in the time of Craffus,
Orodes the Parthian king was well verfed in
the Greek language and Greek learning, and
that Artuafdes the king of Armenia, his contemporary, compofed tragedies, orations, and
hiftories in that language, fome of which are
faid by Plutarch to have been extant in his
time. The fame author relates alfo, that a
part of the feftivities in celebration of the
nuptials between the fon of Orodes and the
daughter of Artuafdes, confifted of the recita-
tion and fcenic exhibition of fome of the
Greek dramatic compofitions. While a diftinguifhed Lydian actor was rehearfing a part
of the Bacchæ of Euripides, a meffenger en-
tered, and laid the head of Craffus, recently

" the Greek literature ; and the latter compofed trage-
" dies, difcourfes, and hiftories in Greek, fome of which
" were extant in the time of Plutarch. A remarkable
" circumftance to this purpofe is related by the writer
" laft mentioned, that, at the inftant when the news of
" the defeat and death of Craffus was brought to the
" court of Parthia, they were engaged in the perform-
" ance of dramatic pieces in the Greek language, and
" particularly of the Bacchæ of Euripides, in the acting
" of which they employed the head of Craffus as if it had
" been that of Pentheus, murdered by his mother A-
" gave." Page 27.

flain, at the feet of Orodes. The actor in-
ftantly applied the occurrence; and, affuming
the character of Agave, bore upon a thyrfus
the head of Craffus, as if it were that of Pentheus, and repeated the appropriate paffages
of the Greek tragedian. The fpectators, it is
faid, applauded the addrefs of the actor, and
felt the happy adaptation of the fiction to the
reality. Nor fhould it be omitted that Su-
rena, the general of Orodes, in order to expofe
the corrupt manners of the Romans, and the
fubject of their thoughts, even at a time when
they were oppofed to an enemy in the field,
exprefsly affembled the fenate of Seleucia, and
produced for their indignant infpection the
licentious volumes of the P Milefiacs of Ariftides, which had been found among the plunder in the military baggage of a Roman officer
of rank.

We are now to pafs to the " ftrangers of
" Rome," and to examine curforily the ftate
of the Greek language in Italy. It is certain.

P Plut. in Vit. Craff. Ovid queruloufly remarks, that,
although Ariftides had written licentioufly, yet he was
not exiled.

Junxit Ariftides Milefia crimina fecum,
    Pulfus Ariftides nec tamen urbe fua.
                                        Trift. ii. 413.

that Italy received many colonies from Greece; but whether after the deftruction of Troy, it is not neceffary to difcufs. The tract of country denominated Magna Græcia was not the only part which was occupied by thefe foreign adventurers. The coaft of Etruria was originally peopled by migrations from Greece, and its Afiatic colonies. Soon after the eftablifhment of a regular fyftem of polity among the Romans, the compilation of the laws of the twelve tables fhews the frequency as well as the facility of their intercourfe with Greece, which might perhaps have originated among the mixed races of the inhabitants of Rome itfelf. We are not to conclude that the ufe of the Greek language was not introduced before the introduction of the Grecian philofophy. There were other caufes, which had led to the acquifition of this language before the ftate of fociety had prepared the Romans for adopting or engaging in philofophical Grecian fpeculations. The ambaffador of Pyrrhus addreffed the Roman fenate in the Greek language three centuries before the Chriftian æra. It appears that Fabricius, who was deputed to confer with Pyrrhus and Cineas, underftood this language fufficiently for every public purpofe. At his interview with Pyrrhus, Cineas

fhocked the fimplicity and purity of character
of the Roman conful by his avowal of the
corrupt doctrines of the Epicurean fyftem.
Cineas directed the converfation to the character of Epicurus, and informed Fabricius,
" that the Epicureans placed the chief end
" and happinefs of man in pleafure; that they
" avoided all offices and employments in the
" ftate, as fo many obftacles to that happinefs;
" that they attributed to the fupreme Being
" neither love nor hate, maintaining that he
" was perfectly regardlefs of men and all hu-
" man affairs, and confined himfelf to an in-
" active life, where he fpent whole ages in the
" full enjoyment of all kinds of pleafure."
The minifter of Pyrrhus found the ftern Roman acquainted with the language, but not
with the enervating philofophy of the Greeks.
" May Pyrrhus and the Tarentines," exclaim-
ed Fabricius, " maintain thefe doctrines as
" long as they are at war with the Romans!"
There is a remarkable contraft between the
two reprefentations which introduced Fabricius and the cenfor Cato to the knowledge of
the tenets of fome of the moft eminent Grecian philofophers. When Tarentum was taken
by Fabius Maximus, Cato, then young, lived
with Nearchus, a Pythagorean. He defired

to hear the nature " of his philofophy, and,
" finding his reflections the fame with Plato's,
" that pleafure is the greateft allurement to
" evil; that the greateft plague and calamity
" of the foul is the body, from which it can-
" not difengage and free itfelf in this world
" but by fuch thoughts and reafonings as
" wean and feparate it from all corporeal paf-
" fions and affections; he was fo much pleafed
" with this difcourfe, that he was ftill more
" determined to adhere to frugality and tem-
" perance." Thefe fentiments might have induced a Roman of this period to cultivate the
language for the fake of fuch philofophy. In
the time of Marcus Marcellus the Romans had
adopted the polifhed manners of the Greeks:
and he himfelf admired fo much the Grecian
learning and eloquence, that he " honoured
" all that excelled in them; but he himfelf
" did not make a progrefs equal to his defires,
" becaufe his other bufinefs and employment
" took him off from a clofe application q."
Cato, however, evidently made a diftinction
between the language and the philofophy of
Greece: for he perufed the writings of the
moft eminent Greek authors, " among whom

q Plut. Vit. Marc.

" he received fome advantage from Thucy-
" dides, but much more from Demofthenes,
" towards forming his ftyle and improving his
" eloquence." When he was at Athens as a
Roman ambaffador, he fpoke to the people
" through an interpreter; not that he was un-
" able to fpeak to them in their own tongue ;
" but his intention was, to maintain the dig-
" nity of the Roman language[r]." When Cato
was old, Carneades the academic, and Dio-
genes the ftoic, came from Athens on an em-
baffy to Rome. This occurrence formed an
æra, not fo much in the ftudy of the Greek
language, as of the ftudy of the Grecian philofophy in that city. The invectives of Cato
were not indifcriminate. He cenfured the
tenets of the philofophers, and directed his
indignant remonftrances againft Carneades,
who adorned the precepts of philofophy with
all the graces of eloquence, and attracted the
Roman youth from their martial fports to

---

[r] It is added, " and ridicule thofe who admired no-
" thing but what was Greek." This was not, and could
not be his intention. He was required to fuftain the
dignity of the people who had deputed him their ambaffador; and the ufe of their language was a point of ceremony, an affumption of official ftate, and an expreffion of
political independence.

liften to the delufive oratory of the Athenian
mafters of wifdom.   It was at this period that
he predicted the evils which would arife from
the admiration of the Greek learning and of
the Greek philofophy, which would produce
the decline of the ancient Roman character.
Even at the clofe of life, when the ufe of the
Greek language was feparated from the Greek
philofophy, he prophetically characterized, in
the language of Homer, the greatnefs of the
younger Scipio.   The fubfequent detail would
occupy too much time if it were purfued
through fimilar inftances minutely.   It may
be fufficient to ftate briefly, that Auguftus addreffed the inhabitants of Alexandria in a
Greek oration, when he explained the reafon
of the pardon which he had granted, after
they had efpoufed the caufe of Mark Antony;
and he is faid to have fpoken in Greek ˢ " in
" order that he might be underftood:" that
" Molo the rhetorician, a contemporary of
" Cicero, declaimed ᵗ in the fenate in Greek;

---

s Καὶ τόνγε λόγον, δι' οὗ συνέγνω σφίσιν, Ἑλληνιςὶ, ὅπως συν-
ῶσιν αὐτοῦ, εἶπε.   D. Caff. lib. li. p. 454.

t See the Appendix before referred to for thefe examples of Molo, Tiberius, and the previous ftudy of Greek,
recorded by Quinctilian.   This is the ufe, to its full extent, which I have made of the Appendix.

" and Tiberius Cæfar examined witneffes, and
" heard pleadings and arguments in Greek, in
" caufes that came before that affembly;"
that it was the language of both focial and
public intercourfe at Rome with ambaffadors
and all foreigners; that " it was ufual to in-
" ftruct the youth in Greek before they com-
" menced the ftudy of Latin." We may add,
that if we pafs the borders of Italy, we find
it among the ᵘHelvetii, who regiftered their
population in the Greek language.

With refpect to the furprife of the dwellers
in Judæa, when they heard the Galileans
fpeak in the tongue wherein they were born,
we do not perhaps underftand how it was
occafioned. We fhould imagine, that a Jew
of Paleftine fpeaking in the Hebrew or Syro-
Chaldee could not be regarded as a miraculous
fact by a Jew of the fame country. Even if
the Galileans had been peculiarly illiterate,
they muft have underftood enough of the lan-

ᵘ Cæfar. Comment. lib. i. c. 18. It has been remarked, that the words *Græcis litteris* may imply only Greek
characters; but I am difpofed to think that we fhall not
be able to find any other inftance, if this be one, of the
ufe of the Greek characters exifting independently of a
knowledge of the language. See a note at the end of
the volume.

guage in which they carried on their various
occupations; but how could their original ignorance in this refpect be fo well known as to
make their facility of expreffing themfelves at
this time appear to be miraculous? This, we
may prefume, was not the meaning of the
hiftorian. The majority of the Jews who reforted to Jerufalem probably ufed the Greek
language in fome of the various dialects of the
countries where they refided. If we fuppofe
that the Apoftles fpoke every variety of language which was ftrictly indigenous in the
feveral quarters of the world, of which the
hearers were refpectively natives, it is fomewhat remarkable that gofpels were not compofed in fome of thefe tongues for the ufe of
thefe profelytes. The period from the communication of the gift of tongues, to the compofition of the Gofpels, was not of fufficient
duration to allow the acquifition of the Greek
language fo generally among diftant nations.
Nor indeed had they any other motive to acquire it, than to qualify themfelves to underftand a gofpel which had been at firft promulgated orally in their native tongue, and was
committed to writing in another. It may be
remarked, that, throughout the whole tract of
the apoftolical miffions, although a native lan-

guage muft be fuppofed to maintain its place and ufe, yet we alfo know that the Greek was fuperadded to the vernacular tongue throughout the fame countries, and more commonly acquired and employed than any modern language that can be named, which has been ever attained for the purpofe of foreign communication.

To the preceding detail it may be objected, that it has been proved only that it formed a medium of intercourfe among the more cultivated and intelligent, and not among that defcription of perfons to whom the Gofpel was to be• preached. There are caufes adequate to account for a ftill more general diffufion of the Greek language than we can at prefent prove to have prevailed from exifting hiftories. It was the language in which the commerce of the ancient world was carried on : if we add to this the difperfion of numerous colonies of Greeks in Afia Minor, Italy, and Sicily; and the effects of the conquefts of Alexander; we fhall find the language eftablifhing itfelf by the influence of fafhion, by the progrefs of the Greek philofophy, and by the moft powerful motives of human action, the interefts of nations and individuals.

If it be an accurate obfervation, that the

Greek language of the New Teftament contains a mixture of oriental idioms, it might
be expected that fuch foreign additions would
be incorporated with the Greek of Paleftine.
But this ftate of the language fhews, that it
had not acquired fuch modes of phrafeology
on a fudden; but that the Greek had been
long enough in ufe in Paleftine, or elfewhere,
to be tinctured with the peculiarities of the
native tongues of thofe who adopted it. The
language of Lycaonia was only a dialect of
the Greek. At what period certain Latin words
began to be introduced into the Greek, it may
not be poffible to afcertain; particularly the
names of things, which were not common in
the ufages or habits of Greece and Italy. This
would prevent the mention of any thing which
was not previoufly known to thofe who inha-
bited the countries in which Greek and Latin
were the vernacular tongues, as no word in
ufe could be found that would exprefs the
meaning. [x] Tiberius, we are informed, when
he enacted a law, forbade the infertion of the
word defcribing the object of the decree, as
being a Greek term, although it could not be

---

[x] D. Caff. lib. lvii. p. 612. Dr. Townfon, I afterwards
faw, had cited the fame fact from another author, Sue-
tonius; and for a different purpofe.

adequately exprefled by any word in the Latin language. Are we not then to expect to
find fuch words as σεδάρια and σιμικίνθια where
the manners and habits of the people did not
furnifh the things themfelves? And yet it is
upon the authority of thefe, and fimilar words,
that we are to pronounce to be forgeries' any
books which contain them before the time of
Trajan. This is an unreafonable ftandard of
authenticity, becaufe it fuppofes that every
word was firft ufed in writing before it was
employed in converfation and general intercourfe. It may happen that terms of this
kind are not to be found elfewhere; when at
the fame time we know, from the nature of
the objects which they reprefent, that they
muft have been ufed from the period of the
invention or adoption of the things themfelves.
Befides, it may not fall within the view of a
writer to mention facts relative to fuch objects; and ftill lefs can we determine that
they were never defcribed, or their ufe noticed
before, fo that the word might remain confined to colloquial ufe becaufe the occafions
of employing it otherwife might feldom occur;
or again we muft fuppofe, that we poffefs
all the writings in which it had ever been introduced.

By this view of the extenfive diffufion of the Greek language we fhall be able to ijudge of an obfervation refpecting the language in which the Epiftle to the Hebrews was written. It is remarked, that y " if this Epiftle had " been fent to Parthian Jews, who became " converts to Chriftianity, the Hebrew ori- " ginal would hardly have been loft; for in " the countries which bordered upon the Eu- " phrates the Chriftian religion was propa- " gated at a very early period." But I have before fhewn, that at the time of Craffus the Greek language was well underftood in Par- thia; nor are we to limit the ufe of the Sep- tuagint verfion of the Jewifh Scriptures to the country where it was executed. If the early eftablifhment of Chriftianity in the countries near the Euphrates were a reafon why any Hebrew writing fhould be preferved, the fame caufe fhould have operated ftill more power- fully in the prefervation of the Hebrew ori- ginal of St. Matthew's Gofpel in Judea and Jerufalem, where Chriftianity was firft pro- mulgated.

It is an affertion not well fupported, that " the greateft part of the inhabitants of Jeru-

" falem were certainly not acquainted with
" Greek." This is contradicted by every argument even from probability. The metropolis of the country, to which perfons of the
fame unmixed defcent reforted annually in
great multitudes to attend their common religious feftivals from almoft every part of the
world, would prefent opportunities of a more
complete communication than could be afforded by any other place in the fame country. It was not an intercourfe between Jews
and ftrangers, but each ftranger recognifed the
other as a member of the fame great family;
and therefore the ufual caufes which create
diftruft, referve, and jealoufy, and a difin-
clination to converfe with foreigners, would
here have no place. It is faid farther, that
even the [z] Jews themfelves called the Greek
the vernacular tongue, and acknowledged it
in this character almoft in Judea itfelf. [a] Jofephus compofed his work on the wars of his
countrymen in Hebrew, which is now loft;
but the Greek verfion of it is preferved. He
has however informed us, that he himfelf
tranflated it, and that he ftudied the Greek

[z] Rumpæus, p. 93.
[a] In Præfat. ad lib. de Bell. Jud.

language at Rome in order to qualify himfelf
to write with more correctnefs, as we may
fuppofe; not that he acquired it there from
its very elements. He defigned his verfion
for the ufe of the Romans as well as the
Greeks; and, as he learnt the Greek language
at Rome, he had the choice of the two languages, but certainly did not prefer that which
was leaft known: and he could have no intereft to write an account of the wars of his
countrymen more intelligibly for the ufe of
the Greeks, than for that of the Romans.

I am not fenfible that this enquiry into the
general prevalence of the Greek language is
defective in the proof of an important circumftance; namely, that it was fo generally fpoken, that the Gofpels, when written
in that tongue, would be eafily underftood
by perfons of almoft every condition. It
would otherwife have feemed to be repugnant to propriety, to the apoftolical practice
and directions, and to the defign of the Author of Chriftianity, that the Gofpel fhould
be preached in the native language of each
people, but publifhed in writing in a language
known to one nation only. On the other
hand, the extent of its diffufion, or the length
of time during which it continued in ufe,

would not prevent the introduction of verfions, wherever they were neceffary. But it
is worthy of remark, that the language of the
originals was fo well underftood at that time,
that it was a fecurity for a faithful interpretation; that one party was able to execute
fuch a work, and another to exercife a controul, which might lead to the knowledge of
the true meaning of Scripture, and tend to
preferve its integrity.

We do not infift upon the adoption of the
Greek language as a fuggeftion of infpiration.
It was neceffary to ufe it even if the writers
had acted only in conformity with prudence
and duty, as it was their object to diffufe
Chriftianity as widely as poffible among the
nations of the world. It has been remarked
indeed, that [b] " the fuppofition that God has-
" chofen in his wifdom the Greek language
" as a vehicle of revelation, becaufe it was
" at that time the language moft generally
" known, will not prove the divinity of the
" revelation." We do not connect the divinity of a .revelation with the language in
which it is communicated, fo as to deduce a
proof of its divine origin from the univerfality
of the language. But we may be allowed to

---

[a] Michaelis, vol. i. p. 99.

admire the concurrence of this fact with the
time and feafon fixed by Providence for the
promulgation of the Gofpel to the world. It
heightened the publicity of the revelation by
enlarging the field of examination, and *immediately* fubjected a religion, whofe effential
characteriftic was, its adaptation to all perfons, to the curious fcrutiny of a larger portion of mankind, and indeed to the whole
civilized world, which would not have taken
place had it been conveyed in a language ufed
by any other of the communities of the earth.
c " No language," it is faid, " is fo widely ex-
" tended as to be underftood by a tenth part
" of the inhabitants of the globe." When
the Gofpel was firft preached, and afterwards
publifhed in writing, the Greek language had
acquired an afcendancy which was not divided with any other. The queftion is, to
what extent is the language known in which
a certain revelation is firft communicated. The
facility of fuch an examination, at the firft
appearance of a divine revelation, will determine its pretenfions to credibility. It is in
vain to urge that "a language may ceafe to be
" a living language in a thoufand years." A
much fmaller period would fuffice for every

c Michaelis.

purpofe of examination, and for the execution
of exact verfions of the alledged revelation.
The language fhould indeed afford as large a
fphere as poffible for the examination of the
facts and documents on their firft appearance
and publication, and the Greek above all other
languages afforded the opportunity of extenfive inveftigation.   It might have feemed, according to a paradoxical foreigner, " not un-
" worthy the wifdom of Providence to have
" chofen the Latin language as the medium
" of revelation." Chriftianity did not require,
but fought greater means of publicity. A
language comparatively little known could
not have been felected confiftently with the
comprehenfive defign of infinite wifdom, or
with the Gofpel, the character of which is,
that nothing was taught or done in fecret.
If we adopt the trite citation from Cicero refpecting the language of his country, compared with the Greek by the ftandard of extenfive ufe, we fhall find, that the former
would have been a defective inftrument for
fpreading a knowledge of the Gofpel, becaufe
it would have limited that indifpenfable fearch
and enquiry, to which every recent revelation
fhould be fully fubmitted, while the latter
correfponds with almoft a providential preci-

fion with the commands of the Author of Chriftianity to his difciples, " to go and teach " all nations;" [d] " Græca leguntur in omni- " bus fere gentibus; Latina fuis finibus, exi- " guis fane, continentur."

I have thus brought the propofed difcuffion to its deftined clofe. I have avoided any re- capitulation of the topics and reafoning, be- caufe it might appear rather as an obtrufive difplay of refearch, than as neceffary to the elucidation of the general argument; becaufe, too, the difputant feems to award to himfelf the advantage in the controverfy; and, laftly, becaufe I remember that there are limits to the indulgence of the moft candid. I cannot characterize the fpirit of " The Diffonance" in more accurate terms, nor conclude with a more juft reprehenfion *of the private and public conduct of thofe, who infidioufly endea- vour to invalidate the beft evidence of which the thing in queftion of any kind is fufceptible,* than is contained in the practical and admoni- tory dogma of the Council of Chalcedon; " Qui " poft femel inventam veritatem aliud quærit, " mendacium quærit, non veritatem."

[d] Cic. pro Arch. Poet.

THE

PROBATIONARY

DISCOURSE,

PREACHED

NOVEMBER 5, 1808.

.

DANIEL ii. 21.

He removeth kings, and setteth up kings.

— ⬩ —

ᵃ ALTHOUGH a superintending Providence be acknowledged to preside over the whole course of affairs, both of particular persons, and those of nations, yet we are disposed to think, from a vain wish to discover its immediate operation, that this controul is more conspicuously displayed in the convulsions and fall of kingdoms, than in the ordinary changes of the condition of the individual. The Deity seems to approach nearer to us in inflicting his judgments, than in dispensing his mercies; and his power is apparently rendered more distinguishable from the efforts and wisdom of man in the destruction, than in the

ᵃ I had not at this time seen an able discourse on the same occasion by the Rev. R. Churton, Archdeacon of St. David's. I can judge of the labour and success of his research. I likewise searched in vain the Bodleian and other catalogues for the book which Dr. Milner has cited under the title of Political Catechism.

T 4

prefervation of ftates. It is from the impreffion, which this fentiment makes upon the
mind, that, when nations commemorate their
deliverances from the rage or the machinations of political or religious factions, they in-
cur fome danger of perpetuating a vindictive
fpirit of animofity againft thofe, who tranfmit
the name, and profefs the opinions of the ancient aggreffors. It is painful, by the acknowledgment of mercies fhewn to ourfelves, to
remind others of the delinquency of their predeceffors; and this facrifice of thankfgiving
may perhaps engage on the fide of devotion
thofe feelings, which without this religious
homage might tend only to renew the refentment of former grievances.

The two great events, the memory of which
the appointment of this feftival was intended
to preferve, have, at different periods, excited
different degrees of intereft in this country;
and the time has again arrived, when the one,
whofe importance feemed to be merged in the
glory of the other, has regained the power of
attracting curiofity, and of ftimulating enquiry.

The neceffity of reviewing a large part of
the hiftory of this event in particular has proceeded from the public affertions of a modern

adverſary of no mean name and rank among his own people. It [b] has been confidently averred, that this ſanguinary ſtratagem was in reality the invention of a Proteſtant Miniſter óf ſtate, to make an oppoſite religious party odious in the eyes of the nation ; ſo that, if this faćt be truly repreſented, our gratitude to Providence has been annually offered up in error for fancied mercies, and a fićtitious deliverance.

Although the Catholics had diſturbed the government of the firſt James at an early period by frequent conſpiracies, yet they had been treated with a lenity, during his ſeparate reign in Scotland, which rouſed the ſuſpicions of Elizabeth, and the jealouſy of his Proteſtant ſubjećts. If the ſovereign Pontiff had been exaſperated, although he might not have been able to prevent by his hoſtile interpoſition, yet he might have obſtrućted by many difficulties the acceſſion of this prince to the throne of England, and might afterwards have continued to haraſs his ſettlement in his new kingdom with the oppoſition of a body of men more numerous, and more aćtive, than thoſe of the ſame perſuaſion in Scotland. As the

[b] See note (A) at the end.

time approached, when it was probable that he would foon be the fucceffor of Elizabeth, his communications with the court of Rome, chiefly relating to his right to the Englifh crown, were frequent and fecret. Of the reality of thefe communications the proof is clear and full; and, if we were to add to them the celebrated letter to Clement VIII. without intimating that the authenticity of this inftrument has not been acknowledged by hiftorians in general, ftill [c] the attachment of James to the Catholic religion would fcarcely appear to be ftronger than before. That he might " de-
" clare in [d] open parliament, that he confi-
" dered the church of Rome as the mother
" Church, although defiled with fome corrup-
" tions ;" that he " might admit the Pope to
" be the Patriarch of the weft ;" that " the
" King's difpofition was for peace and recon-
" ciliation with Rome at the beginning ;" are circumftances, all of which may be conceded to our adverfary, without diminifhing the ftrength of the argument. Such confiderations do not indicate any inclination in the King to

[c] See note (B) at the end.

[d] But in the fame fpeech he very uncourteoufly terms the Pope, " that three-crowned monarch, or rather mon-
" fter." Rapin, vol. ii. p. 166.

grant liberty of confcience to the Catholics, nor is the acknowledgment of " fome degree " of ecclefiaftical fupremacy belonging to the " Pontiff," to be adduced as a neceffary preliminary, or a pledge of that indulgence. If then the zeal of James for the fupport of the Catholic caufe does not, even according to the refearches of an acute adverfary, much exceed this fcanty meafure, why fhould the Minifter be accufed of alienating the regard of his Mafter, or of diverting the current of his benevolence ? If however this accufation comprifed all the odious interference of the Minifter, we fhould not be furprifed, nor think it neceffary to vindicate his ardour. But, when we are further required to believe, that he was the author of a plot, by means of which he chiefly intended to remove a perfon, whofe offence confifted in being a witnefs to the King's ftrong promifes " to fhew indulgence to the " Catholics of England, whenever he fhould " mount the throne of his country," we anxioufly examine the evidence of fuch guilt. Yet how does indignation fupplant every other emotion, when we difcover in a contemporary document, that this man could not be the depofitary of promifes, which, by his own unbiaffed confeffion, were never made. He de-

clared in effect that in his interview with the
King ᵉ" he could not obtain any promife,
" hope, or comfort of encouragement to Ca-
" tholics concerning toleration." We do not
here appeal to the writings of partial and obfcure annalifts, which are now rarely to be
found, becaufe they were originally infignifi-
cant; but to an inftrument of high authority,
of eafy accefs, and of general notoriety. We
are indeed ready to admit that Raleigh's confpiracy, as *this* plot was called, had been afcribed to Cecil before the trial : but as he was
then confronted with the accufed, the latter
would not have hefitated, in his own defence,
to have retorted the accufation upon the fecret
author. When both were prefent, then was
the time to difclofe the real agent. The fact
however is, that Cecil was exculpated from
any participation in this enterprife by the confeffion and trial of the parties themfelves concerned in this confpiracy. But it is alledged,
that " this artful minifter was not long with-
" out finding the means of wreaking his ven-
" geance upon the whole catholic body, and
" (which was his principal object) of diffolv-
" ing the ties by which the King was united

ᵉ State Trials, vol. i. p. 203.

" to them." It does not appear from any hiftorical facts of what kind thofe ties were by
which James was fo firmly attached to the
Catholics. But whatever they might be, they
ftill continued unaltered and unbroken, even
after the difcovery of this atrocious confpiracy.
He acquainted his parliament, that he was
willing to confine the guilt of it to the individuals who were detected in its execution,
and not to involve in a general fufpicion and
cenfure the majority of that perfuafion. Thus
imperfectly was the vengeance of the Minifter
wreaked upon his devoted victims, if the blow
were intercepted in its defcent by the King
himfelf. The number, the weight, and the
characters of the confpirators have been adduced as reafons, why we fhould not attribute
this barbarous project to the Catholics at
large. But this queftion cannot be determined
merely by the confideration of what proportion of perfons ought to be concerned in de-
vifing and executing any plan, fo as to juftify
an obferver in referring it to the body, to
which the individuals, who engaged in it, belonged. This is to change a moral into an
arithmetical enquiry. The fmall number of
the agents is not to be compared with the
number of perfons, of which the fect confifts,

in order to afcertain the proportion which one might bear to the other. We are rather to refer the number of agents to the nature of the deed, to its compatibility with the necef-fary degree of fecrecy, and to the manner in which they were to put it into execution. We do not altogether reject the confideration of an affemblage of perfons numerically, becaufe it may be compofed of fo few, that they would not be employed to effect any political pur-pofe whatever.

It is however admitted, that in the prefent inftance there was another part of the confpi-racy, the execution of which depended upon the fuccefs of the firft. It may be lightly de-fcribed in this manner, that fome of the trai-tors were " only concerned in the fcheme of " an infurrection ;" but a plot and an infur-rection require a very different force to enfure the defired iffue of each. Will not therefore the propofed infurrection, in conjunction with the plot, extend the knowledge and the guilt of this execrable device to a larger proportion of the Catholics, than the plot alone ? We may enquire, in what manner has our adver-fary computed their number ? By what he terms " the act of attainder." By thus re-ftricting our enquiry, we may abridge the

enumeration of the agents, and perhaps contract the fphere of their project : but why
fhould we fuppofe that the law operated fo
exactly as to comprehend all the guilty, or,
that the whole of the guilty were fo impro-
vident in their deliberations, that punifhment
was here commenfurate with criminality ?

They were, it is alfo faid, not only few in
number, but deficient " in weight and cha-
" racter." But what degree of confequence
is it expected that *confpirators* fhould poffefs ?
If we regard the part which they were to act,
we are, on the contrary, furprifed that fo few
of them fhould want the perfonal requifites to
make their treachery to be the effort of mean
and defperate, and unfupported adventurers ?
Some of them were perfons of family and
opulence, none of them were deftitute of education, and others poffeffed amiable qualities
and conciliatory manners. If we add to this
favourable but accurate delineation of their
origin, and habits in general, the counteract-
ing defects, which are formally afcribed to one
or more of them, youth and temerity, we fhall
add all that hiftorical truth can require ; and
yet we add nothing that, with the exception
of their cooperation in this daring attempt,

would otherwife impair their weight, or de-
bafe their character.

Our adverfary is again ready with a com-
plicated and unftable objection, that they were
f " apoftates and outcafts from the body of the
" Catholics;" or, they were " not g Recufants;"
or, they were " nominal Catholics ;" or, " *if*
" any of them were Catholics, or fo died, they
" were known Proteftants not long before."
It is evident from the inconfiftency of thefe
fuppofitions, that the private religious opinions
of thefe perfons muft be inferred from their
actions, where we cannot obtain any precife
and regular declaration of their belief. But
we cannot conclude that they were apoftates
from the Catholic body, and at the fame time
recent and unfteady converts from Proteftantifm. The cafuiftical doubt, which feemed to
perplex one of the chief actors in this enor-
mity, and which related to a difficulty only in
the execution, and not to the principle of the

f Milner, p. 270. note (1).

g Henry Earl of Northumberland was fined in the
Star Chamber " for having admitted Thomas Percy his
" kinfman to be a Gentleman Penfioner without admini-
" fiering the oath of fupremacy, when he knew him to
" be a Recufant." Hiftory of the Gunpowder Treafon,
p. 31.

deed, was refolved ultimately by the fuperior of the Englifh jefuits; and this oracular decifion was confidently appealed to as having fufficient authority to difpel the fame fceptical uncertainty that arofe in the minds of fome of his nefarious colleagues. [h] The counfellors then, to whom he repaired, were Jefuits, who did not hefitate to communicate ther refponfes to an enquiring " outcaft and apoftate." We may ftill further afk, from what religious party are converts in general to derive their characteriftic denomination; from the one which they relinquifh, or from that by which they are received? To which is to belong the diftinction, and to which the difgrace of their choice? To which are the laft virtues,. or the laft vices of their lives to be afcribed? " The " dying behaviour," as it is called, of thefe apoftates is adduced as a proof that " they did. " not act in conformity with the principles of " their religion, even as they conceived it, and " that they did not think the horrible attempt, " in which they were engaged, lawful and " meritorious." [i] Admitting that they clofed their lives with penitence worthy of the pureft

---

[h] See note (C) at the end.
[i] See note (D) at the end.

fyftem of religious opinions, we muft ftill confider whether the principles of their religion,
or the original feelings of human nature, operated moft ftrongly in producing their dubious
concern. Their compunction came too late.
Their fentiments muft have been very different on the profpect of a fuccefsful conclufion
of their enterprife ; and at the time of failure,
difappointment, and death. Did they faulter,
in their career in confequence of the counfel
which they folicited? They prepared their
plan without any interruption from their own
confciences, or thofe of their advifers. Religion did not alarm them with its terrors till
they had firft tried what they could effect.
The contemplation of the attempt was not
attended with any doubts or remorfe which
were creditable to their principles, and their
end was the fame as that of other baffled af-
faffins.—[k] It is to be further remarked, that

[k] " Thomas Winter was fent into Spain, by the joint
" advice of Henry Garnet, and Ofwald Tefmond, jefuit,
" and of Robert Catefby, and Francis Trefham, *gentlemen*
" *of good quality and reputation*, to try what could be
" done for their affiftance, that were ready to facrifice
" their lives and fortunes for the catholic caufe." Hiftory
of the Gunpowder Treafon, collected from approved Authors as well Popifh as Proteftant, 1678.

fome of the principal agents in this plot were the fame perfons who had, in the name of the Englifh Catholics in general, fecretly applied to the court of Spain for affiftance in the time of Elizabeth. The Popifh Plot has therefore been regarded by hiftorians as a continuation of the former; and can we fuppofe that it was calculated to gratify the inclinations of a fmaller number of perfons than the fcheme of the cooperation of domeftic infurgents with the forces of a foreign invader ? There is however proof that the plot was not altogether difagreeable to the Roman Pontiff, although it is faid that the fuperior of the Englifh Jefuits " well knew that he would never "-approve of fo diabolical an undertaking." The Catholics both here and at Rome could neverthelefs folemnly petition Heaven to favour the intentions of the confpirators; and it is affirmed, not by any irritated Proteftant, but by a Jefuit, that the " Pontiff was ac- " quainted with the defign, and had proper " bulls ready to be iffued upon the fuccefs of " it[1]." Such then are the grounds, upon

[1] " It is affirmed by the voluntary confeffion of a Je- " fuit, That at this time there were two bulls procured " from the Pope, and ready upon this occafion, and " fhould have been publifhed, had the powder done the

which we continue to think that this plot has been appropriately defignated by its common epithet, as indicatory of the agents, and of the particular interefts, which it was their object to promote.

We are now to examine briefly the means which the minifter Cecil is faid to have ufed either to fupprefs or to pervert the evidence, by which his agency in this affair might have been detected.—That he permitted four of the traitors to be deftroyed, whofe perfons he might have fecured without facrificing their lives, from the confcioufnefs that they could have expofed his participation in their project, is a fuppofition which will not influence the moft credulous mind, as it requires the previous, or rather the fimultaneous belief of feveral inconfiftent particulars. Is it probable that this participation fhould be known to thofe four perfons only ? Why did not the murderous hireling, who efcaped with wounds only from the arm of the magiftrate, betray their lurking employer ? It ᵐ is urged as an

_____

" intended execution; but, that failing, they were fup-
" preft." Foulis's Romifh Treaf. Vid. Bp. Andrews, Re-
fponf. ad Apolog. Bellarmine, c. v. p. 113.

    ᵐ " Sir R. Walfh having gotten fure trial of their tak-
" ing harbour at the houfe above named, he did fend

article of crimination, that no directions were ' given for employing the milder expedient of apprehenſion, when a delay ſufficient for that purpoſe had intervened; and that it would have been eaſy to have taken them alive. But no directions are ſpecified by hiſtorians relative either to the capture or the death of theſe men. Is it extraordinary that perſons ſhould " not be taken alive who had reſolved " to " break through their oppoſers, and die fighting ⁿ?" Death was the effect of their own choice, not the preconcerted ſtrong reſource of the Miniſter againſt babbling accomplices, who would " have related the ſtory leſs to " his advantage, than he cauſed it to be pub-

" trumpeters and meſſengers to them, commanding them " in the King's name to render unto him, His Majeſties " Miniſter, and knowing no more at that time of their " guilt than was publickly viſible, did promiſe, upon " their dutiful and obedient rendring unto him, to inter- " cede at the King's hands for the ſparing of their lives, " who received only from them this ſcornful anſwer, " That he had need of better aſſiſtance than of thoſe few " numbers that were with him before he could be able to " command or controul them." Gunpowder Treaſon, p. 68.

n " Then ſaid Cateſby to me, (ſtanding by the door " they were to enter,) Stand by me, and we will die to- " gether." Winter's confeſſion, Gunpowder Treaſon, p. 60.

" lifhed." After having thus difpofed of the
living witneffes, we are informed that he publifhed interefted and falfe narratives of this
dark affair, which have mifled " the generality
" of writers." *All* the accounts, which we
have of this affair, did not proceed from the
inventive and fabricating diligence of Cecil,
and his " plot wrights." There is furely one
exception among the documents of the time,
which he neither compofed, nor mutilated,
nor augmented, nor did it require his patron-
age. Did he publifh and circulate the trials
of the confpirators? Did they confefs at his
inftigation, or by his direction? Did he procure perfons to falfify thefe records? Did
he dictate the confeffions of the confpirators
againft themfelves? and by what known means
could he induce them to conceal all that was
unfavourable to himfelf, and relate only all
that was deftructive to their own caufe? Do
not the generality of later writers follow thefe
as much as any other public and contemporary inftruments? We may confidently repeat
the queftion, for it will well bear the repetition, Why did not the Confpirators boldly accufe the Secretary when they had the opportunity? Why did he fo rafhly venture fo often
into their prefence? Why did he appear at

their trials, if he had been confcious thàt he might have been betrayed? Did he confer with thofe traitors only who were killed? Did *they* never fpeak of their illuftrious confederate to others? Is it probable that the Jefuits, Garnet in particular, fhould know fo many other circumftances of the confpiracy, and be ignorant of this? The filence of the Confpirators at this time muft be affumed as a proof that they had it *not* in their power to palliate their guilt by a declaration, which they had every worldly inducement to alledge º.—I have thus examined " the faithful view," as it is denominated, of this confpiracy. It cannot be expected that the detail fhould be completely developed from this place; at the fame time it is not very defective. It is difficult to confine fuch a difcuffion to the limits prefcribed to me on the prefent occafion. There are other topics, which from their minutenefs could not be explained orally, and from their merely fecular character could not be here introduced with propriety.

Another important branch of the enquiry alfo claims our attention. We are now to turn our eyes from the endeavours of fubjects

º See note (E) at the end.

to eftablifh the Catholic religion, to the attempt of a Sovereign to attain the fame object.

It has been fuppofed by no vulgar authority, that the motives of the political conduct
of the fecond James have been mifunderftood
by the earlier hiftorians, from the want of
that private information, which we now poffefs. His moft important actions are thought
to have proceeded from a predominant defire
of abfolute power. But we muft remember,
that he was a bigot long before he afcended
the throne; and can we believe, that it is
confiftent, not with the fact only, but alfo
with the conftitution of human nature, that
this bigotry fhould fuddenly lofe its known
and characteriftic property as a principle; that
it fhould infpire inactivity with a larger fcope
for action, and that it fhould produce no effects with the power of producing the greateft? This is not merely to reject a portion of
the annals of the country, but to mutilate the
hiftory of man. But even thefe contemned
annals do not exhibit any fuch moral anoma-
lies. Were the proceedings of the legiflature
refpecting the *Exclufion* founded on a general
miftake, or merely on a religious prejudice?
They wifhed to prevent the combination in

the fame perfon of certain religious fentiments
with the authority of a Sovereign; and the
event fhewed, that their anticipation of evils
was not a weak and hypothetical foreboding,
and that their deliberations were not the ordinary contention of adverfe parties. Can we
imagine that the King's proceedings in this
place were only the wanton fpeculation of an
arbitrary ruler? that his interference was only
tentative and exploratory, to afcertain how far
he might fhake and controul the independence
of thefe ecclefiaftical bodies; and that the opinions of the refpective perfons, who were the
objects either of his dangerous favour, or of
his contemptible refentment, were otherwife
of no account? That he wifhed to govern his
people without the medium of their reprefen-
tatives was a part, and a part only, of his in-
aufpicious ambition. An attempt of this magnitude makes fo ftrong an impreffion upon
the minds of Britons, that it is with difficulty
we can calmly and difpaffionately regard fuch
an enterprife in the degraded light of means
for the attainment of fome other object, when
it appears to be itfelf that object which would
occupy the powers of the mind exclufively,
and require for its purfuit and attainment
every inftrument, fimilar and oppofite, animate

and inanimate, that could be employed. But do we really difcern any inadequacy in the object, compared with the means, when we fuppofe that this object relates to a general change of the eftablifhed religion of a country? Do we perceive that this could be accomplifhed by expedients of uncertain agency, and by an engine of lefs force? The fubftitution of edicts for laws, intrigues with a foreign ftate to obtain pecuniary fupplies, inftead of a manly application to his own people, and attempts to difpenfe with the execution of ftatutes, are all of them indeed the refources of a defpot; but they alfo mark the neceffary career of a regal bigot, who, if he wifhed to eftablifh his own fyftem of belief, muft either find, or make his fubjects flaves. If however we fet afide thefe abftract arguments, and recur to the fact, we fhall P fee in the authorities themfelves, to which an appeal is made, that the eftablifhment of the Catholic religion was the ftipulated return which was expected for the bountiful aid of the royal ally and coadjutor. But if this be an error, that the bigotry of James is not to be overlooked in the analyfis of his government, it is

P See note (F) at the end.

an error; in which the actors in the great event, which put an end to his machinations and his reign, perfifted ; and they do not feem to have confidered whether it was poffible for a Catholic King to obferve the ancient laws and ordinances of the country, and the new ones, which they intended to devife, but they confidered Proteftantifm as a neceffary qualification for the princely office, and as a better guarantee of their rights and liberties. It was eafier alfo for the people to make a new contract with a new Governor, than to obtain a faithful acquiefcence in the jufteft requifitions from the infidious Monarch on the throne.

 q It has been a fubject of difcuffion, by what name this great fact fhould be perpetuated. This important change, it is faid, we are not to denominate a revolution, and our anceftors have affixed to it an improper appellation. It cannot perhaps be made to correfpond with the definition of the logician ; but is it furprifing that he is unable to bind the meaning of the term with fuch bonds ? We

q The fentiments which I here oppofe may be found in a Sermon, preached before the Univerfity of Oxford on the fifth of November, 1804. by the Rev. H. Phillpott, M. A. now Prebendary of Durham.

may clafs and generalize political events to facilitate arrangement, or to affift recollection: but by what rules fhall we prohibit the ufe of a term, merely becaufe it cannot be reduced under any of the artificial divifions which we have invented ? Is the hiftorian to fufpend the infertion of great actions in the records of fame till the reclufe have found names to ex-prefs their effential diftinctions ? It is in vain to remonftrate, after the lapfe of fo long a period, againft the impofition of a term, the ufe of which has been fanctioned by time [r], confecrated by the opinion of the wife and good, and will be perpetuated by ftrong affo-ciations, and can only be rendered obfolete by the lofs of that liberty, of which it would re-main the melancholy memorial. We are alfo to be reftrained from applying to this event the epithet glorious. We are directed to feek for the glory, of which we boaft, in the cha-racter, and not in the confequences, of this event. Certainly there was no glory in the attempt to fubvert the religion and govern-

[r] The Speaker's reply to the city addrefs: " They " have taken notice of the moft eminent courage and " conftancy the city hath fhewed in the late Revolution." Chandler's Hiftory and Proceedings of the Houfe of Commons, vol. ii. p. 283. 1689.

ment of the country. We do not glory in
the faults or crimes of others. God forbid
that we fhould find in offences againft God, or
man, any fubject of exultation, or wifh, that
fuch offences fhould " come." But we do
derive a manly and rational fatisfaction from
reflecting on the refiftance which was then
made to the arbitrary encroachments of the
Sovereign on the liberties of the people. We
glory indeed in this refiftance; but we do *not*
glory in the caufe which made it neceffary,
and which left no other remedy for the public grievances in the hands of our anceftors.
Whatever moderation however might appear
in the conduct of men who had fuffered fo
much, and might have acted rafhly from a
juft apprehenfion of fuffering much more from
the tenour of the Monarch's proceedings; yet
we are to recollect, that we muft not attribute
to their untried wifdom and moderation that
peaceful termination of the conteft, which
really arofe from the well-timed but ignoble
flight of their Sovereign. But is it ingenuous
to enumerate among the effential conftituents
of revolutions in general, one of the fore judgments of the Almighty, the fword, and to intimate, that it muft *neceffarily* " pafs through
" the land ?" Are men to adapt their forbear-

ance to thefe alarms, and to be fatisfied that; as long as life is fpared, they poffefs all that reafonable men and peaceable citizens can require? This is, as is well known, to eftimate mere exiftence, and the tenure of it, under fuch circumftances, erroneoufly. The value, which is here fet upon it, is too great; but thofe who love their lives *fo* well, muft alfo be content to have their days numbered at the will of an earthly fuperior.—We are alfo further apprized, that the authors of the Revolution did not talk of the rights of men, but of the rights of Englifhmen. That we fhould hear more of the rights of Englifhmen than of the rights of men, cannot be a matter of admiration. Their rights in general were, not for the firft time, afferted. The artificial are alfo more extenfive than the natural rights; and although the former may be agreeable to the fpirit of the latter, yet they could not be deduced from that fource. Trial by jury is the right, and the right by birth, of an Englifhman; but it would be difficult to trace its origin to any natural right. Thefe artificial rights, the creatures of fociety, are, by their peculiar formation, more liable to be invaded than the natural rights. They are not fo eafily nor fo perfectly underftood, and do not

addrefs themfelves fo much to our feelings.
—Thefe might be perhaps fome of the reafons
of the filence refpecting the rights of men.

By this memorable tranfaction the Revo-
lutionifts taught, that .from the rights of one
party flow certain duties of the other; that
the regal ftate is not a fpecies of hereditary
property only, but alfo an office which has
certain relative duties belonging to it; and
likewife, that the regal authority has its limits, but that its limits are identified with
thofe duties. In the cafe of any attempt to
fubvert the government, or, in other words,
to violate thefe fundamental principles of juftice, they rather revived than eftablifhed the
doctrine of refiftance, which is diftinctly recognifed in the s Articles of the Great Charter.
If we confider that the turbulent barons of
that period required the whole community to
obtain, both by defined and by undefined refiftance, the poffeffion of the property of the
Sovereign, till their wrongs were redreffed,
we cannot but admire the delicacy, the gene-
rofity, and the juftice, which dictated a reverence for the perfon of the King, and thofe

s See Articuli Carte Reg. Johann. p. ix. Blackftone's
Law Tracts, ed. 4to.

of all the royal houfe, in the midft of thofe
refolute provifions, which they framed to fecure the fulfilment of the political contract,
and whilft they ftill retained their fwords in
their hands. To revert to firft principles is a
language frequently ufed to denote a recurrence to fome natural right, when thofe rights,
which are derived from the fociety in which
we are placed, are no longer regarded. But
we here fee, that it will either fignify this, or
a recurrence to the ancient forms of the conftitution, where the refiftance of the people
under the calamity of hopelefs tyranny is refolved into the natural right, and received
into its due rank. Hence alfo it appears, that
anciently there was fuppofed to refide in the
monarch a large proportion of perfonal refpon-
fibility, fince violent and unjuft public proceedings were immediately referred to himfelf as the author; and this is not obfcurely
intimated in the precedent of the Revolution,
where, if the deluded James could have tranf-
ferred his guilt and its punifhment to his advifers, he would have been moft eager to
have availed himfelf of any fpeculative fiction,
by which he himfelf could have been declared innocent, and could have obtained a
formal immunity from the effects of the re-

fentment of a people, who had refolved to be free.

What degree of political influence the Catholics in this country may again obtain, feemed at one period to depend on the refult of an enquiry into the prefent ftate of their religious opinions. But it is not eafy to afcertain what tenets they now profefs. Their principal advocate exults in the mifreprefentations of their adverfaries. But whilft they are more ready to declare what they *do not*, than what they *do* believe, whilft they will not direct us to purer or more genuine fources of information, the charge of mifreprefentation on our fide will be converted into that of fubtle and interefted concealment on theirs. If we appeal to a canon of a council, they reply, that its effects were local, and its authority temporary; if we fpecify a doctrine, they intimate, that it is obfolete; if we object the inftitution of the Inquifition, we are affured, that its fires are extinguifhed, and its prifons clofed; and as to the Papal power, its harmleffnefs and its limits are at once illuftrated by its reftriction to fpiritual matters. We are told, that this change of fentiment is to be attributed to the progrefs of general fcience, and the diffufion of learning, and that

the proof of it is to be collected from the declarations of liberal and enlightened individuals, and from the decisions of academical
bodies. But liberal and enlightened individuals do not perhaps constitute a competent
tribunal to determine this question. If it be
to their liberality and illumination that we
are to refer their rejection of what were formerly esteemed some of the most momentous
articles of their creed, as the Supremacy and
Infallibility of the Roman Pontiff, it is probable that the other parts of a religion, which
is founded so deeply on the derived personal
authority of its teachers, retain but a slight
hold on the minds of men thus liberal and enlightened; and that, whilst we seem to have
the opinion of the scientific and literate, we
have perhaps mistaken for it the levity and
relaxed conduct of a band of sceptics and
scoffers. If we examine the characters of the
academical bodies whose decisions we are to
respect, some of them reside in a country
where a great part of their learning consists
of such branches as have been rejected in this,
on account of their inutility, for nearly two
centuries, and is also limited to those foun-
tains, from which alone the Roman Pontiff
previously permits the thirsting multitude " to.

" draw freely." Such an application might indeed inform us what influence the learning, the extenſion of commerce, and the general ſpirit of liberty in our own country might have on the determination of theſe queſtions, and but little elſe has been learnt from the enquiry. It is not ſo much from the operation of ſome principle from within, as from reſtraint impoſed by others from without, that a ſeeming change has been produced in this extraordinary polity. How far a ſyſtem, which has for its baſis the ſubjugation of the mind and judgment, can be improved from the action of principles in its own conſtitution, is not eaſy to conjecture. But can the opinions of individuals, however liberal or learned, or of academical bodies, however illuſtrious, be made the grounds of any legiſlative proceedings reſpecting the enlargement or contraction of the privileges of the Catholics, whilſt the Roman Pontiff is overlooked, whoſe ſpiritual authority is ſtill paramount to every other, and who could confirm, reverſe, or invalidate the deciſions of aſſemblies, which might not be adapted to the real policy of the times? Reſpecting the future ſituation of the Catholics it would be preſumptuous to obtrude any opinion in this place. I would only remark,.

that it may be ufeful to confider how far we
may have miftaken our own ignorance of
their religious opinions for a change of them
on their part.　It would be neceffary for thofe
who have fuch doubts, and there are many
that have, to afcertain whether our adverfaries
ftill think, and ftill teach their children fo,
that they do God fervice in killing thofe,
whom, under the name of heretics, they thruft
out of the fynagogue.　We do utterly deny,
that in recurring to the records of hiftory,
and in enumerating the enormities and cruel-
ties of Proteftants, and comparing them as to
kind and degree with thofe of the Catholics,
it is merely " oppofing hiftory to hiftory, and
" the man of blood to the man of blood."
ᵗ Perfecution is not an article in the Primer of
Proteftants.　It is not a fubject of the early
precepts of our teachers.　*We have no opinions
on which we could found it.*　We do not think
that the Almighty will difpenfe falvation according to the diftinction of churches; or
that there are perfons who have power on
earth to forgive fins, or who can, here in the

ᵗ The queftion is very imperfectly and fallacioufly
ftated, if it is confined to this confideration; which fet of
men is more or lefs difpofed to abufe power, when they
poffefs it.

flefh, bar the doors of mercy, or open the gates of hell.

We do not with decorous affectation condemn a perfecuting fpirit, whilft we teach that there are cafes, where it is a duty, and perfons, who are the appropriate objects of it; but we teach, that it is fo far from refembling a duty, that it is a violation of all others, and moft contrary to the nature of every thing which pretends to be religion. If however upon the moft exact fcrutiny it fhould appear, that oppofite tenets are ftill maintained by our adverfaries, the conclufion would certainly be this; that no Proteftant could wifh to fee *again* fuch perfons, or fuch opinions, among " the many noble" and the " many mighty" " of Cæfar's houfehold."

I fhall be fatisfied with fpecifying one general conclufion, although the fubject might fuggeft many others; namely, that however defirable a ftate of national tranquillity may appear to be in a fpeculative light, yet where the powers of the mind, the emotions of the heart, and the ftrength of the animal frame are permitted, in any country, to produce their full effects in determining and improving the condition of man, there the balance of the political conftitution can never be quiefcent, and where fuch an equilibrium is fuppofed to exift, we find on one fide a defpot, and on the other, flaves.

APPENDIX,

CONTAINING

NOTES AND DISQUISITIONS.

APPENDIX.

IT could not be a doubt whether some notes were necessary, but how far they should extend. I have included
in them several disquisitions, which will enlarge my original plan of confining the discussion to some general
positions contained in " The Dissonance," and will comprehend an examination of the Letter to Dr. Priestley's
Young Man. I have called the whole an Appendix;
but I think that the contingency of perusal is exactly
equal, whether the name Notes or Appendix be used,
when it is necessary to seek for information in any other
place than the page immediately before the eye.

Page 1. *Theological writers.* The elegant author
of " Letters to Soame Jenyns, Esq." has deduced more
from this remark than, I think, the case will justify.
Pag. 31, 32. " He leaves behind him for his disciples
" a few fishermen, and persons in low life, remarkable
" for nothing, while he was with them upon earth, but
" profound ignorance, *natural incapacity,* dulness of ap-
" prehension, and erroneous views of their Master's doc-
" trine, intentions, and kingdom. Now it is by these
" manifestly ignorant, dull, and *incapable* persons, that
" the sublime doctrines and truths of the Gospel are re-
" corded and published. Here, I say, the tenor of the
" argument changes, and here the proof of a superna-
" tural dispensation properly commences. Why? Because

" we have here a real miracle, and miracles alone are the
" direct proof of a commiffion immediately divine." Lett.
by Archibald Maclaine, D. D. It might be objected to
this reafoning, that as we have not a knowledge of all
the powers of nature, fo we have not any ftandard of the
capacities of men; and the Gofpel might poffibly have
been a late invention of man, as well as any of the arts
which he has difcovered. But we are not to collect the
infpiration, or original revelation of the Gofpel, from
reafoning on the narrow extent of the intellectual faculties of the human fpecies. Had the Gofpel been a mere
fyftem of moral and religious precepts, the notion of invention would have been fomewhat plaufible; but fo
many facts relating to its Author are interwoven with
the Gofpel, and on account of that relation have become
parts of its doctrines, as almoft exclude the poffibility of
its invention, as the refult of improved reafon, or indeed
as being in the leaft connected with mere reafon in this
manner.

P. 2. *eloquence and learning.* " Erant hi viri, ple-
" beii, pauperes, illiterati, neque vel artibus, vel dotibus
" illis inftructi, quæ auctoritatem, fidemque apud alios
" parere, mentefque ad temere credendum impellere fo-
" lent; tales autem eos effe volebat, ne quis fructus mu-
" neris et legationis eorum non divinæ virtuti, verum
" *eloquentiæ,* auctoritati, aliifque caufis humanis et natu-
" ralibus adfcribere poffet." Mofheim de Reb. Chrift.
ante Conft. M.

P. 4. *philofophical Greek geographer.* I beg leave to
notice the following paffage in Mr. Carwithen's Bampton
Lectures refpecting this writer : " But if the Grecian
" poet has alfo been dignified by Strabo with the appel-
" lation of the firft and greateft of geographers, becaufe

" he has recounted the names of a few petty tribes en-
" gaged in a temporary alliance for the execution of a
" military enterprife, which he alone has drawn forth
" from obfcurity, and refcued from oblivion, but which
" are now vanifhed from the earth, and whofe place can
" no where be found, &c." I would refer Mr. C. to the
fecond page of Strabo for the reafons why he calls Homer the firft of geographers, and he will not find this
among the number; and alfo to Schoennemann's Com-
mentatio de Geographia Homeri, a prize exercife publifhed at Göttingen, the objeâ of which was, " *orbis ter-*
" *rarum faciem, qualis depingitur ab Homero,* declarare,
" hoc eft, ex utroque poetæ principis opere, tam Iliade,
" quam Odyffea, quicquid iis geographici argumenti con-
" tinetur, diligenter ac plene colligere, *ita, ut Homero*
" *duce, per tres orbis partes eatur."* The knowledge of
Homer, and the judgment of Strabo, fhould not be impugned conjeâurally, but upon a perufal of their refpeâ-
ive writings.

P. 5. *erudition of the fchools of Tarfus.* Michaelis fays,
that " many have fuppofed that St. Paul was endowed
" with a great fhare of profane learning, and have af-
" cribed to him a knowledge of all thofe fciences, which
" might have been learnt in the fchools of Tarfus. But
" this opinion feems *totally ungrounded*; and I fubfcribe,
" on the whole, to the fentiments of Dr. Thalemann, in
" his treatife ' De Eruditione Pauli Apoftoli, Judaica, non
' Græca." Michaelis by Marfh, vol. i. p. 153. The account of Tarfus, and the charaâer of St. Paul, diminifh
very much the probability, that he remained an exception
to the remark of Strabo, or that he confined his reading
to the Greek poets, and negleâed the Greek philofophy.
St. Paul would not deferve attention, if he had fpoken

of the wifdom of this world without being acquainted
with its nature and teachers.

P. 17. *Upon that ground only.* The reader may obferve, that an advantage is here taken of the nature of
this external evidence. It does not, indeed it cannot,
reach to every individual paffage of a book. And this
may be regarded as an advantage; for otherwife it might
interfere with, and perhaps fuperfede the internal. It
would alfo become more of an authoritative declaration,
that fuch and no other was the true archetype of the
Gofpel, than remain what it is, a plain teftimony, which
fuggefts rather than excludes a comparifon of other copies of the facred books.

P. 18. *taught orally.* This topic I have enlarged upon
in another difcourfe. It was fuggefted by the following
paffage in Prieftley's Anfwer to Evanfon, p. 8. " The
" books called the Gofpels were not the caufe, but the
" effect of the belief of Chriftianity in the firft ages. For
" Chriftianity had been propagated with great fuccefs
" long before thofe books were written; nor had the
" publication of them any particular effect in adding to
" the number of Chriftian converts. Chriftians received
" the books becaufe they knew beforehand that the con-
" tents of them were true; and they were at that time
" of no further ufe than to afcertain and fix the teftimony
" of living witneffes, in order to its being tranfmitted
" without variation to fucceeding ages. For what could
" have been the preaching of the Gofpel originally, but
" a recital of the difcourfes and miracles of Chrift by
" thofe who were eye-witneffes of them to thofe who
" were not. The Gofpels therefore contain the fubftance
" of all their preaching." I cannot refrain from fubjoin-

ing an extract from a work by the pious and learned
Richard Baxter. " Yea more, it is paft doubt that a
" man may (in fome cafes or circumftances) be a true
" Chriftian, who knoweth not that there is any Scrip-
" ture, which is God's infallible word. *For firft fo all*
" *believers of the old world were faved, before Mofes wrote*
" *the law. And the Chriftian churches were gathered,*
" *and thoufands converted to Chrift, many years before a*
" *word of the New Teftament was written.*" More Reafons for the Chriftian Religion, p. 22.

P. 19. *This circumftance effentially diftinguifhes,* &c."
The authenticity of the hiftory of Herodotus likewife
was eftablifhed in a peculiar manner not only by the re-
citation of it at the Olympic games, but previoufly in
feveral of the ftates of Greece, according to Lucian.
p. 327. ed. Bourdelot.

P. 20. *authenticity of the whole.* " Now my reafons,
fays the admirable Baxter, " why I take every hiftory,
" chronology, genealogy in Scripture as certainly true,
" and every other word, which is fpoken by a true pro-
" phet and apoftle as by the Spirit, (and not difowned
" by the Scripture itfelf,) but efpecially fuch as you ac-
" cufe in the Gofpel, are thefe; firft, *a priori*, becaufe
" it feemeth to me that the writing of the whole books
" of the New Teftament by them was done in the dif-
" charge of the commiffion given them by Chrift. And
" he promifed his Apoftles his Spirit for the perform-
" ance of all their commiffioned office work. *This writ-*
" *ing is part of the preaching which Chrift fent them for.*
" And no doubt but the Spirit did caufe them to write
" all the fubftantial part: and therefore we have reafon
" to think that the fmalleft parts are from the fame Au-
" thor, and that he affifted them in the leaft as well as

" the greatest." And again; " And though all the rea-
" fons which I have given prove, that the truth of the
" Chriftian religion may be certainly proved, though we
" could not prove every by-expreffion in the Scripture to
" be true; and though we deny not but the penmen
" manifefted their human imperfections in ftyle and me-
" thod; yet if each paffage were not true, it would be fo
" great a temptation to the weak, and make it fo diffi-
" cult to know in fome points what is true, in compa-
" rifon of what it would be, if all be true, that we have
" no reafon to imagine this difficulty ourfelves, while it
" is unproved." More Reafons for the Chriftian Religion,
&c. by R. Baxter. I refer the reader with much fatif-
faction to this treatife, the author of which has been infidioufly called by a modern Archdeacon, who in much
humility calls his own voice, in his own favour, " the
" voice of truth," *a regicide!* This man fhould not
meddle with paft hiftory; himfelf and his own actions
will furnifh a period and events better fuited to his deepeft confideration and timely correction.

P. 32. *Thofe miracles.* Bifhop Bagot has well diftinguifhed the evidences of miracles and prophecy in his
firft fermon at Bifhop Warburton's Lecture, pp. 22, 23.
" The argument from prophecy, thus urged, (in one
" comprehenfive view,) adds a credibility to thofe mi-
" racles, which once carried their own conviction with
" them. In former ages, while the firft defign only of
" prophecy was in view, (namely, to raife hopes and ex-
" pectations in the minds of men, without which no reli-
" gion could have fubfifted in the world,) then was their
" faith in it commonly confirmed by fome miraculous
" work. Of this kind was the immediate change in the
" ferpent's form when our firft parents received the ori-
" ginal promife of a future reftoration; fuch the mira-

" culous birth of Ifaac, and many other like inftances.
" Now in their turn prophecies accomplifhed give an
" affurance to our faith in ,paft miracles, which includes
" one evident reafon why miracles fhould ceafe to be re-
" peated, fince the other, from their nature, muft be go-
" ing on to the end of the world."

P. 33. *With regard to miracles,* &c. It will appear to
the reader, as he proceeds, that I might have extended
my prefent inveftigation to another volume, even if I had
compreffed, as far as perfpicuity would allow, the difcuffion of each topic. The following extract would
furnifh materials for an entire difcourfe. Diffonance, p.
7. " And in the New Teftament, in conformity to this
" criterion given us by Mofes, we are affured upon the
" higheft authority, that ' the teftimony of Jefus is the
" fpirit of prophecy.' Either therefore thofe predictions
" contained in the New Teftament, which relate to the
" prefent time and to times already paft, muft have been
" fulfilled, or elfe the Gofpel itfelf muft be an impofture,
" and of no authority at all. Now the obvious purport
" of almoft all the prophecies of the Gofpel, as they are
" difperfed in different fcriptures of the New Teftament,
" is to predict the circumftances of a moft unhappy cor-
" ruption of the genuine religion of Jefus, which began
" to operate even in the days of the Apoftles themfelves,
" and was to end in an entire apoftafy from the truths of
" the Gofpel, and the eftablifhment of a falfe, fabulous,
" irrational, idolatrous, blafphemous fuperftition, firft by
" the civil power of the Roman empire, under fome fig-
" nal change in its circumftances, and afterwards by the
" civil power of all thofe weftern kingdoms, into which
" that empire, at its diffolution, was to be divided. And
" the fame prophecies affure us, that the true religion of
" Chrift would be no where generally received, till after

" the fame civil powers, which eftablifhed it, fhall have
" abolifhed and deftroyed the Antichriftian church thus
" predicted. Unlefs therefore the teftimony of thefe
" prophecies fails us entirely, and the Gofpel itfelf is
" falfe, the orthodox church eftablifhed by Conftantine,
" which is now, and has been ever fince his time, in fome
" modification of it or other, the only religion eftablifhed
" by the civil powers of Europe, is the very object of
" thefe prophecies, the completion of the predicted apo-
" ftafy; for no other is to be found." It is added in a
note, that ᵃ " if there be, let the zealous advocates of the
" doctrines of that church, and her canonical fcriptures,
" point it out to us ; or, if that be not in their power, let
" them honeftly and candidly yield to the force of argu-
" ments founded upon the infallible word of the God of
" truth." The idolatry, to which Mr. E. refers, is the
worfhip of Jêfus Chrift as the Son of God; and this, in
his opinion, conftitutes the apoftafy which the Apoftle
predicted. We have no comparifon of thefe prophecies
with this alledged fulfilment, but merely an afferted ac-
cordance of one with the other. An opponent therefore
might, on this ground, be excufed from proceeding with
the controverfy. But it is better to examine where this
maze of hypothefis leads. It may be obferved then that
there are two branches of this apoftafy : the idolatry itfelf, and the accommodation of certain entire books, or
parts of certain books, of the New Teftament to this idolatrous fyftem, which accommodation was alfo, it feems,
a fubject of particular prophecy. That part of the queftion
which relates to the corruption or fabrication of books
I have examined in another place. The enquiry whether
the worfhip of Jefus Chrift the Son of God is idolatry, is
determined by affuming, that he was a mere man, and

ᵃ Diffonance, p. 25, 26.

therefore the worſhip of our Saviour is the worſhip of a man long ſince dead, according to the language and interpretation of [b] Julian. Mr. E. has obſerved at what time the adoration of ſaints and martyrs commenced, and has arbitrarily aſſigned the worſhip of our Saviour to the ſame date. There only remains this queſtion, the mere humanity of our Saviour. This it would be preſumptuous to diſcuſs generally, as if it were a new topic. It will be more proper to conſider, as they occur, thoſe arguments, by which Mr. E propoſes to prove it. He ſays, that the apoſtaſy began in the days of the Apoſtles. He ſhould have ſaid, that it began with the Apoſtles themſelves; that *they* ſet the example of the firſt act of ſuch a ſpecies of apoſtaſy, when they prayed to our Lord, as knowing the hearts of all men, to direct their choice in ſupplying the place of the traitor Judas; and Stephen, before his martyrdom, addreſſed our Saviour in language relative to the ſame opinion of his divinity. This was done not long after they had ſeen the ſame Jeſus, whom they then called upon, aſcend, in the human ſhape, into the heavens. This was not the adoration of a man long ſince dead, but a ſimple, plain, and recent teſtimony to his nature.

P. 35. *miracles are diveſted,* &c. The argument purſued by Mr. E. is in conformity with his hypotheſis of an apoſtaſy: he now attempts to ſhew that the deluſion of the profeſſors of Chriſtianity, who apoſtatized, was effected by falſe miracles, " lying wonders," and " all " the deceivableneſs of unrighteouſneſs." He wiſhes to invalidate the teſtimony of eyewitneſſes and hiſtorical evidence in general, by an appeal to certain facts, which he himſelf deems incredible. I therefore propoſe to exa-mine the circumſtances of their ſuppoſed incredibility.

> [b] Mr. E. has repeated more than one argument from Julian.

I. In his Letter to Dr. Prieftley's Young Man, p. 7. he fays, " Be fo good then as to afk this Doctor of eafy " faith, whether he believes the African miracle, fo " ftrongly and judicioufly ftated by Mr. Gibbon, that a " number of the orthodox, whofe tongues their inhuman " Arian antagonifts had cut out, fpoke diftinctly and per- " fectly well, after that cruel operation, without any " tongues at all?" And, p. 8. "He certainly, according " to his own principles, ought to believe it; becaufe the " fact was attefted by great numbers of eye and ear- " witneffes, both in Africa and at Conftantinople, whofe " teftimony is recorded, not only in the writings of pri- " vate individuals, but even in the public annals of the " eaftern empire." The completenefs of this teftimony makes the tranfaction worthy of a minute analyfis. Mr. Gibbon, vol. vi. p. 295. calls the evidence of c Juftinian " fuperfluous;" but it is not fo to others: " Vidimus " venerabiles viros qui abfciffis radicitus linguis fuas pœ- " nas *miferabiliter* loquebantur." Juftinian does not fpeak of it as a miracle, but merely as a fpecimen of the cru- elty of the Vandals, who had fubjugated Africa. d Victor Vitenfis refers the incredulous to " a furviving victim." If any one fhould doubt " of the truth, let him repair to " Conftantinople, and liften to the *clear* and *perfect* lan- " guage of Reftitutus, the fubdeacon; one of thefe glo- " rious fufferers, who is *now* lodged in the palace of the " Emperor Zeno, and is refpected by the devout Emprefs. This Victor " publifhed a hiftory of the perfecution " *within two years* after the event." e Æneas of Gaza, an eyewitnefs, fays, " I faw them myfelf; I heard them " fpeak; I diligently enquired by what means fuch an " articulate voice could be formed *without any organ of*

---

c Cod. lib. i. tit. 27.   d Gibbon, vol. vi p. 294.

e Gibbon, vol. vi. p. 294

" *ſpeech*:—I opened their mouth, and ſaw that the whole
" tongue had been completely torn away by the roots;
" an operation, which the phyſicians generally ſuppoſe
" to be mortal." After all, this is not one ᶠ" of the ſpe-
" cious miracles by which the African Catholics have
" defended the truth and juſtice of their cauſe," and
which is to be " aſcribed with more reaſon *to their own*
" *induſtry*, than to the viſible protection of heaven." The
only queſtion was, whether the tongue is the only organ
of ſpeech; and it is not ſurpriſing, that it was determined
in the fifth century, even by the moſt ſcientific enquirers,
in the affirmative. They only aſcertained, that the faculty of ſpeech was not deſtroyed by a partial or entire
exciſion of the tongue, as they regarded it. But they
did not commit any fraud. They did not pretend that
theſe victims ſpoke by any power committed to themſelves. They did not concert any fictitious occurrences;
and from the ſtate of phyſical knowledge they did not
conclude irrationally, nor aver diſhoneſtly, that this was
an example of a miracle. But they did not aſſume the
credit of the event to themſelves, as the inſtruments by
whom it was performed. This excludes the odious inſi-
nuation of induſtry and fraud, and reſolves itſelf into
opinion and judgment.

II. ᵍ" Yet, Sir," proceeds Mr. E. " the evidence of
" teſtimony to the truth of the miracle of Balaam's aſs
" is far leſs ſatisfactory. For, from the circumſtances
" of the ſtory, it does not appear that *any perſon was*
" *ſenſible of the fact* except Balaam and the aſs herſelf;
" or, *if* the prophet's ſervants, and the meſſengers of
" Balak, were alſo earwitneſſes of the wonderful fact,
" they were very few indeed in compariſon of thoſe who

ᶠ Gibbon, vol. vi. p. 293.
ᵍ Letter to Dr. Prieſtley's Young Man, p. 8.

" attefted the African miracle. Befides, they were all
" Midianites, or Moabites, who at that time were hoftile
" to, and had no communication with the Jews. Yet
" it is a Jewifh hiftory alone in which that *fingular* mi-
" racle is recorded." To thefe cavils it may be briefly
ftated, 1. That, whether the number of witneffes were as
great in one cafe as in another is not any part of the
queftion, where credibility does not depend upon a number of witneffes, nor lefs than a given number. 2. That
Balaam's two fervants were with him, which is a fufficient provifion of evidence, and not to be confounded
with the abfolute want of evidence. 3. That the place
where it happened was " a path of the vineyards ;" a
public road lying between two walls. The " vineyard
" of the man void of underftanding" is defcribed by Solomon, Prov. xxiv. 30. as having " the ftone wall thereof
" broken down;" of which kind, we have a right to fuppofe, was the hedge alluded to by the Pfalmift, Pf. lxxx.
12. " Why haft thou then broken down her hedge, that
" *all they that go by* pluck off her grapes ?" The fcene
therefore of this occurrence was a common track of travellers and paffengers. 4. That the princes of Balak do
not feem by the hiftory to have been prefent when the
angel met Balak, as the expoftulation of the angel concludes with his faying, " Go with the men." 5. That it is
of no ufe to furmife what would have been the teftimony
of perfons, if they had witneffed a certain tranfaction.
6. That although it is recorded in a Jewifh hiftory, yet
we do not perceive that any Jewifh intereft could be promoted by fuch a fiction. 7. That the occafion, as far
as we may prefume to judge, was worthy of the interpofition. 8. That we are no judges whatever of the apparently inferior circumftances which the Almighty com-
bines with the greater means that his wifdom thinks fit
to employ. 9. That the narrative has no moral incon-

gruities or contradictions. 10. That, if it had been recorded by a writer of any other nation, it is probable
that it would have been derived from the Jewish records.
And laftly, that we could not have authority for the authenticity of other books of the fame date, equal to that
which we have for the authenticity of thofe of the Jews.

II. " Afk him," fays Mr. E. " as a philofopher, whe-
" ther he really believes that the fun and moon ftood
" ftill at the command of Jofhua?" the object of which
he ftates to be " only to gratify the Jewish general with
" the pleafure of butchering his flying enemies twelve
" hours longer than daylight would have otherwife per-
" mitted him to enjoy." p. 9. I refer with pleafure to a
very ingenious, and at the fame time the moft correct
explanation of the object of this miracle, inferted in the
Gentleman's Magazine for the month of January 1800.
p. 25, 26. with the fignature C. D. Mr. E. did not remember, that miracles of the Almighty were not defigned for the conviction of the Jewish nation only, but
alfo for warnings and proofs of his power and prefence
to neighbouring idolaters, worfhippers poffibly of thofe
planets.

III. " Amongft the miraculous facts recorded in the
" Scriptures, there are fome which a wary, reflecting,
" and unprejudiced mind might not unreafonably con-
" fider as only uncommon effects of human fkill, or the
" mere illufions of what the ancients denominated the
" magic art, cunning artifice, and a kind of dexterous
" legerdemain. For the very fame *evidence of teftimony*
" which affures us of the miracles wrought by Mofes
" to prevail upon Pharaoh to difmifs the Ifraelites, af-
" fures us likewife, that in the three firft inftances the
" Egyptian magicians performed the fame ; and there-
" fore it is highly probable, that their king fuppofed
" Mofes and Aaron to be only magicians of fuperior

" fkill." As I wifh to abridge the difcuffion of thefe topics, and to avoid the repetition of the arguments of other writers, I fhall briefly obferve, 1. that, in candour, the fame evidence of teftimony fhould have received its proper appellation, the fame hiftory, and it fhould have been remarked, that the apparent fuccefs of the magicians in their attempts is recorded, as well as the miracles of Aaron. 2. Whatever might be the opinion of Pharaoh we cannot tell; but we know what the magicians themfelves thought of the power by which Aaron performed thofe wonderful works, and they declared them to be done by the finger of God. 3. Thefe miracles have the condition of credibility, and authenticity, and reality, which Mr. E. elfewhere affumes as neceffary to eftablifh the general authority of miracles; namely, a previous prophetic promife and fpecification.

Out of refpect to Bifhop Horfley's memory, as a fcholar, it may be proper to notice, although with a view to controvert, his opinion of thefe miracles performed by the magicians. He confiders it (p. 238. vol. i.) " as an " exprefs trial of fkill, if we may be allowed the expref- " fion, between Mofes and the magicians of Egypt, in " the exercife of miraculous powers, in which the magi- " cians were completely foiled. They performed *fome* " miracles, but Mofes performed many more and much " greater.—Now whoever will allow that thefe things, " done by the magicians, were miraculous, i. e. beyond " the natural powers of man, muft allow that they were " done by fome familiarity of thefe magicians with the " devil, for they were done in exprefs defiance of God's " power, they were done to difcredit his meffenger and " to encourage the King of Ægypt to difregard the mef- " fage." pp. 239, 240. I diffent altogether from this view of thefe tranfactions. A trial of fkill implies an independence of each of the contending powers; nor do I fee

how any fatisfaction is to refult from the confideration of
Mofes having performed " more and greater miracles,"
while we are required to admit that, " by their familiarity
" with the devil," the magicians were able to perform *any*
" in exprefs defiance of God's power." Befides, Pharaoh
does not apply to his own magicians, but to Mofes and
Aaron, for the removal of the frogs, which had been
produced equally by the former. What is done in defiance of a certain power is feldom the fame thing which
that power effects and intends, and particularly when
fuccefs would only aggravate the injury already inflicted
by the adverfe competitor. In fuch a cafe then the natural inference feems to be, that one agency controlled
the other, and the magicians appear to have been com-
pelled to be joint authors of the fame miraculous calamities with which the Almighty had refolved to vindicate
his omnipotence. A trial of fkill fuggefts a very degrading notion of the ways of the Almighty, and tends, as I
obferved before, to elevate the power of the devil to that
of an independent being, which is neceffarily implied in
a real competition.

IV. [h] " There are others, which might be fufpected of
" being only the accidental effects of natural caufes faga-
" cioufly obferved, and artfully mifreprefented as the im-
" mediate interpofition of divine power, to anfwer the
" purpofes of the chief actor of the hiftory. Of this
" kind are the extraordinary flight of quails, the fupply
" of manna, the deftruction of Korah and his factious
" party, and *fome others.*"

This reafoning would be more fpecious, if the fupply
of manna had been temporary; but the children of Ifrael
eat it during " forty years," a period rather too long for
the continued and accidental operation of natural caufes.

[h] Letter to Dr. Prieftley's Young Man, p. 9, 10.

In a similar manner, when the Israelites demanded
again flesh to eat, the quails were again sent to satisfy
their desire; and we may be allowed perhaps to argue
from the assemblage of these animals in such vast bodies,
that it was not an accidental effect of a natural cause:
" Shall the flocks and the herds be slain for them," says
Moses, " to suffice them? or shall all the fish of the sea
" be gathered together for them, to suffice them?" Num.
xi. 22. The repetition of one miracle, and the continuation of the other, not to mention how the prophetic particulars ascertained that the manna was the promised
bread, obviate the cavil at once. The destruction of Korah was not an accidental earthquake, for Moses *predicted*
this particular mode of destruction, and therefore the
history is credible according to Mr. E's own criterion.

V. " Nay Josephus, though a Jew, labours to account
" for the passage of the Israelites through the Red sea by
" the favourable concurrence of natural circumstances,
" which happened at that time to occasion a temporary
" dry path in that part of the channel; and intimates that
" similar circumstances have been known repeatedly to
" produce similar effects, in other places, since the time
" of Moses." p. 10. It is a matter of curiosity to examine *how* Josephus " labours" to get rid of this miracle,
and I willingly produce his mode of labouring for this
purpose. " As soon therefore as ever the whole Ægyp-
" tian army was within it, the sea flowed to its own
" place, and came down with a torrent, raised by storms
" of wind, and encompassed the Ægyptians. Showers
" of rain also came down from the sky, and dreadful
" thunders and lightnings, with flashes of fire. Thunder-
" bolts also were darted upon them. Nor was there any
" thing which *is usually sent by God* upon men, as indi-
" cations of his wrath, which did not happen at this time;
" for a dark and dismal night oppressed them." Now

after fome expectation we prepare ourfelves to analyze the circumftances, " which have been known *repeatedly* to " produce fimilar effects, in other places, fince the time " of Mofes." " As for myfelf," fays Jofephus, " I have " delivered every part of this hiftory as I found it in the " facred books : nor let any one wonder at the ftrange- " nefs of the narration, if a way were difcovered to thofe " men of old time, who were free from the wickednefs " of modern ages, whether it happened by the will of " God, or whether it happened of its own accord ; while " for the fake of thofe that accompanied Alexander " King of Macedonia, who yet lived, comparatively, but " a little while ago, the Pamphylia retired and afforded " them a paffage through itfelf, when they had no other " way to go ; *I mean when it was the will of God to de-* " *ftroy the monarchy of the Perfians :* and this is confeffed " to be true by all that have written about the actions of " Alexander. *But as to thefe events, let every one deter-* " *mine as he pleafes.*" There is an effential difference be- tween the paffage of the Ifraelites *through* the Red fea from one fide to the other, and the march of Alexander along *the coaft* of the fea of Pamphylia. I may add from Whifton's note the account of the topography of this march according to Strabo : " Now about Phafelis is " *that narrow paffage by the fea fide, through which Alex-* " *ander led his army.* There is a mountain called Cli- " max, which adjoins to the fea of Pamphylia, leaving a " narrow paffage on the fhore, which in calm weather is " bare, fo as to be paffable by travellers ; but when the " fea overflows, it is covered to a great degree by the " waves. Now then, the afcent by the mountains being " round about and fteep, in ftill weather they make ufe of " the road along the coaft. But Alexander fell into the " winter feafon, and committing himfelf chiefly to for- " tune, he marched on before the waves retired, and fo it

" happened that they were a whole day in journeying
" over it, and were under water up to the navel." Lib.
xiv. p. 666. Arrian's account is this; b. i. p. 72, 73.
" When Alexander removed from Phafelis, he fent fome
" part of his army over the mountains to Perga, which
" road the Thracians fhewed him. A difficult way it
" was, but fhort. However, he himfelf conducted thofe
" that were with him *by the fea fhore*. This road is im-
" paffable at any other time than when the north wind
" blows; but if the fouth wind prevail, *there is no paffing*
" *by the fhore.* Now at this time, after ftrong fouth
" winds, a north wind blew, and that not without the
" Divine Providence, (as both he and they that were
" with him fuppofed,) and afforded him an eafy and
" quick paffage." Thus it feems that the word " repeat-
" edly" defignates *the fingle* inftance adduced by Jofephus; and fo far is he from recurring to natural caufes,
that he confiders Alexander as the agent of the Almighty, and affifted by Him in this particular difficulty;
and thus endeavours, contrary to Mr. E's fuppofition, to
affimilate the cafe of Alexander to that of the Ifraelites,
and not that of the Ifraelites to the tranfit of Alexander's
army.

V. The following objection I fhall confider in a general
view, and not in its application. " [i] Why, fir, young as
" you are, you muft have learned from the four evange-
" lical hiftories themfelves, that to fome of the miracu-
" lous facts they relate, the Apoftles alone could be
" witneffes; that the moft public of them could be feen
" only by part of the inhabitants of Paleftine, chiefly
" in Galilee, or in the neighbourhood of Jerufalem: and
" that of thofe crowds who followed our Saviour, and
" were witneffes to many of his wonderful acts, whether

[i] Letter to Dr. Prieftley's Young Man, p. 11.

" they confifted of thoufands or of myriads, fo very few
" were effectually convinced by them of the divine
" power and authority of his commiffion, that after his
" death the whole number of thofe who believed in him
" amounted only to one hundred and twenty, and of that
" fmall number many were dead before the year fixty-
" two, the date which Dr. P. allots for the publication of
" the earlieft of thofe hiftories." 1. Thofe miracles, which
our Lord performed in the prefence of the Apoftles alone,
were not performed for their advantage, nor had any
other object, than the miracles of greater publicity.

2. The duration of our Saviour's miniftry for three, or
three years and a half, allowed a fufficient fpace for the
repetition of all his wondrous works, particularly if we
confider that his whole employment confifted either of
teaching, or working miracles. The evidence of the divinity of our Lord's miffion would not have been incom-
plete, even if his moft public miracles could have been
feen only by a part of the inhabitants of Paleftine, chiefly
in Galilee, or in the neighbourhood of Jerufalem. But
how are we to learn, which were his *moft* public miracles,
when fo fmall a part of them is preferved in defcription?
Or, can we fuppofe that there was fuch a gradation of
publicity as would affect the fufficiency or validity of this
evidence?

3. We are not any where informed, what numbers of
people believed in our Lord's miffion. To fay that there
were only one hundred and twenty that were to be found
after his death, is not warranted by the paffage in the
Acts, i. 15. where the number of difciples is faid to
be " about an hundred and twenty names." Are we to
infer, that this was the amount of all the believers
throughout all the tract of country, where our Lord had
been teaching; or, can we again fuppofe, that all who
believed every where had immediately after the death of

our Saviour repaired to Jerufalem, and joined themfelves to the Apoftles? Yet thefe aifumptions are all neceflary for Mr. E's argument.

4. Mr. E. proceeds to ftate, [k] " that the moft impor-" tant of all the miracles of the Gofpel, the refurrection " of our Lord Jefus from the dead, we are exprefsly told " by an Apoftle himfelf, was not manifefted to the peo-" ple in general, but only to a *few* chofen witnefses, " who eat and drank, and converfed with him for many " days after his refurrection to life." The witnefses were " chofen" indeed, but not " few." Our Lord did not appear " to all the people," but " he appeared to five " hundred brethren at once," which ought to make fome difference in Mr. E's computation of the numbers of be-lievers after our Lord's death. I am ready to allow, that Mr. E. has received the miracles above referred to, which might be explained away by " reflecting, and wary, and " unprejudiced minds," on the authority of preceding pre-dictions. But was Pharaoh, who might have had a mind of this defcription, acquainted with thefe predictions? It does not appear that he was, nor is his criminal obduracy faid in Scripture to be aggravated by refifting the evi-dence of prophecy as well as of miracles; indeed his ob-ftinacy would not be accounted as criminal in any degree, unlefs the neceflary knowledge of the previous predic-tion had been communicated to him. I argued in a pre-ceding note on the credibility of the miracles without pro-phecy.

P. 79. *had been acquainted*. I had inadvertently adopted the fenfe of this paffage of Tertullian as given by Dr. Prieftley. I believe Mr. E's to be more correct, but it does not amount to " the writer's perfonal knowledge."

[k] Letter to Dr. Prieftley's Young Man, p. 12.

I fhall tranfcribe not merely the ftory, but the reafoning likewife of Tertullian. " *Dividetur autem mors*, fi et ani-
" ma, fuperfluo fcilicet animæ quandoque morituro : *ita*
" *portio mortis cum animæ portione remanebit. Nec igno-*
" *ro aliquod effe veftigium opinionis iftius.* De meo didici.
" Scio feminam quandam vernaculam Ecclefiæ, forma et
" ætate integra funétam, poft unicum et breve matrimo-
" nium, cum in pace dormiffet, et morante adhuc fepul-
" tura, interim oratione prefbyteri componeretur, ad pri-
" mum halitum orationis manus a lateribus dimotas in
" habitum fupplicem conformaffe, rurfumque condita
" pace, fitui fuo reddidiffe. Eft et alia relatio apud nof-
" tros," which fhews that the other was a current anec-
dote alfo. " In cæmeterio corpus corpori jufta collo-
" cando fpatium receffu communicaffe." This is the
whole of Mr. E's extraét. I fhall reft the queftion of
Tertullian's credulity on the reafoning which he immediately fubjoins. " Si et apud ethnicos tale quid tradi-
" tur, ubique Deus poteftatis fuæ figna proponit, fuis in
" folatium, extraneis in teftimonium. *Magis enim cre-*
" *dam* ex Deo faétum, quam ex ullis animæ reliquiis :
" quæ fi ineffent, alia quoque membra moviffent, et fi
" manus tantum, *fed non in caufam orationis.* Corpus
" etiam illud non modo fratri ceffiffet, verum et alias,
" mutatione fitus fibimet ipfi refrigeraffet." This laft explanation, it fhould be remembered, is founded on the
notion, that *all* life was not extinguifhed, and therefore
not fenfation. He is however diffatisfied with what he
had faid. " Certe *unde unde* funt ifta, fignis potius et por-
" tentis deputanda, *naturam facere non poffunt :* mors, fi
" non femel tota eft, non eft : fi quid vitæ remanferit, vita
" eft : non magis vitæ mifcebitur mors, quam diei nox."
De Anima, 51.

P. 96. *Clement of Alexandria.* " Poffemus," fays Le

Clerc in his third Differtation fubjoined to his Harmony,
" hic fubjicere exempla Clementis Alexandrini utentis
" libris apocryphis, non aliter ac Apoftolicis; iis tempori-
" bus, quibus fat notum erat utrorumque difcrimen, nec
" æqualis auctoritas." p. 543. I think I have fhewn, that
he has not unduly raifed the one, nor depreffed the other.

P. 125. *Could not have been diftinguifhed.* Mr. E. feems
to exult in " the conceffions which Le Clerc himfelf was
" forced to make concerning the great number of undif-
" tinguifhable fictitious books, falfely attributed to the
" Apoftles and their followers in the very firft age1."
I had fome curiofity to examine thefe conceffions. Dodwell obferves, as cited by Le Clerc, p. 541. that before
the time of Trajan the canon of the facred books was not
yet determined, nor any certain number of books received in the Catholic church. Le Clerc concedes, " that
" no fynod confifting of members either of all or many
" Chriftian churches had, at this period, made any deci-
" fion on this fubject." And I have elfewhere fuggefted
fome reafons for regarding this filence, as advantageous
to Chriftianity. Dodwell alfo argues, that the true apoftolic writings were fo bound up together, in the fame
volumes, with apocryphal works, that it did not appear
by any mark or public cenfure of the church, which of
them were to be preferred. Le Clerc concedes, that
fometimes the writings of Barnabas, Clement, Hermas,
and others were conjoined with the books of the Apoftles; but it is not yet clear to him, that this was done in
the apoftolic age : and of this combination he again thus
expreffes himfelf; I am unwilling to fuppofe this of the
difciples of the Apoftles, who had received the Gofpel
from their mouth and their writings.

1 Letter to Dr. Prieftley's Young Man, p. 42.

Another conceffion of Le Clerc's, but imperfectly made, may be produced. If I fhould concede, that Clement (of Rome) had not read all the Gofpels, nothing could be inferred againft my opinion, if that epiftle were written fometime before the deftruction of Jerufalem, as many fuppofe, or a fhort time after the appearance of the Gofpels. For then he could not have feen any Gofpel, except that of St. Luke, which he commends. The moft important of all the conceffions is that where he fays he could produce inftances of citations by Clement of Alexandria from apocryphal books, of which he made the fame ufe as thofe of the Apoftles; " utentis libris apocry-" phis, non aliter ac Apoftolicis:" but he does not admit that this was done becaufe the diftinction was not known, or acknowledged, becaufe he adds, " iis temporibus, qui-" bus fat notum erat utrorumque difcrimen, nec æqualis " auctoritas." The ufe therefore which Le Clerc fays that Clement made of thefe books, muft be interpreted with a reference to the above conclufion of the fentence. Such then are the conceffions of Le Clerc, which might be defcribed in lefs fanguine expreffions by Mr. E. than as fuch *as he* " *was forced* to make concerning the great " number of *undiftinguifhable* fictitious books, falfely at-" tributed to the Apoftles and their followers in the very " firft age."

P. 177. *St. Matthew's Gofpel.* It was my original intention to examine fuch parts of " The Diffonance" in thefe notes, as could not be reduced under the general topics, which I had felected for examination in the Lectures, or would have enlarged each difcourfe to an inconvenient length for delivery. I therefore take this opportunity of introducing fome of thefe fupplementary remarks on the objections of Mr. E. to the Gofpels in ge-

neral. With regard to the demoniac of Gadara, mentioned by St. Luke, " there appear to occur ftill ftronger
" objections againft it from the biftory itfelf: and fuch as
" may well warrant a conclufion that the whole paffage
" was interpolated in the fecond century. For in the
" preceding part of Luke's narrative we find our Lord
" was at Capernaum, on the weftern fide of the lake or
" fea of Galilee, and in the eighth chapter he takes fhip
" with his difciples to go unto the other fide of the lake,
" without doubt to preach the Gofpel to thofe parts of
" Paleftine which were fituated on the eaftern fide : but,
" according to this moft extraordinary ftory of the demo-
" niac and the herd of fwine, almoft as foon as he was
" landed on the eaftern fhore, the Gadarenes, terrified and
" alarmed by the injurious though miraculous deftruction
" of their fwine, entreated him to leave their coafts; and
" he accordingly went up into the fhip, and returned back
" again to Capernaum. In Galilee therefore, on the weft-
" ern fide of the lake, he ought to be found in the following
" part of the hiftory: yet in the very next chapter we
" are plainly told, without the flighteft infinuation of his
" having croffed the lake again, that he was on the eaft-
" ern fide of the lake; for from thence he fent out his
" twelve Apoftles, and thither they returned to him
" again, becaufe, immediately on their return, he took
" them afide into a defert place belonging to the city
" Bethfaida, which, we learn from Jofephus, who, having
" had the command of the forces of the Jews in that dif-
" trict, muft have been perfectly acquainted with the
" fituation of every town upon the lake, was on the
" eaftern fide of the fea of Galilee. If then this *very ex-*
" *ceptionable* miracle be an interpolation, and not part of
" the original writing of St. Luke, the narrative proceeds
" confiftently and regularly : but, if it be taken as au-

" thentic, there is fuch a geographical confufion and dif-
" order in this part of the hiftory, as occurs no where elfe
" in this author's works ᵐ." Cellarius confiders this as
one of the moft difficult queftions in facred geography;
and his doubts induced Reland to examine what mode
could be adopted of reconciling the Evangelifts with Jofephus. Reland apologizes for having recourfe to the
fuppofition, that there were two places of the name of
Bethfaida, on different fides of the lake of Gennefaret,
becaufe it is one of the moft trite folutions of fimilar cafes
among geographical writers. Macknight, in the Com-
mentary on his Harmony, p. 256, fays, that " this city
" therefore, being in Philip's jurifdiction, muft have ftood
" fomewhere to the eaft of Jordan. Jofephus has marked
" its fituation diftinctly, Bell. iii. 18. where he tells us,
" that the river Jordan falls into the lake Gennefar behind
" the city Julias," or Bethfaida, the name by which it
was dignified by Philip the tetrarch. " All the circum-
" ftances mentioned in the Gofpels, which ha\e any rela-
" tion to Bethfaida, quadrate exactly wi.h this fituation
" of it." It is neceffary to obferve, that Galilee on this
fide the river Jordan, the lower Gaulonitis, and Peræa
on the other, however various places in thefe tracts might
be affigned to various perfons in the fluctuating diftribution of tetrarchies or toparchies under the Roman emperors, did not undergo any change with refpect to their
feveral boundaries. St. John calls Bethfaida, Bethfaida
of Galilee, as if it were to diftinguifh it from another in
a different diftrict. The Bethfaida of Jofephus was in
Gaulonitis, on the other fide of the river Jordan. Macknight wifhes to reconcile the two by fuggefting, " that
" Bethfaida being fituated hard by the Jordan which
" according to Jofephus divided Galilee from Gaulonitis,

ᵐ Diffon. pp. 47, 48.

z

" it might be called a town of either country. Perhaps
" it belonged fometimes to the one, and fometimes to the
" other." Of this there is no evidence. Nor is the fubfequent reafon to be admitted. " Farther; although when
" Jofephus wrote Galilee did not extend beyond Jordan,
" the boundary of Herod's dominions, the Scriptures give
" the name of Galilee to the whole region lying north of
" the fea, (Matth. iv. 13—15.) and particularly to the
" tract which Jofephus names Gaulonitis; for, Acts v. 37.
" Gamaliel calls him Judas of Galilee, whom Jofephus
" names Judas Gaulonitis. Nay the latter calls him
" fometimes Judas of Galilee." All that can be inferred
from the coincidence of the two writers is, that they had
the fame reafon for calling him Judas of Galilee, not that
the facred writers give the name of Galilee to the tract
which Jofephus diftinguifhes by the name Gaulonitis.
Hudfon ingenioufly intimates in a note, page 792, that
Judas might receive a double appellation, one from the
place of his birth, and the other from the place of his
education, or refidence. Aldrich, Hift. Jofeph. p. 1060.
is perfuaded, that the firft paffage is corrupt in which
Judas is defcribed as a Gaulonite from the city Gamala,
and remarks, that there was a Gamala in Galilee as well
as in Gaulonitis; but this correction is furely unneceffary.
There is no neceffity for difturbing the geography of Jofephus to fuch an extent, when a man, who changes his
abode, may naturally derive a local defignation from the
place where he either paffed the greateft part of his life,
or where he moft diftinguifhed himfelf by certain actions,
without any reference to the length of the period during
which he remained there. Since however Macknight
has affirmed, that the collocation of Bethfaida upon the
eaftern fide of the lake of Galilee quadrates exactly " with
" all the circumftances mentioned in the Gofpels which
" have any relation to it," it is proper to examine the

paffages from which its true fituation can be collected. Our Saviour paffed twice from the eaftern fide of the lake to Bethfaida, directly. It is worthy of attention to ob- ferve by what track, upon another occafion, he arrived on that fide of the lake.[n]. He firft departed into the coafts of Tyre and Sidon, and then directed his courfe to the fea of Galilee; but St. Mark informs us, that it was " through the midft of the coafts of Decapolis." He then took fhip and came into the " coafts of Magdala," or, according to St. Mark, " into the parts of Dalma- " nutha," on the weftern border of the fea of Galilee. He then returned with his difciples to the eaftern fide, and repeated the miracle of the provifion of food for the multitude. St. Mark is the only Evangelift that notices his fubfequent removal to Bethfaida : " And he cometh " to Bethfaida." I fhall purfue the line of our Saviour's journeying from this point, although it is a digreffion from the argument. We next find our Saviour, in the accounts both of St. Matthew and St. Mark, in the coafts of Cæfarea Philippi, which will accord very well with the return to Bethfaida. At this time it was that he "abode" with his difciples " in Galilee ;" that " they " paffed through Galilee," or traverfed a large tract of that country, and " would not that any man fhould " know it," as St. Mark adds; and St. John (ch. vii. 1.) relates, that " after thefe things Jefus walked in Galilee, " for he would not walk in Jewry, becaufe the Jews " fought to kill him." It is on his return to the fouth from the upper parts of Galilee that we find him again at Capernaum, which place he left, and " departed from " Galilee, and came into the coafts of Judea beyond Jor- " dan," the Peræa. After fome ftay in this diftrict, he afterwards, as his time approached, journeyed towards

---

[n] *See* the map of Paleftine in D'Anville.

Jerufalem. The brief expreffions of St. Mark, " and he " cometh to Bethfaida," may be beft explained by a pre- vious account of our Saviour's croffing the lake to the fame place. St. Matthew (ch. xiv. 22.) has not given all the particulars ; and it may be ufeful to compare the lefs full with the more enlarged detail. " And ftraight- " way Jefus conftrained his difciples to get into a fhip, " and to go before him unto the other fide, while he " fent the multitudes away. And when they were gone " over, they came into the land of Gennefaret." St. Mark inferts fome material information, " to go to the " other fide before unto Bethfaida." " And when they " had paffed over, they came into the land of Gennefaret, " and drew to fhore." This teftimony places Bethfaida not only in Galilee, but in the land of Gennefaret, the *ager Gennefareticus.* Macknight therefore feems to be incorrect in his chorography, when he refers every tranf- action connected with Bethfaida to the eaftern fide of the lake ; and the Evangelifts had as much reafon to fpeak of Bethfaida of Galilee, as Jofephus had to notice that in Gaulonitis.

P. 147. *copyifts.* Mr. E. proceeds to obferve [o], that " if the plain exprefs dictates of the Lord Jefus himfeff " could not efcape free from material alterations and ad- " ditions, by the pens of copyifts of thefe books in the " third, fourth, or fifth centuries, what other parts of " them can we fuppofe fecure from their daring interpo- " lations, whenever they hoped to ferve by them the " caufe of their particular religious fyftem ?" The player dictated by our Lord to his difciples, as preferved by St. Luke, is faid to be " interpolated out of the Gofpel " called Matthew's ;" and the authority of Griefbach is

---

* Diffonance, p. 53.

adduced for this affertion. I think the word *interpolation* is a very harfh one; and it is ufed by Griefbach, as well as by Mr. E. They are not additions flowing from the imagination of the copyift, and fhould therefore be diftinguifhed from the produce of human invention, directed to a certain object and purpofe. I do not underftand how " the caufe of their particular religious fyftem" could be ferved by transferring to St. Luke the words which " affign a local habitation to God in heaven," or thofe which contain the petition for deliverance from the evil one. It is not remarked by Mr. E. that "the learned " and diligent" Griefbach did not difcover any reafon for rejecting thefe fame claufes from the prayer, as recorded by St. Matthew. Mr. E. rejects, on the ground of " the " evangelical hiftory of St. Luke being made more con- " formable to that attributed to Matthew by the fame " copyifts," the baptifm of Jefus, " his forty days faft- " ing, his temptation, and the transfiguration." I hope I may be excufed, if, having obferved that the arbitrary affignment of motives to thefe unknown copyifts is not fupported by any proof, I merely fhew how Mr. E. would have proceeded, had he belonged to this affociation of ancient tranfcribers. " It well deferves our notice," fays Mr. E. (Diffonance, p. 55.) " that *if we pafs from* the " account of John's imprifonment by Herod, Luke iii. " 20. to iv. 14. *and read,* ' Then came Jefus,' *inftead of* ' And Jefus returned,' the hiftories both of John and Je- " fus proceed *regularly,* and in order." This admirer of Griefbach will not find any various reading in this paf- fage. The word ὑπέςρεψεν is written " with an iron pen " and lead, in the rock, for ever." Mr. E. has explained his own fyftem, and we fee how he can audaciously dif- figure by mutilation, in the face of that fame criticifm, whofe affiftance he can fo complacently ufe, when in his own favour, the latter periods of the hiftory of the chofen

people of God, and of the divine Author and Finisher of
a new difpenfation, under the impofing objection of want
of probability, or confiftent connection; but in reality,
becaufe it is irreducible, when entire, to his views of orthodox Socinianifm. It is not however intended to fubftitute this remark in the place of an examination of the
reafons for rejecting the hiftory of the baptifm of our
Saviour. " With what propriety," it is afked, p. 56.
" could he, who knew no fin, receive fuch a baptifm?
" or, the deftined Meffiah attend the preaching of his
" own precurfor, to be prepared by him for the coming
" of himfelf?" The Baptift himfelf, well knowing that
his own was a baptifm unto repentance, hefitated in com-
plying with the intention of our Lord, who came in order to be baptized by him; " I have need to be bap-
" tized of thee, and comeft thou to me?" Our Lord did
not explain himfelf further than by replying, " Suffer
" it to be fo now, for thus it becometh us to fulfil all
" righteoufnefs." This is all the fatisfaction which Mr.
E's queftion can receive. In what Gofpel did Mr. E.
learn that our Lord " attended the preaching of his own
" precurfor?" It is fufficient to expofe *this interpolation*
of the fcoffer himfelf, nor is it neceffary to repel otherwife the deiftical mockery with which the object of that
attendance is expreffed. " And what probability," continues he, " is there, that our Lord would have ftudi-
" oufly avoided calling himfelf ' the Son of God' during
" his whole miniftry, and forbidden his difciples before
" his death to announce him as fuch to the Jews, if God
" had miraculoufly declared him to be fo by a voice from
" heaven, in the audience of fo great a multitude?" I
was prepared to fpeak harfhly of the affertion, that our
Lord was baptized in the prefence of a great multitude,
and that a great multitude heard the voice from heaven;
but I reftrained my diffent within other limits, when I

obferved that the able author of " Illuftrations of the
" Gofpels," Mr. Jones, has fpoken twice of the prefence of a multitude upon this occafion, p. 38. and 359.
The language of the Evangelift does not feem to authorize fuch an interpretation. St. Luke fays, iii. 21.
" Now when all the people were baptized, it came to
" pafs, that Jefus alfo, being baptized, and praying, &c."
The original is, ἐν τῷ βαπλισθῆναι ἅπαντα τὸν λαόν : but
thefe expreffions do not imply that this multitude was
prefent when our Saviour prayed. My objeôtions to the
above fuppofition are thefe : 1. It weakens the teftimony
of the Baptift, " And I faw and bare record that this
" is the Son of God." 2. St. John alone was prepared
by prophecy to recognize our Lord ; " He that fent
" me to baptize with water, the fame faid unto me,
" Upon whom thou fhalt fee the Spirit defcending and
" remaining on him, the fame is he which baptizeth
" with the Holy Ghoft." 3. Would our Saviour have
prayed, contrary to his fubfequent praôtice and injunctions, not in fecret, but before a great multitude ?
4. But even fuppofing that a multitude were prefent,
they were probably ignorant of the charaôter of the perfon who was baptized. " I baptize with water," faid
the Baptift to the enquiring Pharifees; " but there ftand-
" eth one among you, whom ye know not ;" and he repeats it of himfelf, fo as to attraôt attention, " and I knew
" him not." And with a reference to this circumftance
I imagine thefe words are to be explained : " but that he
" fhould be made manifeft unto Ifrael, therefore am I
" come baptizing with water." The manifeftation to Ifrael did not confift in receiving the rite of baptifm publicly, but in the record of John refpeôting the nature of
the perfon who was baptized, which had been previoufly declared to him by the Spirit, and had been con-

firmed by the voice from heaven. Mr. E. continues, that our Lord forbade his difciples, before his death, to announce him as the Son of God to the Jews. St. Luke has given this as a reafon of the injunction of filence at this time, which our opponent would extend to every fubfequent period. " He ftraitly charged and " commanded them to tell, no man that thing, faying, " The Son of man muft fuffer many things, &c." He knew what effect fuch a communication would have as the period of his death approached, and, at the time of this converfation with his difciples, he was on his way to the north of Galilee, in order that he might avoid thofe who fought to kill him, before all things were accomplifhed. He did not enjoin filence on this fubject as relative to particulars that were not true, or indifferent, but the declaration of which at this juncture would have accelerated an event, which had its appropriate feafon. There is an exception to the remaining affertion, that our Lord " ftudioufly avoided calling him-" felf the Son of God during *his whole miniftry*" in the miraculous reftoration of fight to the man who was born blind. " Doft thou believe on the Son of God?" was our Saviour's queftion. " Who is he, Lord, that I might be-" lieve on him? Thou haft both feen him, and it is he " that talketh with thee," was the unambiguous language in which he afferted the union of both natures. The " account of the transfiguration is fo directly con-" tradictory to the repeated doctrine of the Gofpel, that " Jefus was the firft man whom God raifed from the " dead, that it *cannot be a true authentic ftory.* For, " whatever may be thought of Elias, Mofes, we are ex-" prefsly affured, died and was buried : if therefore he " was alive in the reign of Tiberius, and vifited our Sa-" viour on the mount, Mofes, and not Jefus, muft have

" been the firſt fruits from the dead [a]." This is not any inſtance of a refurrection from the dead. Moſes indeed died, and was buried: but is there any reaſon to conclude from this viſion, as it is called, that this appearance at the transfiguration was either in the place of a refurrection, or the confequence of it? Mr. E. next objects to the whole of the two firſt chapters of St. Luke's Goſpel. One improbability in his opinion is, that " an-" gels, like men, ſhould be diſtinguiſhed from each other " by proper names." To this it certainly is not eaſy to give a direct anſwer, except indeed that no one perſon is furniſhed with any peculiar information reſpecting the nature of this order of beings. It is however not repugnant to our conceptions to ſuppoſe, that as the angels are not perfect, their allotted places and functions, as miniſters of the Almighty, may neceſſarily be denoted relatively to their own capacities by certain names; at leaſt theſe names may have a relation to the perſons to whom they have been occaſionally directed to communicate the will of God. I muſt alſo obſerve, that although the angel predict a miracle, which was accompliſhed, yet this conformity to the criterion of credible miracles has not reſtrained Mr. E. from rejecting the account as a forgery. I willingly tranſcribe the reaſoning on this miracle from a very able letter to Mr. Stone, by the Rev. E. Nares, p. 26. " But, Sir, if you doubt " the veracity of Mary and Joſeph, from the extreme " privacy of the tranſactions, why doubt the viſion of " Zacharias, ſo immediately connected with them in all " its circumſtances? This, if it happened in private, was " yet attended with circumſtances of conſiderable pub-" licity. For though, indeed, it was in the inner part " of the ſynagogue that the angel appeared to Zacha-

[a] Diſſonance, p. 57.

" rias, yet ' the whole multitude of the people' was
" praying juft without; and, after an impatient expecta-
" tion of his appearance, the inflant he came forth, it
" was the people in waiting who difcovered, by his
" looks and manner, that he had feen a vifion. What
" fay you, Sir, to this annunciation? Remember the
" two vifions (or miracles, if you pleafe, for the truth
" of the latter depends on the former) are clofely con-
" nected, and cannot indeed be feparated: and mark
" the character of Zacharias; he was not only a good
" man, and righteous before God, but he was by no
" means a credulous man; the reverfe indeed to a fault,
" v. 20." It may be added, that he was to remain ju-
dicially dumb " until the day that thefe things" were
" performed;" fo that the continuance of the miracle verified the antecedency and reality of the prediction to
others, who were not fpectators of the effect, as foon as
it was produced. Dr. Prieftley, in his Letter to a
Young Man, p. 47. fays, that Mr. E. has " fuggefted
" feveral new and valuable arguments againft the mira-
" culous conception, for which I and others think our-
" felves greatly obliged to him." Some of thefe we are
next to examine. Mr. E. objects to the defignation of
Elizabeth as " not only of the tribe of Levi, but of the
" daughters of Aaron," becaufe " *it is in the higheft de-*
" *gree improbable*" that the Levites, and " more efpe-
" cially the family of Aaron, who were feparated from
" all the other tribes and families, and peculiarly fancti-
" fied and appropriated to the rites and offices of their
" religion," fhould " intermarry with any other tribe."
The fact, even without much confideration, appears to
be this; that a female defcendant of a Levite married
into another Levite family, for Elizabeth certainly did
not marry into another tribe, becaufe Zacharias, as a

prieft, muft have been of that of Levi. But " the family
" of Aaron" was " feparated from all other tribes and
" families." Zacharias is exprefsly faid to be of " the
" courfe of Abia;" and how did it happen that he was
of this courfe, unlefs he alfo had been a fon of Aaron?
The fons of Aaron were divided into the four and
twenty courfes. " Thefe were the orderings of them in
" their fervice to come into the houfe of the Lord, ac-
" cording to their manner, under Aaron their father, as
" the Lord God of Ifrael had commanded him, 1 Chron.
" xxiv. 19." It will be faid, that no mention is made
of the return of the family of Abia from captivity.
That may be; but ftill there was lefs danger of confufion
among the facerdotal families, than among any others.
Since however St. Luke fpecifies the courfe of Abia, the
courfes of the fervices of the priefts muft have been reftored after the captivity; and if Zacharias had his place
in that of Abia, we may prefume that there was as
valid a reafon for fuppofing that he was one of the defcendants of Aaron, to whom thefe courfes were peculiarly affigned, as there was for afferting that Elizabeth's
defcent was from the head of the fame family. If I
may not be permitted to fuppofe this part of the chapter
to be genuine, its want of authority does not arife at
leaft from the inconfiftency imputed by Mr. E. There
is another improbability of Mr. E's, which I fhall leave
with nearly an unreferved acknowledgment of my ignorance. " Neither is it at all probable," fays he, " that
" the providence of the Almighty fhould deftine the
" Jewifh prophecies refpecting the Meffiah and his pre-
" curfor to be accomplifhed in two perfons, related
" by confanguinity to each other." As brevity is my
object, I wifh merely to obferve, that there is one
decifive circumftance to which we may appeal, that
was fubverfive of any benefits to be expected from

fuch a petty affociation of confederate relatives. The
miniftry of the Baptift terminated before any utility
could refult from fuch an union of interefts, and before
any private or fecular objects of the individuals themfelves, if it were poffible for fuch to have exifted, could
be promoted. We have next an inftance of the facility
with which Mr. E. rejects his own canons of fufficient
or infufficient evidence of the credibility of miracles, in
impugning the account of St. John, in which he records the teftimony of the Baptift refpecting our Saviour. Mr. E. avers, and argues at fome length, that the
Baptift knew our Saviour by traditions and anecdotes
preferved in his own family, while the Scriptures declare
that he was prophetically inftructed how to diftinguifh
him from other perfons, who reforted to his baptifm.
I pafs on to another inconfiftency alledged by Mr. E.
between the caufe affigned in the account of the annunciation of the birth of our Saviour, why he fhould " be
" called the Son of God," and that which the Apoftles
adduce, who, he fays, do not refer to any circumftances
of his carnal birth, but to his being raifed from the dead
" to a new and fpiritual life, by the immediate power
" of the Almighty;" and he adds, that " St. Luke, as if
" he meant directly to contradict the heavenly annun-
" ciator, *except in the acclamations of fome lunatics*, never
" once mentions him by any other appellation than the
" Son of Man, or Son of David, till after his refurrection.
" *Then indeed he fpeaks of him as being commonly and*
" *publicly called the Son of God.*" I only remark, that
the queftion is here artfully examined, as if it related
only to the date of the acquifition of a name, and not
to that of the affumption of a certain nature. It is
fomewhat remarkable, that thefe lunatics fhould acci-
dentally have anticipated the application of a title to
our Saviour, which, according to this theory, originated

in the fubfequent event of the refurrection. Did thefe lunatics forefee this event, and the introduction of a new defignation of our Saviour ? The teftimony of thefe lunatics, as they are called, is too fingular a fiction for ordinary fabricators. The more frequent ufe of this name by the Apoftles after the refurrection is to be afcribed to another caufe. The teftimony to our Lord's nature was then perfected, and the exclamations both of the demoniacs, and of St. Peter, were anticipations of the conclufion, which would indeed naturally follow from the view of the whole of our Saviour's life, but which was premature at the periods of his miniftry, when thefe declarations were made, and before all the Scriptures concerning him could be fulfilled. The intention of the paffages which fucceed, relative to " our " Lord's examination before the Jewifh council," has been fo ably examined in a work, entitled, " An Illuftra-" tion of the Method of explaining the New Teftament " by the early opinions of Jews and Chriftians concern-" ing Chrift, by W. Wilfon, B. D. Fellow of St. John's " College, Cambridge, 1797," that I could only repeat what I find there, and this repetition is contrary to my defign. Dr. Horfley's book in reply to Dr. Prieftley has been termed a model of controverfy. I think that it has only a third place ; the two former may be juftly affigned to Dr. Burgh and Mr. Wilfon. Paffing forwards to another objection of Mr. E's, which, from its brevity and portable form, rather than from its importance, merits notice, we fee it ferioufly advanced, though not profeffedly infifted upon, that there is an inconfiftency in the ftories the two firft chapters of St. Luke contain " of the Prophet Simeon and the Prophetefs " Anna, with the well known hiftoric truth, that there " never was a prophet amongft the Jews from the time " of their return from their captivity to the preaching

" of John the Baptift." There was no prophet, whofe
predictions were faid to be committed to writing, nor
perhaps whofe office it was to utter predictions, if any
fuch there were, which were not recorded; but the
name of prophet muft have belonged to many in the
Jewifh polity, to whom the events of futurity were never
revealed. Still however, when the Almighty vouchfafed
to make known his purpofes, they were ufually, as occafion required, communicated to his people through perfons of this clafs. To thefe remarks may be fubjoined
an extract from Dr. Horfley's firft fermon on the fubject
of prophecy. " Under this name," he obferves, " is not
" to be included every thing that might be uttered by a
" prophet, even under the divine impulfe; but the word
" is to be taken ftrictly for that which was the higheft
" part of the prophetic office, the prediction of the
" events of diftant ages. The prophets fpake under the
" influence of the Spirit upon various occafions, when
" they had no fuch predictions to deliver. They were,
" in the Jewifh church, the ordinary preachers of right-
" eoufnefs; and their leffons of morality and religion,
" though often conveyed in the figured ftrains of poetry,
" were abundantly perfpicuous. They were occafionally
" fent to advife public meafures in certain critical fitua-
" tions of the Jewifh ftate. Sometimes they gave warn-
" ing of impending judgments, or notice of approaching
" mercies, and fometimes they were employed to re-
" buke the vices, and to declare the deftiny, of indivi-
" duals. What they had to utter upon thefe occafions
" had fometimes, perhaps, no immediate connection with
" prophecy, properly fo called; and the mind of the
" prophet feems to have been very differently affected
" with thefe fubjects, and with the vifions of futurity."
P. 18, 19. vol. ii.

It is a curious, although not an agreeable employment,

to follow Mr. E. in his application of certain prophecies in St. Luke refpecting the church. He remarks, that in the fifth chapter, verfe 35. the humiliated, fuffering, and afflicted ftate of the Chriftian church is delineated by the fafting of our Saviour's difciples after the bridegroom was taken away; but that the orthodox church eftablifhed by Conftantine " hath experienced none of " thefe prophetic marks of the true difciples of Chrift, " that fhe hath wantoned in the enjoyment of temporal " honours, opulence, and power;" and " that fhe hath " been the chief means of accomplifhing thefe prophe- " cies upon the *confcientious difciples of Jefus* and his " Apoftles by the confifcation of their property, the im- " prifonment and punifhment of their bodies, the depri- " vation, in numberlefs cafes, of their lives, and, in all, " of their natural rights as men, and denizens of their " native countries;" and that " the predicted period of " her prefumptuous triumph, and of their own ftate of " degradation and oppreffion, haftens faft to its conclu- " fion." My reader will be fatisfied with one additional fpecimen of the interpretation of prophecy. The pro- grefs of the Gofpel is compared in the thirteenth chapter of Luke to a fmall feed gradually becoming a large tree, and to a fmall portion of leaven pervading the kneaded mafs. Hence Mr. E. reafons, that as the tree cannot decreafe in magnitude, nor the mafs become unleavened, fo the Gofpel, when once eftablifhed, cannot be fup- planted. " On the credit of thefe prophetic fimilitudes," he fays, " we may pronounce with certainty, that the " religion, which fpread fo rapidly in the third and " fourth centuries, was not the religion of the Gofpel " of Chrift, becaufe it was fuperfeded by the Mahom- " medan fuperftition." We are alfo informed, that there is fufficient " reafon for God's fo confpicuoufly declaring " his preference of the Mahommedan to the orthodox

"a fuperftition." The caufes of this preference are ftated
to be, the prevention of idolatry by inculcating the
unity of the Deity, and the improvement of morality
by prohibiting in the Koran the ufe of ftrong drink;
" whereas in Chriftendom the conftant copious ufe, and
" very frequent, intemperate, and exceffive abufe of
" fermented liquors," now mark the new conclufion,
" has effects fatally pernicious to the bodily health
" and morals of its inhabitants." This effect is as
ftrongly admonitory of the impropriety of this indulgence, as any precept in the Koran. But what is the
reafon, why the fuperftitious drunken believer of the
church of Conftantine drinks on without any attention
to thefe effects on his health and morals? It is, gentle
reader, becaufe he believes in the doctrine of the Atonement; and obferve, whether we do not correctly draw our
conclufion from this extract. " It is true, the orthodox
" church preaches the pure ethics of the Gofpel, and
" *the virtue of temperance amongft the reft: but fhe has,*
" *at the fame time,* ingenioufly and impioufly contrived to
" render her own, and, what is ftill worfe, all the preach-
" ing of the Gofpel of none effect, by her doctrine of the
" death of Jefus, confidered as a propitiatory facrifice of
" infinite efficacy, and an univerfal atonement for fin b."
I do not think it neceffary to examine all the reafoning on prophecy, but fhall content myfelf with making
a few remarks on Mr. E.'s objection to the fign of the
Prophet Jonas, and to the firft two chapters of the book
infcribed with his name. " Whofoever," he fays, " com-
" pares the geographical fituation of Nineveh with re-
" fpect to the Mediterranean fea, will be convinced, that
" nothing tranfacted upon that fea could fall under the
" notice of the inhabitants of Nineveh, nor, confequently,

b Diffonance, p. 109.

" be any fign to them at all." That the inhabitants of
Nineveh could not fee from their city to the Mediterra-
rean, does not require abundance of geographical proof.
The miracle was of a perfonal nature, and intended as a
judicial punifhment of the Prophet's difobedience. He
was commanded to repair to Nineveh, and he defigned
to avoid. the miffion by embarking at Joppa in a veffel
bound to Tarfhifh. In their courfe to this place, but at
what diftance from Joppa the hiftory does not inform us,
the tempeft arofe, which was appeafed by the fuppofed
death of the Prophet. If by any accident the Ninevites
could have queftioned the idolatrous mariners refpecting
the ftory of Jonas, they could only have related, " that
" they took on board at Joppa a ftranger ; that a ftorm
" arofe, which, after their cuftom, they proceeded to ap-
" peafe by a trial of lots, which among their number
" fhould be caft into the water ; that the lot fell upon
" this ftranger, who, as he told them, was a Hebrew ;
" that he acknowledged how juftly it was thus deter-
" mined that he fhould die, but that they afterwards con-
" tinued to attempt to reach the land by rowing, but to
" no purpofe ; that they at length caft the Hebrew into
" the fea, and faw him no more." Can we imagine that
the Ninevites were lefs curious than the mariners, who
enquired of Jonas, " What is thine occupation, and
" whence comeft thou ? What is thy country, and of
" what people art thou ?" Would Jonas have waited for
fuch an enquiry ? Would he have been received without any other credentials of his authoritative warning
than the mere fubject of his preaching ? Would he forbear to tell them the confequence to himfelf of his firft
refufal to come to their city ? The hiftory is moft beauti-
fully related, and has every character of credibility which
nature can give to it ; and her teftimony in this, as in

many other inftances, affords a fufficient preponderance againft all the reafon contained in the argument of the Deift.

P. 171. note. " the ftudy of geometry." I requeft the reader to eftimate the candour of the Author of the Free Enquiry into the authenticity of the firft and fecond Chapter of St. Matthew's Gofpel, when he affirms, "what " is worthy of remark, they will find, that it was not " unufual in thofe days, i. e. in the fecond century, *to* " *call any man a heretic, who excelled in, or ftudied philo-* " *fophy, logic, geometry.*" P. 32. firft edit.

P. 177. " Two firft chapters of St. Matthew's Gofpel." Michaelis remarks : " But were the objection unanfwer- " able, it would affect, not the New Teftament in general, " but merely the two firft chapters of St. Matthew, which " may be feparated from the reft of the Gofpel ; becaufe " it is *ftill* a queftion, whether they belong to it or not." P. 50. vol. i. The reafons why fuch a fact fhould yet remain queftionable may be, either that our information refpecting it is very fcanty, or that the whole of it has not hitherto been collected, or that it is fo obfcure that it will not admit an uniformity of conclufion. The facts are few and fimple, and relate, as we may divide them, to the genealogy, or either to the two firft chapters of St. Matthew. We have the teftimony of Epiphanius, that the Hebrew Gofpel of St. Matthew contained the ge- nealogy, and it is at prefent found in all the Greek MSS. with the exception of one, which is imperfect. We have the teftimony of Epiphanius likewife, that the Hebrew ftemmata according to Matthew were either the genea- logy detached, or a name for the whole Gofpel, but more

probably the former. To trace the formation of arguments is fometimes to refute them; and I fhall try this
experiment upon fome of thofe in the Free Enquiry, as
I am not acquainted with any reply to that book. "It
" was neceffary," fays the Author, " to give fome ac-
" count of the particular fentiments held by thefe an-
" cient fects of Chriftians, becaufe they received a copy
" of St. Matthew's Gofpel which had not the genea-
" logy, or indeed, by all that appears, either the firft
" or fecond chapters." p. 33. The Cerinthians received that part of the Gofpel of St. Matthew which
contained the genealogy, and they received it for that
very reafon, as Lardner has proved by comparing the
words of Epiphanius in this paffage with what he relates
of Carpocrates. The portion which they rejected is not
fpecified. The Ebionites " ufed a gofpel," it is alledged,
" which began with thefe words : ' It came to pafs in the
" days of Herod, King of Judæa, &c.' From hence it
" appears, that the Gofpel of St. Matthew, which they
" received, began at what now is called the third chap-
" ter." p. 37. Free Enquiry. " Epiphanius," fays Lardner, " informs us that the gofpel of the Ebionites begins
" thus : ' It came to pafs, &c.' And he there fays ex-
" prefsly, that their gofpel called according to Matthew
" is ' defective and corrupted." It is true indeed that
Epiphanius does fay this : Ὁρα δὲ—πῶς πάντα χωλὰ, λοξὰ,
ἠ ἐδεμίαν ὀρθότητα ἔχοντα, but he fays more. Carpocrates and Cerinthus, he fays, ufed the fame gofpel as the
Ebionites, and " wifh to fhew from the *beginning of the*
" *Gofpel according to St. Matthew, by means of the ge-*
" *nealogy,* that Chrift fprung from the feed of Jofeph
" and Mary. But thefe perfons (the Ebionites) have
" other opinions; for, having cut away the defcents in
" Matthew, they begin as I have before mentioned ;"
ἄρχονται τὴν ἀρχὴν ποιεῖσθαι is the language of the origi-

nal. This teſtimony reſpecting the practices of the Ebionites will not juſtify any writer in merely declaring that their Goſpel began in ſuch a manner, becauſe the queſtion is, in what ſtate the ſect received it from others, not what particulars they themſelves eraſed or inſerted. It is uſeful indeed to know the date of theſe alterations, but we might on the ſame principle take the Goſpel of the Evanſonians, conſiſting of one mutilated book, as authority for an ancient Goſpel exiſting in the 19th century. The author of the Free Enquiry aſſerts, that " we " have *undoubted* evidence that they (the deſcents) were " *wanting* in ſome very ancient copies of St. Matthew, " which were reckoned of conſiderable authority. Mr. " Toland in his Nazarenus mentions an Iriſh copy of this " Goſpel that he had ſeen, which had not the genealogy, " for it began at verſe 18." Upon referring to Toland's Nazarenus, which I had not an opportunity of examining till I wrote this note, I obſerve, that his language and his concluſion are in conformity with thoſe of the author of the Free Enquiry. " In an Iriſh MS. of the four Goſ- " pels, of which I ſhall give you an account in my next " letter, the genealogy of Jeſus is inſerted apart, among " certain preliminary pieces ; and the firſt chapter of " Matthew begins at theſe words, ʻ Now the birth of " Jeſus was on this wiſe." p. 18. In his ſecond letter, Mr. Toland deſcribes this MS. more minutely : " It is " not only very remarkable and valuable for being a re- " lique of the ancient Iriſh church, but moreover for " being one of the correcteſt copies I have ever ſeen, and " finely written in Iriſh characters ; as alſo for various " readings of ſome importance, for ſome very ſingular " obſervations, and for a Catena Patrum on the Goſpel " of St. Matthew, (interſperſt with a few notes in the " Iriſh tongue,) that deſtroys the credit of certain cor- " rupt editions of the Fathers, wherein ſome of thoſe

" paffages being manifeftly depraved, it probably follows,
" that many more are fo. There is an interlineary glofs
" of little worth in another hand, and fome odd feparate
" pieces, among whom the genealogy of Chrift, which I
" told you in my laft letter did not begin the firft chap-
" ter of Matthew." p. 2. In a third paffage he ftates
the circumftances in this manner, after obferving that
" Tatian left the genealogy out of his gofpel,—fo that
" the *want* of this genealogy in the Irifh copy of Mat-
" thew is not fo ftrange a thing as it may feem at firft
" fight." p. 19. In "a moft venerable exemplar of the
" four Gofpels of St. Jerom's verfion with the prefaces
" and canons of Eufebius," " the genealogy of our
" bleffed Saviour appears to be diftinct and feparated
" from St. Matthew's Gofpel. The following words in
" two independent lines occurring after the 17th verfe
" of that chapter, *Genealogia Hucufque. Incip. Evangl.*
" *Secd. Matth.*" There is the fame diftinction in the
" famous copy of the four Gofpels, formerly belonging
" to King Æthelftan," and alfo " in the Latin Gofpels
" written with red ink, about the beginning of the 11th
" century, and in the Anglo-Normanic character." The
Irifh MS. is " a Latin MS. copy." Nazaren. p. 1. lett. ii.
As the author of the Free Enquiry has argued from the
mode of placing the genealogy in various MSS. I think
myfelf at liberty to confider likewife the manner of tranfcribing it, which may afford as much light at leaft as
the preceding circumftance refpecting its authority; and
the preface to the fecond edition of the Enquiry will
furnifh, I prefume, the neceffary information. Among the
fame Harleian MSS. is found, N°. 1802, " Genealogia
" D. N. I. C. five initium Evangelii fecundum Matthæum
" cum notis, fol. 3. b." " This," fays Mr. Wanley, " is
" written feparately from the reft of the Gofpel, and
" *amongft other prefaces, as being looked upon as a pre-*

" *face. I have seen other antient copies of the Evangelists,*
" *written in Ireland, or coming from books written by Irish*
" *men, wherein this sacred genealogy was not rejected, but*
" *misplaced.* There would neverthelefs appear a great
" diftinction between it, and what followed. The words
" Χρι autem generatio *being illuminated again,* as if the
" Gofpel began there." Pref. p. 17. The genealogy, it
feems, participated equally in the fame honorary embel-
lifhments of the artift. Another MS. N°. 2795. of the
Harleian collection contains the four Gofpels. " In this
" MS. *the genealogy is in gold capitals,* till generatio
" fic erat, *which words are alfo in gold capitals :* the reft
" is written in red letters." This MS. is fuppofed to be
of the 11th century. Is there any indication here that
the tranfcriber, or his employers, wifhed " to get rid"
of the genealogy ? " Among the Cottonian MSS. in the
" Britifh Mufeum there is a quarto volume marked Tib.
" A. 11. *finely illuminated at the beginning of St. Mat-*
" *thew's genealogy, written in gold letters on a blue ground*
" till *omnes ergo generationes ab Abraham,* and afterwards
" *it is written* in plain letters of that age, that is, towards
" the beginning of the tenth century." Pref. p. 20. " In
" that ancient MS. (the Dublin MS.) *part of the genea-*
" *logy is wanting ;* but it is evidently owing to the tearing
" or wearing of the vellum, becaufe the laft part of it is
" ftill legible. I think it begins about the 13th verfe,
" but there are marks of the vellum being torn off."
Pref. p. 21. The Author here obferves, " that *no* infor-
" mation concerning our enquiry can be derived from
" this manufcript." I am not of this opinion. The information is of this extent. Part of the genealogy ftill
remains legible ; and if all the vellum had been preferved,
we fhould have had all the genealogy. But if the commencement were never written, I do not know how to
account for the objection to its appearance ceafing at the

13th verſe. The inference of the Enquirer is moſt bold. " The account of MSS. above given is intended only to " ſhew, that the genealogy of St. Matthew ſeems to have " been of dubious authority for many centuries, In- " deed it ſeems to have been ſuſpected in very early ages." Pref. pag. xxii. What external proof of ſuſpicion exiſts? " The Harleian MS. No. 1802. ſeems *plainly* to ſhew, " that St. Matthew's genealogy was not held in much " eſtimation in 1139, for it is ſeparated from the reſt of " the Goſpel by prologues, notes, and old poems." It may indeed be ſeparated, but it ſtill has reference to the place which it occupied, and had engaged the attention of ſome perſon ſo much as to induce him to comment upon it. " Genealogia D. N. I. C. *five initium* Evangelii " ſecundum Matthæum *cum notis*." Or is it pretended, that the object of theſe notes is to caution the reader againſt its reception, by demonſtrating its want of authen‑ ticity ?

With reſpect to the two firſt chapters of St. Matthew, Dr. Marſh obſerves, " Epiphanius expreſsly ſays (Adv. " Hæreſ. xxx. 13.) that the Hebrew Goſpel uſed by the " Ebionites *began* with the words, Ἐγένετο ἐν ταῖς ἡμέραις " Ἡρώδε τῶ βασιλέως. *Their* Goſpel therefore contained no " part of Matth. i. ii." Vol. iii. part. ii. p. 136. Epiphanius accuſes them of having *cut away* the genealogies. But this is not evidence againſt, but in favour of, the exiſtence of this introductory portion of St. Matthew's Goſpel in the Hebrew. It is clear that the Goſpel was not deli‑ vered into their hands with this deficiency, and therefore their practice affords a period to aſcertain the uſual ſtate in which this book had been tranſmitted. Dr. Marſh's ſtatement is, to ſay the leaſt of it, incautious. Cerinthus *retained* the genealogy; whence appears the difference between the original of the Cerinthians, and arbitrary mutilation by the Ebionites.

Pag. 181. " Tatian's Diateffaron." Dr. Williams, in his Free Enquiry, is not at a lofs to convert either the fury or the forbearance of the orthodox Chriftians to his own advantage. Theodoret fays of the two hundred copies of Tatian's Diateffaron, " *all which I took away, and* " *laid afide, in a parcel.*" On which words there is this note; " Others, moft probably, did the fame, which will " very naturally account for Tatian's genuine works being " foon loft." But who are thefe others? and what influenced them? The reader however will fee, that if a book were burnt, it was not orthodox; and if it were merely neglected, it contained nothing fo contrary to general opinion as to be efteemed dangerous. " But if this Har " mony was a dangerous work, one might rather expect " that the whole two hundred would have been com " mitted to the flames." Thus is the Father's moderation changed into a teftimony in favour of the book, although he fays, that the perfons who ufed it did not perceive " the fraud of the compofition." Dr. W. is offended that the Father fhould have only configned to fome oblivious recefs what he condemned as a fraud, and therefore the fentence of the Father refpecting the contents of this " parcel" is thought to be at variance with the execution of it.

Page 184. " wifhed to get rid of it." " Confequently," adds Dr. Marfh, " it is highly uncritical to take *their* " manufcripts even into confideration." But can it be fhewn, that the writers of thefe " few Latin MSS." were embarraffed in reconciling the two genealogies, and that the writers of the Greek MSS. were able to reconcile them, and therefore inferted that of St. Matthew as the commencement of his Gofpel? The reafon here affigned for the difference between fome of the Latin MSS. and thofe of the Greek tranfcribers, would have produced an explanation. The difficulty in queſtion was not ſo recent as theſe Latin MSS.

P. 186. " Hebrew ſtemmata." I was firſt ſtruck with Jones's tranſlation of the word φυτὸν, and turned to the paſſage in Epiphanius, but did not conſult the annotators, as the paſſage did not ſeem to be obſcure. I have ſince ſeen Toland's Nazarenus, in which he remarks, " Nay, " he (Epiphanius) farther acquaints us, how in the fourth " century, while Conſtantine the Great reigned, this ge- " nealogy, with other curious pieces in Hebrew, was " found by a certain Joſeph in a cell of the treaſury at " Tiberias, which he honeſtly broke open to ſteal ſome " money; and that this odd accident was the chief reaſon " of his becoming a Chriſtian. But whether the word " there ſignifies the Genealogy by itſelf according to Pe- " tavius, or the whole Goſpel of Matthew according to " Fabricius, it is certain that Tatian left the Genealogy " out of his Goſpel." I did not copy my own opinion from Petavius or Fabricius, for I had not ſeen their notes. The expreſſions of Theodoret, that the Chriſtians uſed the Diateſſaron of Tatian ſimply as a compendious work, make it probable, that theſe Chriſtians knew that there exiſted other more minute Goſpel hiſtories, of which either they had then no copies, or very few in compariſon of thoſe of Tatian's work. We are to conſider, that two hundred MSS., even when MSS. were ſo commonly diſ- perſed, would conſtitute a large proportion, if not the whole of the means of their religious inſtruction. The con- duct of the Father was highly commendable. The entire Goſpels were properly placed in the hands of Chriſtians, that they might know and examine to what parts the op- poſition of adverſaries was directed, and that their faith might be expoſed to all the trials of the times.

P. 187. " This goſpel." Toland is of opinion, but I

am not difpofed to agree with him, that Epiphanius has confounded the Gofpel according to the Hebrews with that of St. Matthew. " But yet," fays he, p. 19. Nazarenus, " Epiphanius, who confounds every thing, (as par-
" ticularly this Gofpel of the Hebrews with that of Mat-
" thew,) tells us, &c.' Epiphanius fpeaks of this Gofpel of Matthew ufed by the Ebionites as alfo denominated " according to the Hebrews, the Hebrew Gofpel," Adv. Hæref. t. i. p. 127. et 137. I have faid, that it had one name from the " Jewifh party who received it." I might have faid, from the perfons to whom it was particularly addreffed.

P. 188. " evidence of the ancient Father." Epiphanius has been feverely cenfured by Dr. Horfley ; but if his authority be really impugned by the arguments of that learned Prelate, it is ufelefs to produce it in any café whatever. " Epiphanius," fays Dr. Horfley, " expreffes " a doubt of their heterodoxy (the Nazarenes) upon the " article of our Lord's divinity, in fuch terms as ought to " leave no doubt upon the mind of his reader of their or-
" thodoxy in that particular." p. 145. I do not difcern the caufe of this animadverfion. Dr. H. allows that the words of Epiphanius are, " I am not *informed* to fay, " whether they too, carried away with the impiety of the " afore-mentioned Cerinthus and Merinthus, think him " a mere man." Nor was he acquainted with the ftate of the Gofpel which they ufed. The Father, however, alludes to thefe Nazarenes in another paffage, and perhaps Dr. H.'s affertion may appear to be rafh. Epiphanius is fpeaking of the caufes which induced St. John to write his Gofpel. Διὸ καὶ ὁ Ἰωάννης ἐλθὼν ὁ μακάριος, καὶ εὑρὼν τὸς ἀνθρώπες ἠσχολημένες περὶ τὴν κάτω Χριϛῦ παρϱσίαν, καὶ τῶν μὲν Ἐβιωναίων πλανηθέντων διὰ τὴν ἔνσαρκον Χριϛῦ γενεαλογίαν ἀπὸ Ἀβραὰμ καταγομένην καὶ Λϱκᾶ ἀναγομένην ἄχρι τῦ Ἀδὰμ,

εὑρὼν δὲ τὰς Κηρινθιανὰς καὶ Μηρινθιανὰς, ἐκ παρατριβῆς αὐτὸν λέ-
γοντας εἶναι ψιλὸν ἄνθρωπον, καὶ τὰς ΝΑΖΩΡΑΙΟΥΣ καὶ ἄλλας
πολλὰς αἱρέσεις, κ. τ. λ. p. 746. Adv. Hæref. I have not confounded the Nafareans with the Nazoreans, who, Dr. H.
fays, were the Chriftian Nazarenes, Ναζωραίοι. p. 132. It
is not to my purpofe to purfue this argument. I have
proved all I wifhed to prove, that Dr. H. might have
here ufed with propriety lefs violent terms in fpeaking of
the Father, and perhaps too of Dr. Prieftley, on the fubject of the opinions of the Nazarenes. I do not apprehend, though I fpeak with diffidence, that Epiphanius intended to mention any others befides thofe who profeffed
heretical tenets.

P. 207. "St Matthew's Gofpel." Mr. Evanfon has alledged another inftance of ignorance of the geography of
Paleftine in this Gofpel, which I fhall give at full length,
becaufe the anfwer to it is very fhort and decifive. "In
" the account he has thought fit to give us of the caufe
" of his dwelling at Nazareth in Galilee, he has betrayed
" an ignorance of the geography of Paleftine, which can-
" not be attributed to Matthew, nor to any other native
" of that country. He tells us, that Jofeph, on his return
" out of Ægypt, after the death of Herod, finding that
" his fon reigned in his ftead, was afraid to go into Judea,
" and therefore, by divine admonition, ' turned afide into
" the parts of Galilee.' Here the reader is requefted to
" remark, firft, that Galilee having been as much under
" Herod's jurifdiction as Judea, and his kingdom having
" been divided amongft his fons after his death, it was a
" fon of Herod who reigned in his ftead in Galilee, as
" well as in Judea; confequently the child Jefus could
" be no fecurer in one province, than in the other. He is
" next defired to caft his eyes upon the map of Paleftine,

" and obferve, *how impoffible* it was for Jofeph to have
" gone from Ægypt to Nazareth without travelling
" through the whole extent of Archelaus's kingdom, un-
" lefs he undertook a long peregrination through the de-
" ferts, on the north and eaft of the lake Afphaltites, and
" the country of Moab, and then either croffed the Jor-
" dan into Samaria, or the lake of Gennefareth into Ga-
" lilee, and from thence went to the city Nazareth ; and
" *if it were at all credible* that the latter were the cafe,
" with what propriety could fuch a tedious journey have
" been denominated, ' *turning afide into the parts of Ga-*
" *lilee.*" Diff. p. 160. To the firft remark it may be fufficient to reply, that however unwilling Jofeph might be
to return to Judea, yet he was commanded in a dream to
go within the limits of the jurifdiction of a new governor,
although he were a fon of Herod. The word " turned
" afide" is a mere inaccuracy of our verfion, and Mr. E.
has not argued from the original word ἀνεχώρησεν. In
examining Schleufner, I found a reference to Herodian ;
and the paffage is fo much to the purpofe, that I fhall
produce it. Ἦσαν δέ τινες, οἳ διαδράντες πρὸς τὸ παρὸν ἀνακε-
χωρήκεσαν δέει τῆς παρουσίας τοιȢτȢ βασιλέως. Lib. i. c. 3.
§. 13. I add a part of Irmifch's note ; " Conf. Thuc. Ind.
" negligente P. hic, ubi, ut et 7, 2, 6, et 10. de iifdem
" Germanis fignificat, receffiffe in terras fuas interiores, et
" maxime in filvas, tum ibi commodius pugnaturos, tum
" falutis caufa, ut tutius laterent ; ut ἀναχ. dicitur proprie
" de iis, qui fecedunt fecuritatis et incolumitatis ergo.
" Conf. Lœfner." The term will denote the mode of
paffing unobferved from Ægypt to Galilee through Judea,
which cannot be better defcribed than in the language of
holy writ, Judges v. 6. " In the days of Shamgar the
" fon of Anath, in the days of Jael, *the highways were*
" *unoccupied, and the travellers walked through by-ways.*"

When Jofeph had arrived at Nazareth, the contempt in which that place was proverbially held might be the fecurity of the infant Jefus.

Mr. E. is fond of this fpecies of objection, for he adduces another. " In verfes 13, 14, 15, we have another " remarkable inftance," he fays, " of the author's very " imperfect knowledge of the geography of Paleftine, " which cannot be fuppofed of any native of the coun-. " try; as well as another direct contradiction to the " much more probable account given us by Luke. As " if he imagined the city of Nazareth was not as pro- " perly in Galilee as Capernaum was," (which indeed feems implied alfo in the fecond chapter, where he tells us, Jofeph went afide, not into Galilee, but into the parts or coafts of Galilee) " he informs us, that, after John's " imprifonment, our Saviour departed into Galilee, and, " leaving Nazareth, came and dwelt at Capernaum in or- " der to fulfil a faying of Ifaiah's refpecting the country " beyond Jordan in Galilee of the Gentiles. Now to " Ifaiah, or any inhabitant of Judea, the country *beyond* " muft be the country *eaft* of the Jordan, as Gaulonitis, or " Galilee of the Gentiles, is well known to have been ; " whereas Capernaum was a city on the *weftern* fide of " the lake of Gennefareth, through which the Jordan " flows." Diff. p. 164. It is here affumed as " well " known," that Gaulonitis was on the eaftern fide of the Jordan, and it may be admitted ; but it was not fynony- mous with " Galilee of the Gentiles," for no part of Ga- lilee was on the eaftern fide of the Jordan. Neither do we know whether Ifaiah denominated Galilee of the Gentiles with refpect to his own fituation in Judea. All the principal part of Canaan was called the country be- yond Jordan, before. it was occupied by the Ifraelites. It might have the appellation relatively to thofe nations who had hitherto fat in darknefs and in the fhadow of death. But how fhall we be able to difpofe of the tribes of Zebulon and Naphthali, the limits of whofe territories never extended to the eaft of Jordan. To this place may be referred an objection of Mr. E's to the authenticity of the Epiftle to the Romans, fince an anfwer to this objection is furnifhed by an appeal to a geographical writer. " I cannot " forbear remarking farther the inconfiftency of this wri- " ter," fays Mr. E. p. 310. Diff. (which indeed muft gene- rally be difcernible in all falfifiers,) " in making Paul per- " fonally acquainted with fo long a lift of members of the " church at Rome, where he had never been; amongft " whom we find Aquila and Prifcilla, and even his own mo- " ther, to whom he fends falutation in the laft chapter, " v. 13. Of the two firft Luke tells us, that, about, or rather " before, the pretended date of this epiftle, they had left " Rome, being Jews, in obedience to an edict of Clau- " dius.   And if there is any reafon to believe that Paul's " mother was then living, is it credible that an old wo- " man of Tarfus in Cilicia, whofe fon was fo wonderfully " appointed to preach the Gofpel, and who was occupied " in that commiffion in Afia and Greece, fhould leave her " native country, and fuch a fon, and ramble after other " preachers of the Gofpel, at fo advanced an age, to the far " diftant metropolis of Italy ?"   We may invalidate fome of this conjecture by ancient facts. Rome was the great re- fort of the natives of Tarfus and Alexandria; for Strabo in- forms us, Μάλιϛα δ᾽ ἡ Ῥώμη δύναται διδάσκειν τὸ πλῆθος τῶν ἐκ τῆσδε τῆς πόλεως φιλολόγων· Ταρσέων γὰρ καὶ Ἀλεξανδρέων ἐϛὶ μεϛή. Lib. xiv. p. 675, or 962. But it was not Rome only which they vifited. They had a turn for general *rambling* to places where they could improve themfelves, and they were all φιλόλογοι. Οὐδ᾽ αὐτοὶ, fays Strabo, μένϝσιν αὐτόϑι, ἀλλὰ ϗ τελεϝνται ἐκδημήσαντες, ϗ τελειωθέντες ξενιτεύϝσιν ἡδέως, κατέρχονται δ᾽ ὀλίγοι. Lib. xiv. p. 674, or 961. Hence it is not improbable that Prifcilla and Aquila might have been known to St. Paul before they were at Rome; and the affectionate term of mother, which he applies to some matron at Rome, confirms the suppofition, that she might be a native of Tarfus, and had been not merely ufeful, but had shewn a tender regard for him in some of his sufferings, or during his abode at Tarfus. Nothing contradicts the suppofition, that many of the persons at Rome may have been personally acquainted with him before their refidence there; and many arguments make it probable, that there were many natives of Tarfus at Rome, who, whether known or unknown to him, would befriend him, as a fellow citizen, in his appeal to Cæfar. It is not unpleafant to be able to reprefs the licentioufnefs of infidel conjecture.

P. 209. It is neceffary to explain the caufes of the defects of this difcourfe, which however originate in the want of materials. The want of direct information, and the fmall proportion even of that which is collateral, muft be my defence againft any imputation of incoherence and defultory obfervation. Mr. E. is recurring unceafingly to his abufe of the Church as eftablifhed by Conftantine. It may be fufficient to extract the following paffages from Mofheim's work, De Reb. Chrift. ante Conft. Magn. " Qui Conftantini religionem oppugnant oftendere volunt " dominandi cupiditatem tantum apud animum ejus po- " tuiffe, ut fe Chriftianum fimularet, aut viam eum fibi ad " fupremum imperium per fictam religionis Chriftianæ " profeffionem munire voluiffe. Ego quidem, ut de me " aliquid prædicem, Hiftoriam illorum temporum, qua " fieri potuit diligentia infpexi ac confideravi, neque ta- " men perfpicere potui Chriftianam religionem defide- " rium ejus fine focio regnandi, quo eum flagraffe infitiari " nolo, vel juviffe, vel juvare ac promovere potuiffe. Fe- " liciter ille ac cum gloria regnaverat nondum Chriftianus,

" et nulli religioni addictus; et eadem felicitate ad fupre-
" mum imperium pervenire, atque magnas res gerere po-
" tuiffet, fi vel in magorum religione perfeveraffet, atque
" Diis fervire perrexiffet." p. 969, 970. "Conftantinum poft
" victoriam de Maxentio non Chriftianam religionem fu-
" pra reliquas omnes evexiffe, atque unice veram judi-
" caffe, verum Chriftianis tantum poteftatem conceffiffe,
" religionem fuam profitendi, *pacem vero facultatem om-*
" *nibus, nulla prorfus excepta, fectis et religionibus tri-*
" *buiffe;* neque etiam idem perpendit multitudini ac nu-
" mero Deorum cultores illo tempore Chriftianis longe
" fuperiores fuiffe, licet ubique Chriftiani verfarentur."
p. 670.

P. 265. note. A doubt was fuggefted to me by a
learned friend, the accuracy and extent of whofe knowledge on any point of ancient erudition I do not intend
to queftion, whether *Græcis literis* denoted more than
the Greek characters. Davies, the editor of Cicero's philofophical works, contends, that this is the meaning of
the words. Cæfar fays, " In caftris Helvetiorum tabulæ
" repertæ funt litteris Græcis confectæ, et ad Cæfarem per-
" latæ ; quibus in tabulis nominatim ratio confecta erat,
" qui numerus domo exiffet eorum, qui arma ferre poffent;
" et item feparatim pueri, fenes, mulierefque." Cæf. de
Bello Gallico, lib. i. In the paffage relating to the Druids
the fame words are ufed; which, it is afferted, fignify the
ufe of the Greek letters only, and not of the Greek language. " Neque fas effe exiftimant ea literis mandare,
" quum in reliquis fere rebus, publicis privatifque rationi-
" bus Græcis literis utuntur." In confirmation of this opinion, (having previoufly admitted that the word *Græcis*
is to be found in all the MSS.) Pliny's teftimony is produced : " Gentium confenfus tacitus primus omnium con-
" fpirarit, ut Ionum literis uterentur." Nat. Hift. lib. vii.

c. 57. This relates to the ancient form only of their letters. We fhall examine how this fenfe of mere characters will agree with the tenor of Cæfar's letter to Q. Cicero. " Tum cuidam ex equitibus Gallis magnis præmiis
" perfuadet, uti ad Ciceronem epiftolam deferat. Hanc
" Græcis confcriptam literis mittit, ne, intercepta epiftola,
" noftra ab hoftibus confilia cognofcantur." Now if the preceding paffage of Pliny is well applied, it may be fhewn
that the object of concealment would not have been attained by the ufe of the Latin language and Greek characters; "Veteres Græcas fuiffe eafdem pene quæ nunc funt
" Latinæ, indicio erit Delphica tabula antiqui æris." This
is a continuation of the fame fubject; and although the
extract is diftinguifhed as another, but ftill a fubfequent
chapter or fection, yet it is evidently feparated only ac-
cidentally from the preceding. 2. Cæfar reprefents the
Druids as familiarly acquainted with the Greek language; and yet Davies obferves, that Divitiacus, one of
the Druids, addreffed Cæfar in an interview through an
interpreter, which was unneceffary, if he himfelf had underftood Greek. Perhaps this may be explained. Cæfar had remonftrated with the Ædui before a convention
of their chiefs, that he could not obtain fupplies for his
army. Lifcus, who prefided over the political magif-
tracy, intimated, that this difficulty arofe from Dumno-
rix, the brother of Divitiacus; " Cæfar hac oratione Lifci
" Dumnorigem Divitiaci fratrem defignari fentiebat; fed,
" quod *pluribus præfentibus eas res jactari nolebat,* celeriter
" concilium dimittit; Lifcum retinet. Quærit *ex folo* ea,
" quæ in conventu dixerat. Dicit liberius atque audacius.
" Eadem *fecreto* ab aliis reperit effe vera." He afterwards
wifhed to obtain farther information from Divitiacus himfelf : " Itaque, prius quam quidquam conaretur, Divitiacum
" ad fe vocari jubet, et, *quotidianis interpietibus remotis,* per

" C. Valerium Procillum, principem Galliæ provinciæ, fa-
" miliarem fuum, cui fummam rerum omnium fidem habe-
" bat, cum eo colloquitur; fimul commonefacit, quæ, ipfo
" præfente, de Dumnorige fint dicta, et oftendit, quæ fepa-
" ratim quifque de eo apud fe dixerit." It is evident that
Cæfar commenced the conference, and felected the language in which it fhould be conducted; and we are not
to be furprifed that he fhould prefer the native language
of a perfon who was to be examined refpecting affairs
in which he might be induced to mifreprefent his own
conduct, and that of his brother. Strabo defcribes the
Gauls as φιλέλληνας. We might therefore argue, that, if
the account of Strabo be correct, Cæfar fhould not have
had either his ordinary or extraordinary interpreters of
the Celtic, fince it may be prefumed that the Greek
language prevailed extenfively at leaft among thofe with
whom Cæfar might be obliged to communicate. There
were occafions, when it was more proper to ufe one
language than the other; although either could have
been employed, and certainly the native language would
be preferred, where we can fuppofe it to have been a
matter either of political ceremony, or of political pre-
caution. It muft be remarked, that the inftance of the
Helvetii might have been erafed without any injury to
the argument of the difcourfe; but every example was
impugned where the words *literæ Græcæ* were ufed
to defcribe the fact. The philological part of the queftion without doubt favours my deductions, and the fame
phrafeology is found in the Greek language. The connection of Gaul with Afia Minor by a migration and fettlement of a colony is well known.

P. 271. " vernacular tongue." Francifc. Burmann. Ex-
ercit. Academ. b. ii. difp. 4. Immo ipfos Judæos **pro**

vernacula linguam Græcam apud fe, fere in ipfa etiam
Judæa, agnoviffe adductis e Judæorum magiftris tefti-
moniis confirmat Rumpæus.

I much wifhed to have confidered the origin and application of the apocryphal gofpels, and the hiftory of
the latter Platonifts : but thefe topics muft be referved
for another opportunity, if another fhould ever occur.

$\mathbf{P}$AGE 89. " Adapting the Gospel of St. Luke." Mr. Evanson, Diffon. p. 140, 141. has taken a most unwarrantable liberty with a paffage of Chillingworth, in order to vindicate his own affumption of one Gofpel, as fufficient for the ufe of Chriftians. The conclufion of the quotation from Chillingworth is this ; " When you have " well confidered thefe propofals, I believe you will be " very apt to think (if St. Luke be of credit with you) " that all things neceffary to falvation are certainly con- " tained in his writings alone." Then comes Mr. Evanfon, and cuts off what he does not like, for fuch reafons as leave no authority for the remainder, which he exempts from profcription, and tells us, that St. Luke's Gofpel is fufficient for Chriftians ; as if Mr. E's Gofpel of St. Luke and Mr. C's were the fame books.

P. 95. " The martyr Juftin." Le Clerc has cenfured Juftin Martyr for afferting, that at Rome capital punifhment was ordered to be inflicted upon thofe who read the books of the Prophets, Hydafpes, and the Sibylls. But it is not improbable that this might have been the cafe, although no other writer has recorded the fact. We have no complete collection of the edicts of the Prætors. Befides, the Prophets, Hydafpes, and the Sibyll, would all fall under the clafs of *libri vaticini*. Livy has recorded : " *Quoties* hoc patrum avorumque ætate ne- " gotium eft magiftratibus datum, ut facra externa fieri

" vetarent ?—*vaticinos libros conquirerent comburerent-*
" *que ?*" We may furely believe that they would prohibit the reading of fuch books, fince in the perfecution
of Dioclefian they burnt the books of the Chriftians, or
in their place, or together with them, the refractory poffeffors themfelves; and, as Bifhop Watfon has well remarked, " the very expedient of forcing the Chriftians
" to deliver up their religious books, which was prac-
" tifed in this perfecution, and which Mofheim attributes
" to the advice of Hierocles, and you (Mr. Gibbon) to
" that of the philofophers of thofe times, feems clear to
" me, from the places in Livy before quoted, to have
" been nothing but an old piece of ftate policy, to which
" the Romans had recourfe as often as they apprehended
" their eftablifhed religion to be in any danger." Apology for Chriftianity, p. 168, 169. ed. 12mo. The queftion, whether thefe books were alike genuine, or alike
fpurious, was not difcuffed by the Roman politician; but
he read them, and anticipated the ufe to which they
might be applied.

P. 114. " St. Paul." This Apoftle fays to Timothy,
" The things that thou haft heard of me among many
" witneffes, the fame commit thou to faithful men, who
" fhall be able to teach others alfo." The effect of oral
teaching was meant to be the fame in both thefe inftances; and we have the beft defence of the want of a
declaration, that St. Matthew's Gofpel was written by
the perfon whofe name it bears, in the example of Galen,
referred to by Wetftein. The true caufe of the omiffion of the name of the writer was this; it was unneceffary. Galenus de libris fuis : Φίλοις γὰρ ἢ μαθηταῖς ἐδί-
δοτο χωρὶς ἐπιγραφῆς, ὡς ἂν οὐδὲ πρὸς ἔκδοσιν, ἀλλ' αὐτοῖς ἐκεί-
νοις· γεγονότα, δεηθεῖσιν, ὧν ἤκυσαν, ἔχειν ὑπομνήματα — ἐγὼ
δὲ ἁπλῶς διδὺς τοῖς μαθηταῖς οὐδὲν ἐπέγραψα. Wetftein. That

which was written had previoufly been fpoken in both cafes before many witneffes.

P. 120. I fhall here reprint my remarks upon St. Luke's preface to his Gofpel, which were not recommended to Dr. Marfh's perufal by any patron of mine, but which I refolved to republifh in confequence of that important recommendation. The cautions to the readers of the Introduction of Michaelis were abfolutely neceffary. I would afk, whether thofe, who have perufed that work, have not fometimes forgotten that the fubject of it was any thing efteemed facred. I have fuperftition enough, if it fhould pleafe any perfon to call the feeling by that name, to be offended with the familiarity and confidence of critics, in fpeaking of the books of holy writ; and I am difpofed to think that critical habits may in many inftances be regarded as the true fource of prejudices againft the opinion of infpiration, or fupernatural aid, being afforded in the compofition of our holy books. The licentious employment of probabilities is peculiarly unfavourable to the belief, that man has accomplifhed with divine affiftance, and according to divine promife, that which the critic flatters himfelf he can place by the help of his art within the fphere of mere human ability.

Since the preface of St. Luke is the only evidence of the exiftence of narratives of the life and actions of Chrift, prior to his own, it is the foundation of the whole of Dr. Marfh's hypothetical fyftem of documents, and therefore I wifh to fee whether it be " rock," or " fand."

According to Dr. Marfh's hypothefis, a Hebrew document exifted, which was the bafis of the feveral Gofpels of St. Matthew, St. Mark, and St. Luke; that it was copied by the former Evangelift, and tranflated by the two latter. I fhould be induced to infer from this character of the document, that its authority was greater than that of the writings of the perfon who copied it, and of thofe who tranflated it; and therefore ought to have been, from fuch pretenfions, acknowledged, by the conduct of the Apoftle Matthew, the original Gofpel. It was, however, " drawn up from communications made " by the Apoftles," p. 197; " a fhort narrative contain- " ing the principal tranfactions of Jefus Chrift from his " baptifm to his death," p. 196.

" The perfon, or perfons, who drew it up, might en- " title it ' A narrative of thofe things, which are moft ' furely believed among us, even as they delivered them ' unto us, which from the beginning were eye-wit- ' neffes and minifters of the word,' " a title, which St. " Luke himfelf has quoted in the preface to his Gof- " pel," p. 197.

This title I fhall confider in another place.

We muft obferve, that the conjecture of the title of the fuppofed document is returned in the next fentence to its owner Leffing, after Dr. M. has ufed it; and he de- fires the reader to notice, that the application is the in- tereft which he has in it; and that neither Leffing, nor Storr, who approved the conjecture, thought of this ap- plication of it—an affertion, which I fuppofe the reader will immediately believe.

That this conjecture is not ill founded, Dr. M. main- tains by thefe arguments.

1. " After St. Luke had written," ' Forafmuch as many ' have undertaken to fet forth in order,' " he would have " ufed the word narrative," (declaration in our verfion) " not in the fingular, but in the plural number; if by " this word he had meant, as it is commonly fuppofed, " to exprefs narratives written by thefe ' many." The queftion in this place does not relate to an idiom, to any

peculiar conftruction of words, or to any mode of phrafeology of the Greek language ; but to a form of fpeech,
which muft be examined by the principles of grammar,
common to all languages ; and therefore we may be allowed to feek for an analogy in our own. I did not
defpair of difcovering an example in the firft hiftorical
work which lay upon my table. The following paffage
from Hampton's Polybius, p. 32, vol. i. 8vo. will fhew
that St. Luke might have ufed fuch an expreffion, without intending to denote what Dr. M. and the German
theologians fuppofe, and without occafioning any ambiguity. The word was currently ufed for feventeen centuries, and fuggefted nothing of the kind. It was not
fufpected that any hidden meaning was involved in fo
plain a phrafe ; or that any one could hefitate about the
number of authors, and the number of their narratives.
Hampton fays, " There are *many* indeed who have
" written *an account* of particular wars, and among them
" fome, perhaps, have added a few coincident events."
I do not imagine that any other perfon would infer from
St. Luke's words, that the narrative was the joint compofition of the ' many ;' nor from thofe of Hampton,
that the ' many,' who wrote different accounts of particular wars, neverthelefs compofed one account only
amongft them. The critic that fhould cenfure the tranflator's accuracy, and accufe him of confounding the meaning, would be thought to have very faftidious and finical
notions of propriety. St. Luke, indeed, has been more
precife ; for he is fpeaking of accounts of the fame
facts.

2. " The word ' fet forth in order' is not fynonymous
" in the original to write a narrative ; for it does not
" fignify to write a new narrative, but to arrange a nar-
" rative already written."

Againft Dr. M.'s interpretation are Grotius, Cafau-

bon, Raphelius, Wolfius, Alex. Morus, and Dr. Townfon, who refers to thefe writers; but let us try Dr. M.'s
fignification.

' Forafmuch as many have undertaken to *re-arrange*
' a narrative of thofe things, which are moft furely be-
' lieved among us, even as they delivered them unto us,
' which from the beginning were eye-witneffes and mi-
' nifters of the word.' We muft obferve, that Dr. M.
fays, p. 197. that this narrative was " drawn up from
" communications made by the Apoftles," and therefore
that it was not only " a work of good authority, but a
" work which was worthy of furnifhing materials to any
" one of the Apoftles, who had formed a refolution of
" writing a more complete hiftory," " a fhort narrative,
" containing the principal tranfactions of Jefus Chrift,
" from his baptifm to his death;" " not a finifhed hif-
" tory, but a document containing only materials for
" a hiftory."

Firft, then, many of the Apoftles contributed to this
" fhort narrative;" fecondly, it was the work of many
perfons (whether Apoftles or not, or infpired, Dr. M.
entirely forgot to *fuppofe*) to " re-arrange" it. Who
was fit to undertake to re-arrange the communications
of the Apoftles? But we muft proceed yet further. This
document was very defective, it feems. " In procefs of
" time, as new communications from the Apoftles, and
" other eye-witneffes, brought to light either additional
" circumftances, relative to tranfactions already recorded
" in the firft Hebrew document, or tranfactions which
" had been left wholly unnoticed;" thefe were added in
the MS. by the poffeffors of the firft Hebrew document,
" and thefe additions in fubfequent copies were inferted
" in the text," page 200.

The work, then, to which St. Luke is thought to
refer, was firft written by no body knows whom, and

yet poffeffed fuch a claim to authority, as to induce St. Matthew to copy it; but yet written irregularly and without any method, fo that it required a new arrangement. It muft appear very ftrange that the Apoftles fhould furnifh their materials by piece-meal, in fuch a defultory and capricious manner, at various times, and in detached portions. I fhould maintain that a work fo framed was *not* " worthy of furnifhing materials to any " one" (much lefs to any) " of the Apoftles." The narrative was drawn up by an unknown perfon or perfons (their names are not mentioned, but Dr. M. fuppofes them to be Apoftles; yet as we are not informed of their names, we cannot judge of the fuppofition) from the communications of the Apoftles, then re-arranged by another fet of unknown perfons.

The bufinefs which Dr. M. affigns to St. Luke was to tranflate this Hebrew document, " enriched by addi- " tions," " and to adhere to it throughout in the *arrange-* " *ment* of the facts, becaufe he was not an Apoftle and " eye-witnefs," p. 205.

But what does " write" mean in St. Luke's Preface ? I fhould think it meant " a new narrative." The " many" re-arranged an old narrative. What did St. Luke do as diftinguifhing his labour from theirs ? He " wrote;" and fo fimple a word cannot, I maintain, by all the fophiftry and utmoft torture of perverfion, be brought to fignify all that Dr. M. defcribes, without imputing to St. Luke unworthy motives and corrupt views.

I adopt then, with the great authorities before mentioned, the plain and obvious meaning " compofe;" and at any rate it was not a proper term to exprefs his fhare in the narrative, (if he did no more than Dr. M. *fuppofes,*) as contrafted with the work of the " many."

3. " If thefe had been St. Luke's own words, he muft

" have faid ' as they delivered them unto them,' " and
" not as they ' delivered them unto us ;' for " although
" we may fay of other perfons, that they have under-
" taken to write a hiftory, as eye-witneffes have related
" the facts to them, we cannot well fay that they have
" undertaken to write a hiftory, as eye-witneffes have re-
" lated the facts to us," p. 198.

Dr. M. is proud of this thought. " No commentator,
" as far as I know, has made this remark, although it
" appears to be a very obvious one."

This is not the only inftance, I apprehend, where Dr.
M. has the imaginary advantage of appearing alone
amongft the commentators. But to proceed : when
writers compofe narratives of events contemporary with
themfelves, is it not ufual for readers to compare the
written relation with the account of eye-witneffes ; and
what greater commendation can a work of that kind
receive, than that it is confirmed by fuch teftimony ?

4. " If fo many perfons had written narratives of
" Chrift's tranfactions, and had written only what eye-
" witneffes to thefe tranfactions had related, there was
" the lefs neceffity for St. Luke to write a Gofpel ;
" and Theophilus might have known the certainty of
" thefe things, if St. Luke had not written."

I cannot accede to this argument : the number of accounts is little to the purpofe. All the perfons, who received thefe various narratives, were not acquainted, probably, with the circumftance, that they agreed with the
evidence of eye-witneffes. St. Luke could not promife
greater certainty upon this ground than the " many."
He could only relate what he knew himfelf; and I am
difpofed to believe he was an eye-witnefs of all he
relates. But let us admit, that he only related what
he received from eye-witneffes. What then diftinguifhed
his narrative from thofe of the " many ?" I conclude

that there was a defect in the authority of the writers. Their ftory turned out to be true upon enquiry, but it wanted confirmation. St. Luke's character was a fufficient fecurity for the reception of his Gofpel: "It feemed "good to me alfo." If I might be allowed to indulge in a conjecture, I fhould fay, that he oppofes his own well known character and biftory to the uncertain qualifications of the "many."

I have been lefs ftruck with the verbal harmony of the Evangelifts, than with another coincidence—that out of the exuberance of matter which the life of Chrift muft have fupplied, and where we cannot fuppofe for a moment that any felection was made upon the ground of one event, or one miracle, or one parable, or one precept, being more worthy of infertion than another; where what was omitted could be omitted for no other reafon but that God thought what was recorded was fufficient for his high purpofes; that fo many facts are mentioned in common by the Evangelifts, than that fo little matter has been added.

I folemnly proteft againft the application of the critic's laws refpecting biography and hiftory to the life of Chrift, as related by the Evangelifts. It is not fimply a piece of biography. The life of Chrift was the Gofpel itfelf, the glad tidings of falvation; and Dr. M. obferves, that the "good tidings," or Gofpel, was ufed, after the firft century, as fynonymous with the "Life of Chrift," p. 197, note. The life of Chrift was a new religious difpenfation. The death and refurrection of Chrift were not only facts, but likewife points of doctrine. Shall I prefume thus to decide upon the defects or excellence of compofitions which I never faw, of which nothing remains; or upon the merits of writings, which were defigned to introduce into the world a new fyftem of religion? I dare not.

5. " All the objections are removed by the fuppofition,
" that the words from ' a declaration to minifters of
' the word' are " nothing more than a Greek tranflation
" of a Hebrew title, which had been adopted by the
" writer or writers of the Hebrew document."

. Long titles, *if any*, are not characteriftic of other ancient Oriental writings, and therefore I fhould apprehend Dr. M. and his German affociates have not imi-
tated in this fuppofition the. ancient Hebrew coftume.
I am not provided with the means of profecuting this
enquiry, but I believe my affertion is not groundlefs.
" In the interval, which elapfed between the compofition
" of this document and that of St. Luke's Gofpel, many
" perfons had attempted to re-arrange and new model
" the Hebrew narrative, by making in it additions, tranf-
" pofitions, &c. in fhort, re-arranging * the narrative;
" and that as not all the additions which had been made
" by thefe many writers were drawn from the beft
" fources, St. Luke, who had accurately traced every
" tranfaction from the beginning, refolved to compofe a
" narrative, of which he made (as others had done) the au-
" thentic document the bafis, but introduced only fuch ad-
" ditions as he knew were confiftent with the truth ; that
" Theophilus, for whofe immediate ufe he wrote, might
" know the certainty of thofe things in which he had been
" inftructed." Saint Luke then, it feems, ufed a document, which was fo corrupted, by the time it came to
his hands, that it contained falfehoods ; for if St. Luke
introduced only fuch additions as were confiftent with
truth, the many muft have inferted what was not confiftent with truth. Dr. M. indeed foftens the obvious in-

---

* Here Dr. M. ufes the Greek word, which he fays fignifies *re-*
arrange, although he extends the meaning far beyond what the primitive fenfe *re-arrange* will juftify. Arrangement relates only to order,
but addition relates to defects and omiffions.

ference, by faying, " they had undefignedly blended ac-
" curate with inaccurate accounts;" that is, confounded
the true and the falfe together, did not know how to diftinguifh one from the other; and yet they were Apoftles,
or eye-witneffes, as we fhall fee. But how came thefe
additions not to be " drawn from the beft fources?"
The fuppofed firft Hebrew document with the fuppofed
additions is otherwife defcribed by Dr. M. p. 200. " In
" procefs of time, as new communications from the Apo-
" ftles and other eye-witneffes brought to light either ad-
" ditional circumftances relative to tranfactions already
" recorded in it, or tranfactions which had been left
" wholly unnoticed, thofe perfons who poffeffed copies
" of it added in their MSS. fuch additional circum-
" ftances and tranfactions; and thefe additions, in fubfe-
" quent copies, were inferted in the text." If I am miftaken, the reader of Dr. M.'s work will decide; but if
there are any better fources than Apoftles and eye-witneffes, our Saviour has left the momentous and awful
fcenes of his death and refurrection to be recorded by
perfons ill qualified for the tafk, or we have not the beft
evidence of thefe facts; and our Saviour could not, as
he declared, " bear witnefs of himfelf." Thefe better
fources would be likewife a fingular difcovery, even in
this difcovering age.

Dr. M. has not attributed to the Evangelift any extraordinary merit in faying that he introduced nothing but
what was confiftent with truth. To fay that an infpired
writer tells truth, is not the moft extravagant flattery;
nor is it the higheft office of infpiration to prevent the
infertion of falfehood, or to watch over a perfon who
might ignorantly or wilfully relate it for truth, unlefs he
was thus watched. I do not ufually build arguments
upon the fignifications of words, but I may remark, that
the term ἀσφάλειαν does not relate to truth as oppofed to

falfehood, but as certainty oppofed to doubt ; and St. Luke's Gofpel appears to poffefs the advantage of truth combined with the authority of the writer. The accounts of the ' many' had truth on their fide, but the writers appear to have wanted authority.

Dr. M. appears to have expofed Chriftianity to many ferious objections, in his attempt to folve a few and unimportant difficulties, which do not affect its truth. I can believe the accounts of the Evangelifts, upon the old grounds of belief; but if I did or could think that Dr. Marfn's hypothefis had any foundation whatever, I would not cull an extract or two from St. Luke with Marcion, but I would reject the entire hiftories of the Evangelifts. I conclude with the fentiments, which I had, in fact, anticipated, of the author of the pamphlet to which I have referred—

" I admit, then, of a common document, but that do- " cument was no other than the preaching of our bleffed " Lord himfelf," p. 34.

NOTES

THE PROBATIONARY DISCOURSE.

*To many readers the following notes will appear tedious;
and by thofe who hold the opinions of Dr. Milner, they
will be thought to be fufficiently brief. The argument
indeed might have been included in a few deductions
from the Trials of the Confpirators; but I was willing
to follow Dr. Milner through the ftrange confufion of
hiftory and hypothefis, of hiftory perverted or mifunderftood, and of hypothefis licentious and contradictory.
There are occafions, when the enquiry might have abruptly concluded in the language of juftifiable indignation; yet, to an adverfary, I might have appeared to
conceal ignorance in contempt, while on the other hand
expreffions of refpect, where none can be felt, argue an
infincere or a timid opponent. I may obferve, that, as
the objections chiefly relate to facts, the fubjoined reply
frequently confifts fimply of a citation, and the reader
himfelf is left in moft cafes to examine and to infer.*

Note (A), p. 281.

THIS is an old accufation revived. It appears, but
probably not for the firft time, in the Calendarium Ca-
tholicum, publifhed in the year 1662. See the Pref. to

the book entitled " The Gunpowder Treafon," repub-
lifhed by Bp. Barlow in 1679. Dr. Milner fays, " I have
" proved, that this was an exprefs contrivance of the Se-
" cretary of State." p. 346. See alfo pp. 267, 271, 278,
283, 302, of " Letters to a Prebendary." 1807. " This
" account of the Powder Plot, which places it in fo dif-
" ferent a light from that in which Dr. S. with the ge-
" nerality of other writers exhibit it, this gentleman has
" not thought proper to conteft in a fingle particular."
p. 347. It is not my intention to permit an adverfary to
deduce a furrender from filence on any particulars which
I have the means of examining.

I wifh to apprize the reader, that I had not an opportunity of referring to Foulis's Hiftory of Romifh Treafons, or to the works entitled " The Gunpowder Trea-
" fon," and " The Hiftory of the Gunpowder Treafon,"
till the Difcourfe was compofed and delivered.

NOTE (B), p. 282.

Dr. Milner profeffes to colle&t various proofs of the
friendly difpofition of James towards the Catholics *at
the time of his acceffion,* in order to fhew how much his
opinions were fubfequently influenced by his minifter
Cecil. But it muft be obferved, that thefe proofs are
taken from political circumftances of various dates.

1. The firft is, the conference with the French Envoy,
the Archbifhop of Ambrun. The Englifh Catholics had
been treated with great feverity by James, and had applied to the French Monarch to intercede in their favour. The King of France, apprehending that they
might prevent the Pope from granting the difpenfation
neceffary for the marriage of his daughter with a Proteftant prince, difpatched the Archbifhop of Ambrun as
the mediator. Whatever fentiments James might exprefs in this conference with the Archbifhop, we may

reafonably refer to the fame apprehenfion, which the King of France entertained refpecting the obftruction of the marriage. At any rate, they admit the fame interpretation as thofe articles, fo highly favourable to the Catholics, which were inferted in the treaty of marriage itfelf, and they were explained in the following manner, when the Marquis de Blainville remonftrated, and demanded their execution. " Mais qu'il plaife auffi au " Roy Trefchreftien, et à fes Miniftres, de fe reffouvenir " que les plus obligeans et exactes termes et mots, com- " pris es dictes articles, furent propofez de la part du " Roy Trefchreftien, feulement aux fins de donner au " Pape telle fatisfaction que la Difpenfation s'en puit en- " fuivre." Rymer, tom. xviii. p. 224. We muft in the next place note that this conference took place in 1624!

2. The letter of James to Clement VIII. was a forgery of Sir Edward Drummond, coufin of the Secretary Elphinfton Lord Balmerinoch, who was tried and condemned upon his own confeffion, and afterwards pardoned. He was not charged with this offence till the year 1608. " The Secretary was brought before the " council, and charged with the fault; which the Lords " did aggravate in fuch manner, as they made the fame " to be the ground of all the confpiracies devifed againft " the King fince his coming into England, efpecially of " *the Powder Treafon.* For the Papifts, faid they, find- " ing themfelves difappointed of the hopes which that " letter did give them, had taken the defperate courfe, " which they followed to the endangering of his Ma- " jefty's perfon, pofterity, and whole eftates." P. 508. Spotfwood. It appears however what James's fentiments were at this period, when the letter was fent. " The " treatife" (Bellarmine's, in which he charged James with inconftancy, objecting the letter to Clement) " com- " ing to the King's hands, and he falling upon that paf-

" fage did prefently conceive that he had been abufed by
" his Secretary, *which he remembered had moved on a*
" *time for fuch a letter.*" P. 507. Spotfwood. The Secretary in his confeffion faid, " As he wifhed God to be
" merciful to his foul in that great day, his Majefty was
" moft falfely and wrongfully charged with the writing
" of that letter to the Pope, and *that he never could move*
" *him to confent thereto.*" P. 511. Spotfwood.

3. " The Secretary of State, Cecil," fays Dr. Milner,
" repeatedly affured the Catholics, that the King would
" fulfil his promifes of granting them liberty of con-
" fcience. He gave affurances of the fame nature to the
" Spanifh ambaffador. The fubfequent event fhews, that
" his intention in thus raifing their hopes was to provoke
" their indignation, when they fhould find themfelves
" difappointed." P. 265. I do not wifh to prefs the author in this obfcure allufion to an hiftorical fact; but I
muft enquire, when did Cecil give thefe affurances to the
Spanifh ambaffador ? I cannot difcover on what other
occafion than the projected marriage of Prince Henry
with the Infanta, that he had any opportunity to introduce thefe affurances, in his conferences with the Spanifh
ambaffador. " Cecil Earl of Salifbury, the great ftatef-
" man of that time, purfued and drove the matter to that
" point, that the Duke of Lerma finding no evafion, dif-
" claimed the being of a marriage treaty. Neverthelefs
" the Spanifh ambaffador, to acquit himfelf to this ftate,
" and to clear his own honefty, at a full council pro-
" duced his commiffion, together with his letters of in-
" ftruction given under the Duke's hand." Rufhworth,
vol. i. p. 1. Cecil's name is affixed to the treaty of peace
concluded with Spain in 1604, but no mention is made
of the Catholics in any of the articles. I cannot connect
thefe affurances of Cecil refpecting the Catholics with a
" fubfequent event" peculiarly unfavourable to them,

without fome violent derangement of the chronology of ,the hiftory. Dr. M. is not therefore entitled to conclude in this manner his review of James's early opinions. " Such were the genuine fentiments and inclinations of " this King, *particularly when he firft fucceeded to the* " *Englifh crown.*" P. 266. The perfon who raifed the hopes of the Catholics was not Cecil, but the prieft Watfon. " Touching the firft, (Watfon,) no man can fpeak " more foundly to the point than myfelf; for being fent " into the prifon by the King to charge him with this " falfe alarm only two days before his death, and upon " his foul to prefs him in the prefence of God, and as he " would anfwer it at another bar, to confefs directly, " whether at either or both thefe times he had accefs " unto his Majefty at Edinborough, his Majefty did give " him *any promife,* hope, or comfort of encouragement " to Catholics concerning toleration ; he did there pro- " teft, that he could never win one inch of ground, or " draw the fmalleft comfort from the King in thofe de- " grees ; nor further than that he would have them ap- " prehend, that as he was a ftranger to this ftate, fo till " he underftood in all points how thofe matters ftood, " he would not promife favour any way. He did con- " fefs, that in very deed, to keep up the hearts of Ca- " tholics in love and duty to the King, he had imparted " the King's words to many in a better tune and a higher " kind of defcant, than his book of plain fong did di- " rect."

" For this he craved pardon of the King in humble " manner,—and feemed penitent as well for the horror " of his crime, as for the falfehoods of his whifperings." State Trials, vol. i. p. 203.

Note (C), p. 289.

I fhall in this place examine Dr. Milner's defence of

the Jefuits who were concerned in this conspiracy. Tefmond, or "Greenway," or Greenwell, as he is also
called, "escaped abroad; but his case was exactly the
"same with that of F. Garnet, who suffered on this occa-
"sion, and was peculiarly hard. These men were both
"successively consulted as divines, and under conscientious
"secrecy, concerning the lawfulness of the plot, and they
"both strongly condemned it, intreating that infatuated
"wretch to lay aside the thought of it." P. 269. Note
(1).

1. If Greenwell were first acquainted with the conspiracy by the confession of Catesby, he maintained afterwards more intercourse with the conspirators than can
be reconciled with any original disapprobation of the
design.

2. " They both strongly condemned it, intreating that
" infatuated wretch to lay aside the thought of it." Greenwell did not however condemn the plot, when it was a
second time revealed to him in confidence by Catesby's
man, Bates, who " went to confession to the said Tesmond
" the Jesuit, and in confession told him, that he was to
" conceal a very dangerous piece of work that his master
" Catesby, and Thomas Winter, had imparted unto him,
" and said he much feared the matter to be utterly un-
" lawful, and therefore therein desired the counsel of the
" Jesuit; and revealed unto him the whole intent and pur-
" pose of blowing up the Parliament-house upon the first
" day of the assembly. But the Jesuit, being a confede-
" rate therein before, resolved and encouraged him in the
" action, and said that he should be secret in that which
" his master had imparted unto him, for that it was a
" good cause. Adding moreover, that it was not dan-
" gerous unto him, nor any offence to conceal it; and
" thereupon the Jesuit gave him absolution; and Bates
" received the sacrament of him in the company of his

" master Robert Catesby, and Thomas Winter." State
Trials, vol. i. p. 196.

3. Nor was Garnet informed of the conspiracy through
the means of confession alone. " For the main plot, he
" confessed, that he was therewithal acquainted by Green-
" well particularly; and that Greenwell came perplexed
" unto him to open something, which Mr. Catesby with
" divers others intended: to whom he said, he was content-
" ed to hear by him what it was, so as he would not be
" acknown to Mr. Catesby, or to any other, that he was
" made privy to it. Whereupon Father Greenwell told
" him the whole plot, and all the particulars thereof;
" with which he protested, that he was very much dis-
" tempered, and could never sleep quietly afterwards, but
" sometimes prayed to God that it should not take effect."
State Trials, vol. i. p. 215. It is evident that the knowledge of the conspiracy was not communicated under the
seal of confession to Garnet; " nay himself (Greenwell)
" *hath clearly delivered under his hand*, that the powder
" treason was told him (Garnet) not as a fault, but by
" way of consultation and advice." Vol. i. p. 217. So
little reason is there for Dr. Milner's assertion, that " nei-
" ther from the declarations of the conspirators, nor from
" his own at his trial or his execution, could any evidence
" be procured of his having any knowledge of the plot,
" except in the way of confession." P. 273. note (1). The
above declaration of Tesmond was cited at Garnet's trial.

4. If Garnet condemned the plot to Catesby, and dis-
suaded him from the prosecution of it, he changed his
opinion, for " *he had confessed to the Lords*, that he had
" offered sacrifice to God for stay of that plot, unless it
" were for the good of the Catholic cause." State Trials,
vol. i. p. 215. " Then Garnet began to use some speeches,
" that he was not consenting to the powder treason.
" Whereupon the Earl of Salisbury said, Mr. Garnet, give

" me but one argument that you were not confenting to
" it, that can hold in any indifferent man's ear or fenfe,
" befides your bare negative. But Garnet replyed not."
State Trials, vol. i. p. 217.

5. " Garnet, when he found that his arguments were
" ineffectual, by way of gaining time, and in the end
" defeating the villainy, begged of Catefby to fend a
" meffenger to confult the Pope concerning it; knowing
" well that the latter would never give his confent to fo
" diabolical an undertaking." Milner, p. 275. note (1).

" The Earl of Salifbury replyed to Garnet, I muft now
" remember you, how little any of your anfwers can
" make for your purpofe, when you would feek to co-
" lour your dealing with Baynham, by profeffing to write
" to Rome to procure a countermand of confpiracies,
" and yet you know when he took his journey towards
" Rome the blow muft have been paffed, before the time
" that he could have arrived to the Pope's prefence, (fuch
" being your hafte and his zeal for any fuch prevention,)
" as it was about the 20th of our October, when he
" paffed by Florence towards Rome. To which Garnet
" made no great anfwer and let it pafs." State Trials,
vol. i. p. 215.

6. " Father Garnet, whofe guilt was fuppofed to be
" the deepeft in this bufinefs, was not *indicted and exe-*
" *cuted for having taken any part in the treafon,* but
" barely for having concealed his knowledge of it."
Milner, p. 273. The indictment is as follows: " The
" faid Henry Garnet, Ofwald Tefmond, John Gerard and
" other Jefuits, did malicioufly, falfly, and traitoroufly
" move and perfuade as well the faid Thomas Winter,
" &c. &c. That our Sovereign Lord the King, the No-
" bility, Clergy, and whole Commonalty of the Realm
" of England (Papifts excepted) were heretics, and that
" all heretics were accurfed and excommunicate, &c.

" To which traitorous perfuafions the faid Thomas Win-
" ter, &c. traitoroufly did yield their affent, And that
" thereupon the faid Henry Garnet (here follows the lift
" of the Confpirators) traitoroufly amongft themfelves did
" conclude and agree with gunpowder, as it were with
" one blaft, fuddenly, traitoroufly, and barbaroufly to
" blow up &c."

7. It is faid that he was " feverely and repeatedly tor-
" tured on the rack," p. 273. and that " to make him
" appear diftracted at his trial, he was kept without fleep
" fix nights and days previous to it." Milner, p. 274.
" We are told by a late confident author of their own,
" that Garnet was kept waking fix days and nights toge-
" ther, and that Hall was put to extreme torture for fif-
" teen hours fpace together in the Tower." Hift. Miff.
Anglic. p. 315, 334. But a greater than he, (Thuanus)
one of their own perfuafion doth affure us, that " the
" King to avoid calumny did purpofely forbear any thing
" of that kind of rigour." Hiftory of the Gunpowder
Plot.   This account is well fupported by the State Trials.
" Of which impudent calumnies the ftate is fo tender, as
" you do beft know, Mr. Garnet, that fince your appre-
" henfion, *even till this day*, you have been as chriftianly,
" as courteoufly, and as carefully ufed, as ever man could
" be of any quality, or any profeffion : yea, it may truly
" be faid, that you have been as well attended for health
" or otherwife as a nurfe-child.   Is it true, or no ? faid
" the Earl (*of Salifbury*). *It is moft true*, my Lord, faid
" Garnet, I confefs it." State Trials, vol. i. p. 216. " Let
" it not be forgotten, that this interlocution of your's
" with Hall, overheard by others, appears to be digitus
" Dei: for thereby had the Lords fome light and proof of
" matter againft you, which muft have been difcovered
" otherwife by violence and coercion, a matter ordinary in
" other kingdoms, though now forborn here; but it is

" better as it is for the honour of the ſtate." " His Ma-
" jeſty and my Lords were well contented to draw all from
" you without racking, or any ſuch bitter torments."
State Trials, vol. i. p. 216. I ſhall here cloſe this examination with the teſtimony of Lord Stafford, the victim of faction, whoſe trial no one can read without the deepeſt ſor-
row, and ſcarcely without tears. " My Lords, I have heard
" very much of a thing that was named by theſe gentle-
" men of the Houſe of Commons, and that very pro-
" perly too, to wit, of the Gunpowder Treaſon. My,
" Lords, I was not born then, but ſome years after I
" heard very much diſcourſe about it, and very various
" reports; and I made a particular enquiry, perhaps more
" than any one perſon did elſe, both of my father, who
" was alive then, and my uncle, and others; and I am
" ſatisfied, and do clearly believe, by the evidence I have
" received, that that thing called the Gunpowder Treaſon
" was a wicked and horrid deſign (among the reſt) of
" the Jeſuits." " Beſides, my Lords, I was acquainted
" with one of them that was concerned in it, who had
" his pardon, and lived many years after. I diſcourſed
" with him about it, and he confeſſed it, and ſaid he was
" ſorry for it then : and I here declare to your Lord-
" ſhips, that I never heard any one of the Church of
" Rome ſpeak a good word of it; it was ſo horrid a thing,
" that it cannot be expreſſed or excuſed." State Trials,
vol. ii. p. 620. We thus aſcertain the reality of the plot,
who were the authors of it, and what were the ſentiments
which it excited in the honeſt and worthy among the
Catholics themſelves.

Note (D), p. 289.

" I ſhall only obſerve to you, that after the diſcovery
" of this plot, the authors of it were not convinced of the
" evil, but ſorry for the miſcarriage of it. Sir Everard

" Digby, *whofe very original papers and letters are now in*
" *my hands,* after he was in prifon and knew he muft
" fuffer, calls it the beft caufe; and was extremely trou-
" bled to hear it cenfured by Catholics and priefts, con-
" trary to his expectation, for a great fin: ' Let me tell
" you,' fays he, ' what a grief it is to hear that fo much
" condemned, which I did believe would have been other-
" wife thought of by Catholics.' And yet he concludes
" that letter with thefe words : ' In how full joy fhould
" *I die,* if I could do any thing for the caufe, which I
" love more than my life.' And in another letter he
" fays, ' he could have faid fomething to have mitigated
" the odium of this bufinefs, as to that point of involving
" thofe of his own religion in the common ruin: ' I dare
" not,' fays he, ' take that courfe that I could, to make
" it appear lefs odious; for divers were to have been
" brought out of danger, who now would rather hurt
" than otherwife. I do not think there would have been
" three worth the faving, that fhould have been loft.' And
" as to the reft, that were to have been fwallowed up in
" that deftruction, he feems not to have the leaft relenting
" in his mind about them. All doubts he feems to have
" looked upon as temptations; and entreats his friends,
" to pray for the pardoning of his not fufficient ftriving
" againft temptations, fince this bufinefs was undertook."
Tillotfon's Sermon on the fifth of November, 1678.

I fhall contraft this extract with one from Dr. Milner,
Letter to a Prebendary, p. 268, 269. " Amongft thefe
" (the fixteen perfons accufed) it does not appear, that
" more than feven individuals were acquainted with the
" worft part of it; the reft being only concerned in the
" fcheme of an infurrection, *or barely* knowing it, as a
" confcientious fecret, *which they ufed every means in their*
" *power to difcourage and prevent.*" Of thefe feven, Sir
Everard Digby is faid by Dr. M. on the authority of

Stow's Continuat. and Patinfon, " to have pleaded guilty
" to his indictment, and to have fuffered death with great
" compunction ; *declaring at the fame time, that he was*
" *not let into the whole foulnefs of the plot ; which if he*
" *had known, he would not have concealed it to gain the*
" *whole world.*"

Note (E), p. 295.

We are to return to the evidence that Cecil was the
principal perfon concerned in the invention and direction
of this plot.

1. " Cecil did not carry on his fchemes fo fecretly, but
" that fome of his own domeftics got a general notion of
" them.　Accordingly, one of them advifed a Catholic
" friend of his, of the name of Buck, to be upon his
" guard, as fome great mifchief was in the forge againft
" thofe of his religion.　This was faid two months before
" the difclofure of the powder plot." Milner, p. 275.　I
can confider this merely as an indication of a want of
other evidence, and fhall not think it neceffary to fay
more of it, than that " the general notion" of the domeftic muft have been more minute than Dr. Milner's
hypothefis allows ; which implies, that as fome great
mifchief was in the forge, he muft have defcribed by its
magnitude the Powder Plot ; that although it was often-
fibly directed againft the Proteftants, yet that his mafter
was able to controul the actors in this confpiracy ; that
he did not intend that it fhould take effect, and that it
was folely a pretext for fome fevere treatment of the Catholics, and that therefore this perfon was to be upon his
guard.　If he referred to the Powder Plot in his advice,
he muft have known all this.　Thefe are two many particulars to conftitute " a general notion," whilft the cold-
nefs of the caution betrays the want of precife information.　The fact is, he alluded to other circumftances.

2. " Certain it is, that *thefe reafons* have had equal
" weight with many intelligent Proteftants, as with Ca-
" tholics. One of them calls it ' a neat device of the Se-
' cretary." Ofborne's Memoirs of James I. p. 275. I am
of opinion that the writer here cited fays no fuch thing.
He is fpeaking of the difcovery of the plot. " The dif-
" covery appeared no lefs admirable than the treafon, to
" fuch as took the printed account for authentic, that a
" letter was fent to the Lord. Morley, and from him to
" his Majefty, &c. A neat device of the Treafurer's to
" fetch him in, to whofe eftate, or perfon, if not both, he
" had a quarrel. He being very plentiful in fuch plots,
" writing a book, a little after, wherein to magnifie his·
" zeal to religion and the ftate, he publifhed a libel,
" where they threaten to kill him, with a well penn'd
" anfwer, both thought to fmell of the fame ink." Ofborne's Memoirs of James I. vol. ii. p. 117.

3. The Earl of Salifbury is fufpected of having written
the letter to Lord Monteagle, becaufe " he had been
" trained up by his father Lord Burghley and his col-
" leagues in the arts of counterfeiting letters, and pri-
" vately conveying them to Catholics, and of employing
" fecret emiffaries to draw them into dangerous prac-
" tifes;" and we are required to " obferve that Babington
" was firft drawn into the plot, for which he fuffered, by
" fuch a letter delivered to him by an unknown perfon."
Milner, p. 276, note 3.

1. The author of the letter to Lord Monteagle was
concealed. 2. The hand writing was unknown. 3. Its
purport was to declare the fudden approach of the cata-
ftrophe of a confpiracy, and does not feem to be calculated
to enfnare others for this reafon ; that as the plot was fo
far advanced, it was implied, that a fufficient number of
perfons was already employed to execute it. 4. The author of the letter to Babington was the Queen of Scots.

5. It was written in a cypher familiar to Babington. 6. The object of it was to engage Babington to efpoufe her party, and to manage a private correfpondence to advance her interefts. 7. The two cafes agree in this circumftance only, that the letters were delivered by an unknown perfon. 8. Babington afcribed, in his confeffion, the origin of his confpiracy not to the letter above mentioned, but to Ballard the prieft. State Trials, vol. i. p. 106.

4. There ftill remains another fuppofition not lefs licentious than the reft, to try the patience without exercifing the mind. " He (Trefham) was well acquainted with " Cecil, and is known to have had fome communications " with him concerning the affairs of Catholics. Trefham " was upon fuch terms with Cecil, that he had accefs to " him at all hours, not only of the day, but alfo of the " night. Goodman Bifhop of Gloucefter, quoted by Fou- " lis in his Popifh Treafons, exprefsly fays, that Trefham " wrote the letter to Lord Monteagle. If fo, it cannot " be queftioned, who dictated it." Note to p. 278. As Dr. Milner affumes, that this obfcure letter was of fuch a kind as to inveigle other Catholics to join the Confpirators, it is of importance to conjecture, who might have been the author of it. But how it was to produce this effect, is ftill more difficult to conceive. It is deficient in every characteriftic of an invitatory nature. It neither allures, nor folicits, nor exhorts, nor convenes the votaries of Catholicifm. If the object of Cecil were to " en- " tangle" " perfons of that rank, as he might find it expe- " dient," p. 279. this letter is a fingular inftance of a ftatef- man having fo far mifunderftood the means of effecting this, as not to fuggeft any topic, which could influence the mind in that manner. This contrariety between the fuppofed object of the writer, and the letter itfelf, muft, where we have no facts, fatisfy an enquirer of the futility

of the hypothefis. That Cecil fhould delay the develop-
ment of the plot that it might " run to full ripenefs," and
to fee whether any other nobleman would receive fimilar
advertifement, was conduct both prudent and natural;
but to interpret Cecil's words, as if it were " to allow
" him time to fend *frefh letters* to perfons of that rank
" (whom moft of all he wifhed to entangle) if he found it
" expedient," p. 279. is quite unneceffary, unlefs the " frefh
" letters" were very different from the fpecimen fent to
Lord Monteagle.

5. " Trefham it feems died of poifon," Dr. Milner fays,
" before any trial or examination of him took place."
Wood's account is this; " He was taken and committed
" prifoner to the Tower of London, where he died of the
" ftrangury, fay fome, others, that he murthered himfelf:
" yet a venerable author tells us, that he being fick in the
" Tower, Dr. Will. Butler, the great Phyfician of Cam-
" bridge, coming to vifit him as his fafhion was, gave
" him a piece of very pure gold to put in his mouth; and
" upon taking out of that gold, Butler *faid he was poi-*
" *foned.*" Athen. Oxon. vol. i. p. 282.

Was it incumbent upon Cecil to procure Trefham to
be poifoned, in order to conceal the author of the letter
to Lord Monteagle?

Note (F), p. 298.

" I have alfo a fufficiently high opinion of the fincerity
" of the King of England in the profeffion, which he
" makes of the Catholic Religion, to induce me to believe
" he will employ all his authority to eftablifh its free ex-
" ercife, without it being neceffary to excite him to it by
" a premature advance of money, and which ought not to
" be employed if the Parliament grant him the revenues
" enjoyed by the late King, and confent alfo to the eftablifh-
" ment of the free exercife of our religion." P. 67. The

King to Barillon. Speaking of a certain fum of money,
" which I wifh you to preferve only to be difpofed of in
" the event of the King of England not being able to ob-
" tain from his Parliament a continuation of the revenues,
" or on his finding fuch obftacles to the eftablifhment of
" the Catholic Religion, as may compel him to diffolve it,
" and employ his authority and arms to bring his fubjects
" to reafon." P. 67, 68. The King to Barillon. " He (the
" Earl of Sunderland) will in future enjoy a large fhare
" of his mafter's confidence, fhould his union with your
" Majefty continue, and he perfevere in his defign of
" eftablifhing the Catholic Religion." P. 71. Barillon to
the King. " So that, after having given proofs of my zeal
" for *the re-eftablifhment* of the Catholic Religion in
" England, and of my friendfhip towards this Prince, by
" the fuccours I am at this time tranfmitting to you, I
" may not, in the event of his entertaining finifter inten-
" tions, contribute further towards placing him in a con-
" dition to act contrary to whatever I could defire."
P. 84. Extract of a letter from the King to Barillon. " As
" I find with pleafure, that the Englifh Parliament con-
" tributes liberally to all his Majefty's wants, and that he
" will meet with no obftacles to *the re-eftablifhment* of
" the Catholic Religion, when he fhall undertake it after
" the difperfion of the remains of the rebels; I have
" thought proper to recall the fums, which have been
" tranfmitted to you for the purpofe of fupporting, in
" cafe of need, the defigns this prince might have in fa-
" vour of our religion." P. 98. The King to Barillon.
" This minifter (Lord Sunderland) faid to me, ' I know
" not whether things are feen in France as they are here;
" but I defy any one, who views them clofely, not to
" know, that the King my mafter has nothing more at
" heart, than a defire to eftablifh the Catholic Reli-
" gion.'

" I fee clearly the apprehenfion entertained by many
" people of a conne&ion with France, and the efforts that
" will be made to weaken it : but no one will be able to
" do it, unlefs there be a wifh for it in France : this is a
" matter upon which you muft diftin&ly explain yourfelf,
" and fhew that the King your mafter wifhes fincerely to
" affift the King of England in permanently eftablifhing
" the Roman Catholic Religion." P. 104. Barillon to the
King, and p. 106, 107, 114.

I would only remark, that much more than even an
univerfal toleration was intimated by the expreffions of
the King o Barillon, who does not ufe the fimple term
eftablifhn: :nt, but the re-eftablifhment of the Catholic Religion—rétabliffement de la Religion Catholique. See
p. 88, and 102. of the French Appendix. This word cannot be reduced to the meaning of a toleration of any extent.

FINIS.

ERRATA AND CORRECTIONS.

Page 153. line 19. *for* " initiation" *read* " imitation"
Page 192. line. 10. *for* " fcuptural" *read* " critical"
Page 237. line 2. *dele from* " and" *to* " Chrift."
Page 240. line 24. *dele* " and irregular"
Page 276. line 4. *for* " fuis" *read* " fuis"
Page 304. line 5. *dele* " a"